CHINESE WOMEN SPEAK

Born in Sydney, Ellen Dymphna Cusack (1902–81) was a descendant of two pioneering families who went to Australia in the 1840s. She became the author of many award-winning novels and plays, as well as travel books. And of all Australian writers, she was one of the most travelled and most translated. In 1969 she was named by the Australian national daily paper as being among 'the one hundred opinion-makers of Australia'. Famous for novels such as *Come in Spinner, Say No to Death* and *Heatwave in Berlin*, she also achieved the status of being the most popular contemporary author in Russia—where she is read in translation.

First published in 1958, *Chinese Women Speak* was received by the Chinese themselves as a 'classic'. It was the first in-depth study of Chinese women, and Dymphna Cusack wrote it only after spending eighteen months travelling over seven thousand miles through 1950s China: a voyage of discovery which enabled her to become the mouthpiece of the Chinese women she met in their hundreds. A sympathetic interviewer, she was admitted into their private lives and here she retells their intimate stories, from peasant to Manchu princess, and including factory-workers, housewives, former prostitutes and beggars.

This is a book of unparalleled human interest where the China of the past comes to life in testimonies of existence before Liberation—when child-selling and foot-binding were common practices. And because the author meets such a wide age-range of Chinese women, she is able to present this feudal lifestyle in contrast with the communism of modern China—where it is the ubiquitous 'street committees' who oversee the general social and moral welfare.

CHINESE WOMEN SPEAK

Dymphna Cusack

CENTURY HUTCHINSON LTD
LONDON

First published in 1958 by
Angus & Robertson Ltd
This edition published in 1985 by
Century Hutchinson Ltd,
Brookmount House, 62–65 Chandos Place,
London WC2N 4NW

ISBN 0 7126 0456 1

The cover shows a Chinese poster

Reprinted in Great Britain by
Richard Clay (The Chaucer Press) Ltd, Bungay, Suffolk

TO

THE WOMEN OF CHINA

CONTENTS

Contents

*The decorations are taken from
Chinese paper-cuts.*

CHAPTER I

Arrival

IKNEW the first week I was in China I would write a book about it, though I hadn't come with that intention. I'm not a travel-writer. I'm neither interested in nor capable of writing political or economic studies. I'm interested only in people. But, without a knowledge of the language, how could I get close enough to people to write about them as I like to write about them?

Something of the ancient magic of the country touched me as our plane, leaving behind the blistered monotone of the Gobi Desert, soared over the ranges west of Peking—improbable as the mountains of the moon—and dipped to show us the writhing dragon that is the Great Wall.

Fields on mountainside and valley formed intricate rust-coloured patterns like wind-ripples in sand against the sun-baked dust. Mud huts were distinguishable from the fawn earth only by the shadows they cast. Dark distorted pines enclosed the ancestral graves.

"I don't believe it," my companion said flatly, face against the window. "It's too like a Chinese painting."

More and more like a painting the sapphire clefts of the Western Hills with their pagodas and temples; the lake at the Summer Palace mirroring the many-arched marble bridge, the golden-tiled palaces. . . .

Privately, I didn't believe it either!

That evening, as I lean on the balustrade of the hotel terrace, nine storeys up, the sense of unreality deepens. To add to it, my Chinese companion tells me that this attractive, comfortable hotel was built in forty days! His words come to me through a sound like that of aerial wood-winds that rises and falls above me.

"Pigeons," he says in answer to my query.

"Do Peking pigeons sing?" I ask, prepared for anything.

"No. But they wear whistles affixed to their bodies. Look, you

can see them. There are more than a hundred kinds of whistles
—of bamboo and reed and calabash."

Sweet and mellow the sound crescendoes as the flock sweeps
downward to the south.

On the southern horizon, gilded by the low light, a parachute
tower, the scaffolding of a huge building, a pagoda, factory chimneys, and, seeming to float in the brilliant air like three giant
inverted hibiscus blossoms set one within the other, the roof of
the Temple of Heaven.

At our feet stretches Peking, revealed by our height in its
ancient formal pattern: its heart, the Forbidden City enclosed
by its own walls and moat, then the walls of the Imperial City,
both surrounded by the six-hundred-year-old wall; beyond it,
like the top bar of a T, the Southern City lies within its own
walls.

From street-level Peking is a secret city, its narrow streets
bounded by high grey walls that enclose courtyards with one-
storeyed houses whose curved roofs one can barely glimpse. It was
forbidden to build higher lest the Emperor be overlooked. But
secrecy has gone with height and from here I see a receding vista
of grey roofs—their long cylindrical tiles looking like caterpillars
laid side by side—surrounding courtyards each with its green
plume of a tree unmoving in the windless air.

Beyond them the golden tiles of the Forbidden City catching
the last sun, triple-curved eaves black against the pale sky. Modern
buildings mushrooming above the ancient, and away to the west
the mountains I had crossed a few hours before, insubstantial as
an old print against the apricot glow.

A pedlar calls in the lane, his cry rising and falling repetitively;
a car hoots; a donkey brays; the Angelus rings; cymbals clash.

Again an air of unreality. To be looking over Peking on a
summer evening soft as silk under this high arching sky belongs
to the world of fantasy!

I had always wanted to visit China—"always" going back to a
time when I was about five and had an experience of Chinese
tolerance from the gardener on an Australian sheep-station far
inland.

Ah Fong lived across the river and used to bring the vegetables
up to the homestead each day across a swinging bridge of wire
and planks. My sister and I discovered a most amusing game. We
would wait till Ah Fong, bamboo pole across his shoulder, laden
baskets dangling from it, was in the centre and then rush out
from hiding and jump up and down on the bridge. It would rock

and sway perilously and Ah Fong, clinging to his precious baskets, would appeal to us in language we little monsters found extremely funny.

At last it got too much for him. He told my father. We were lectured and sent to bed without any tea. It was my father's favourite punishment and would have been effective if someone in the kitchen had not taken pity on us. Cups of warm milk and pieces of bread and butter came in surreptitiously and two thick slices of the first ripe watermelon Ah Fong had brought up specially for us. We were ashamed!

Indeed, for us in Australia, China was never the "Far East", though it is sometimes forgotten that the same ocean that washes our shores washes China's. Back in the early days convicts, having no maps to guide them, used to say that "beyond the hills lies China", and runaways tried to find a way there by land, while others set out in small ill-equipped boats in the hope of reaching its shores and freedom.

Besides, there were too many Chinese scattered round the countryside for us to have many misconceptions about the inscrutable Orientals. Some of them, solitary new-comers, worked hard and lived "on the smell of an oil-rag", sending most of their money home, saving only enough to buy a coffin and pay for its transport so that their bones might lie among their ancestors.

Others were settled families with a reputation for probity, whose grandfathers had come there in the days of the Gold Rush and who were Australian like ourselves, talked like us, played like us, lived like us.

My earliest memories recall my mother's bamboo fan, the tea-chest with its strange characters, the calendar from the Chinese drapers with the very mountains I had seen from the plane. Presents from sea-going friends who travelled up and down the Pacific—kingfisher-feather brooches, red-lacquer boxes, cloisonné vases with multicoloured dragons, exquisitely embroidered silk underwear—all, for me, tainted by the tales of abysmal poverty and misery and human abasement.

Learning to use chopsticks and appreciate Chinese food in a Campbell Street restaurant. Chinese history and art and novels and plays: a world of millennial culture opening up.

Friends going off to China to teach in mission schools or be medical missionaries. Millennial misery.

Tales of horror: of war-lords, of bandits, of Japanese atrocities, of famine and flood, and fatalism. Women with bound feet, infanticide and forced marriage and concubines and sing-song girls and ineradicable conservatism.

What was left of this China, I wondered as I leant on the balustrade of the hotel terrace nine storeys up.

"Built in forty days," my companion repeats unnecessarily, along with a lot of other figures I don't really listen to. I dislike statistics nearly as much as the picturesque for what they blind us to.

Now I ask myself, behind the picturesque survivals and the forty-day buildings, what am I going to find?

The air of unreality persists next day when I visit the Temple of Heaven where for more than five centuries the Emperors went to worship the Supreme Ancestor.

The architects and astronomers and doctors of magic who combined to design it gave it a setting that enhances its beauty. Three miles of high walls, glowing a rich cornelian red and topped with glazed green tiles, enclose a vast park. Here five thousand knotted, twisted, five-hundred-year-old cypresses surround inner walls of equal magnificence, beyond which rises the triple lapis-lazuli roof that had mesmerized me the night before.

Today, though it is a weekday, there are many visitors, for now all the once Forbidden Places are open to the public. I wonder what the Emperor would think of the groups that cluster round the guides—peasants and soldiers and students and factory workers, all listening absorbedly, with that thirst for knowledge typical of China today. Out on the terraces children in bright shorts and frocks play "tip" round the six-foot-high incense burners. Mothers in gay floral trousers and coloured tunics carry fat babies like little burnished buddhas, sensibly naked in the heat. Bound-foot grandmas totter up steps after their laughing charges, walking with a stiff-kneed Chaplinesque walk on their tiny wedge-shaped feet.

Old men in long black robes, ivory faces, scanty beards, sit sipping tea and fanning themselves reflectively like the sages in ancient prints. Down in the park scantily-clad butterfly hunters leap shouting after their fluttering prey.

Cicadas are shrilling in the thick cypresses that line the royal-processional way to arched marble gateways, strangely airy with decorations that look like wings in flight opening on to the full glory of the enormous elevated marble altar. Dazzling white in the sunshine, awe-inspiring, its grandeur and isolation make it an altar unique in the world.

There is also a remarkable echo that tempts you. As I go down the marble steps a group of children come whooping along the avenue, sucking ice blocks on bamboo-sticks.

"Where are you from?" they ask, with that uninhibited friendliness that marks Chinese children.

"O-ta-lee-a," Lao Chang explains.

And, after sticky handshakes, they go whooping away up the ceremonial steps and I hear the echo from the highest platform come back, faint but clear: "O-ta-lee-a! O-ta-lee-a!"

I try to visualize the gorgeous scene of sacrifice as I stand looking up at the Pray for Good Harvest Shrine, its three tiers of circular blue eaves topped with gold, towering ninety-nine feet on its man-made hill. (The Good Spirits fly at one hundred feet, it was believed, and must not be impeded.) It stands in the centre of three levels of marble terraces, up which the Emperor's sedan chair was borne over the central ramp of deeply-carved marble.

The guide's voice interrupts me, saying, "No woman—not even the Empress herself—could come here."

As though to challenge the age-old prohibition, two women pass me, one thin and shrivelled, with the stamp of ancient privation on her face, wearing a long, old-fashioned black tunic over tight-legged trousers and walking uncertainly on her mutilated feet, the other young and strong, glossy black hair framing her face and falling to her shoulders. She wears a white cotton tunic printed in rose over sky-blue trousers, and walks with long strides in modern sandals. Slowly the older woman hobbles up the marble steps where once only the feet of the Emperor's bearers trod. Pitiful feet. . . . Her daughter takes two steps at a time.

Half-way up they pause and turn. Small granddaughter is insisting on crawling the hard way up over the spirit-walk where deeply carved dragons and phoenixes, mountains and cloud and waves riot. It is forbidden, but the guardians are tolerant of children. It is hard going, even in long cotton pants, split in the Chinese fashion so that her plump bare bottom shows where once only the Emperor's shadow passed.

Over her sleek black head I meet the eyes of her grandmother. We smile and suddenly there are no gaps between us, either of race or language. I go up the steps and stand beside her, asking the child's name and age. She is Little Plum-blossom, aged two and a half.

I comment on her tenacity.

"My daughter was like that," the old lady says proudly. Then her face saddens. "I had another girl older than she but I had to sell her in the famine when she was no bigger than that."

At my exclamation of horror she says quickly, "But it's not like that any more. No one has to sell a child any more." She nods towards her daughter who, deciding that Little Plum-blossom's trousers and knees have had enough wear and tear, lifts her protesting from the ramp.

"She goes to kindergarten—my daughter is a tram-driver—and when she grows up she can be anything she likes."

We are photographed together and when I leave Little Plum-blossom, at mother's direction, shakes my hand rather reluctantly, and at grandmother's, gives me a stiff little bow.

It is then the germ of my book settles in my mind.

CHAPTER II

Decision

O^{N THE} way to the opening of Parliament we drive through a slanting silver curtain of rain across the city. Downpours, tropical in their violence, punctuate Peking's hot summer days.

The water sprays out from our wheels, the roads are rivers, the gutters awash. Pedi-cab drivers bow over their handle-bars, hats like inverted basins above sulphur-yellow rain-capes, passengers protected by waterproof sheets. Policemen in hooded fawn raincoats direct the traffic.

Blue blinds flap on the red trams; a horse and donkey linked with rope harness bow their heads against the rain. Each has a "tail-bag" conveniently attached—double-purpose: to keep the streets clean and save precious manure!

A file of soldiers, each carrying a large oiled-paper umbrella—scarlet and gold and blue and green—halts laughing as our car hoots and slows.

Trees lash, sprinkling with acacia blossoms the ground at the foot of the walls of the Forbidden City, once Pompeian red, now faded to old rose.

The balustrades of the five curved marble bridges that span the Golden Water River glisten against the rich red of the newly painted Tien An Men—the Gate of Heavenly Peace, the gatehouse that guarded the entrance to the Palace. Enormous, massive, its curved roof is covered with golden-yellow tiles above double-curved eaves, and the people sheltering in its arches are reduced to pygmies by the high brass-studded gates.

Once, only the Emperor's yellow processional sedan chair passed beneath these arches. Yellow and red were sacred to the Emperor. Now the national emblem shines in the centre under the uptilted eaves and two inscriptions in characters of gold run the length of the walls on either side: "Long live the People's Republic of China!" and "Long live the great unity of the peoples of the world!"

Our car turns in through a high gateway up an avenue lined with acacia-trees and an occasional late-flowering mimosa.

China's Parliament meets in a setting of beauty and colour probably unequalled in any other country. The vast hall, built over five hundred years ago, was once part of the Imperial Palace —a palace which consisted of scores of separate palaces.

We pass through a flower- and palm-filled forecourt now covered at a lofty height with woven matting as a protection against the fierce summer sun (or rain!) into the enormous chamber where Parliament assembles. It has been carefully modernized without losing any of its splendour. High lacquer-red pillars surround the body of the hall, above them intricately carved woodwork. Lanterns of delicately carved wood and silk hang symmetrically from the ceiling and, high up, giant recessed bowls that look like inverted lotus-flowers give daylight lighting.

Focus of all, the stage, flanked by the same vermilion pillars; above, an exquisite traditional design in green and gold and red. At the back, silver-grey velvet hangings—a setting fit for a gorgeous opera! But sharp contrast: against it, the business-like desks at which the Presidium sits.

In the body of the hall up-to-date desks for the deputies, each with its earphones: over a thousand deputies, twelve per cent of them women, are already seated. Women in Parliament are impressive anywhere, but remarkable in a country where, so few years ago, women had no civic rights at all. Eight of these women deputies are Ministers or Vice-ministers.

Movie-camera men and press-photographers are busy setting up their apparatus. Klieg lights are strategically placed. A woman press-photographer in a smart grey suit tries out a position on a small step-ladder. Everywhere there are ushers—young girls with long black plaits, in tunic and trousers.

The murmur of voices ceases: the members of the Presidium are filing on to the platform amid a hailstorm of clapping. Among them I can distinguish Chairman Mao Tse-tung, Premier Chou En-lai, and Madame Soong Ching-ling, widow of Dr Sun Yat-sen and one of China's Vice Prime Ministers.

A band of the People's Army plays the Chinese National Anthem, *"Chi-lai"*—"Arise all ye who refuse to be slaves". Lights dazzle us. Cameras flash.

Congress is open. Beside me my interpreter whispers the gist of the formal proceedings. On the other side a young girl in a flowered tunic and blue cotton slacks translates in French for her neighbour. Behind me I catch words in Italian, German, Russian, as the young Chinese girls—they all seem so young—interpret for their charges.

Speeches . . . flutterings of fans on the Presidium.

Formal opening over, the House votes for a brief adjournment. I can study the deputies as they file past. Men and women of all ages and types and classes. Men in high-necked tunics—blue, grey, the khaki of the army. A man in the latest Western clothes, obviously a business-man. A typical scholar, Chi Pai-shih, the famous ninety-five-year-old painter, with a meagre beard falling over a long silken Manchu robe. Mei Lan-fan, famous star of the Peking opera, in a striped summer suit.

Old women with the seamed tan faces of peasants. Pale, elegant women fashionably dressed. Others in the *chi-pao*, the straight elegant Chinese robe, split up the side. Others, again, in trousers and tunic, still others in skirt and blouse. All the colours and patterns in the world, for China has gone colour-crazy this year.

A dark-faced man in a pink turban, representative of one of the minorities, a Tibetan in a red-lined brown robe over a white tunic. A giant Mongolian, resplendent in a wine-and-gold robe, baring one massive brown shoulder, an old man in a black robe holding a long cigarette holder. He might have served as the model for the ivory statues we see in the street of the antiques. A Buddhist lama in saffron. He smiles and bows over his two hands raised in the attitude of prayer.

Then two women come towards me. They might have walked out of an exotic travelogue: the older one in black trousers and white tunic, her sleek black hair drawn into a tight chignon low on her neck; the younger one, not typically Chinese, a girl with fine olive skin, small pointed face, delicate nose, dancing eyes, on her head a high circular turban of dark blue and white and hooped silver ear-rings, hoops of silver round her neck, royal-blue tunic above black trousers covered by an apron beautifully embroidered in red and blue falling to the knees, a vivid sash of woven coloured wools.

We smile at each other. They stop and hold out their hands. Will I walk with them? I go, their arms linked in mine, the interpreter following. In the crowded foyer with its richly carved furniture, its thick embossed carpets of old gold, its long, low tea-tables, we talk.

Li Yu-hsin, the older woman, comes from Kiangsi Province, where she is chairman of the Agricultural Producers' Co-operative of her village. It has taken her two days by car and three days by train to come to Peking via Shanghai.

I want to know something of her life and she sums it up for me in a sentence: "Four years ago I was illiterate. Last year I was selected to go to a women's conference in Switzerland."

The gap is too wide for me to bridge and I ask for details.

"There is no time here," she says. "You must come and visit me in Kiangsi and I shall show you what has happened to my village and my family. Our village is a flourishing co-operative of eighty-seven families. My children have been given education and have good jobs."

"And what was your life in the old days?" I persist.

"When I was a young woman my home was plundered and burnt to the ground by Chiang Kai-shek's armies. My husband was murdered. I fled to the mountains with my four children and we lived on wild roots. I brought up my children by the work of my own hands. Sometimes we had nothing but rice gruel in our bowls from one year's end to the other. And now we all eat rice every day out of good china bowls."

She turns to the younger girl. "But now it is Wu Tse-chuin's turn."

Wu Tse-chuin laughs and a dimple shows in her cheek. Her light voice runs on rapidly.

She comes from Kweichow—actually farther away than Kiangsi, though her journey has taken only two days by car and two and a half days by train, since there is now a direct line. She is a Miao, one of the minority nationalities which, in some districts, was almost exterminated under the old régime.

I ask what she does, prepared to hear anything but her answer: "I am a welfare worker! My work is among the women of my village, who are very backward because for so many centuries the Miaos lived withdrawn as far as possible into our mountains to escape the systematic attempts at extermination by the major race, the Hans. Now the New Constitution gives all the minorities equal rights."

Her eyes sparkle. "Imagine what it meant to us to learn that henceforth there would be no discrimination against us—we who for centuries had known only oppression! In 1943 when I was a child the Kuomintang came and for no reason killed thousands of my people and burnt more than two thousand huts. We were forbidden to speak our own language. Women had to burn their national costumes. We were ashamed to go out because we had nothing left to wear. Now we have full rights. We now have a written language of our own. We were so backward we never had one in all our history."

A tall, proud girl passes us, something faintly Arab in her

face. She wears a long, swinging dress of purple satin richly embroidered; exquisitely worked gold medallions tinkling from her head-dress. Wu Tse-chuin calls to her and I am introduced; she is a deputy from another minority, but I do not catch her name or her race. I find only that she confirms Wu Tse-chuin's story of race-discrimination and attempted "Sinization".

"But today we are free to be ourselves," she says, and the medallions tinkle as she throws back her head.

Now it is their turn to ask me questions. Where do I come from? Why am I here?

When I tell them I should like to write a book about Chinese women Li Yu-hsin impulsively throws her arms round my neck and our cheeks touch—the typical Chinese embrace. Wu Tse-chuin takes my hand between hers and presses it. We stand smiling at each other, deeply moved. Movie-camera men and press-photographers converge on us. The interpreter gives up trying to translate the rapid questions that flow out. Never have I so deeply regretted the lack of a common language.

The interpreter touches my arm and I turn. Premier Chou En-lai has come up to us. We are presented to him.

I am so frustrated by having to say everything through an interpreter that, remembering that Chou En-lai spent years in France, I begin to speak in French.

He replies in the same language, telling me that, alas! he has forgotten his French. "But I am learning English," he adds.

The warning bell rings for the resumption of the session.

"You must come and visit us," they cry, one after another, pressing my hand between theirs in the traditional Chinese handshake. "Come and see for yourself how Chinese women have stood up!"

Weeks spent seeing the wonders of Peking—ancient Peking that famous travellers ranked in beauty with Ispahan and Rome.

Looking down from Chingshan, the highest of its man-made hills, on the Forbidden City whose moat surrounds old-rose walls enclosing palaces that are among the wonders of the world: a sea of fantastically beautiful roofs, their golden tiles glittering in the sun, upswept eaves bearing the mythical animals that once were thought to protect them from fire. Palaces too numerous to count, each a gem in itself with its marble steps and balustrades, its cross-beams richly decorated in gold and green and blue, its vermilion pillars upholding the splendour of its ceiling.

Boating on the lakes that Kublai Khan had excavated eight hundred years ago when he was Emperor of Peking: the curve of milk-white bridges, pavilions with fluted roofs of peacock blue, with tilted eaves frilled like the skirts of a ballet-dancer.

Out into the countryside past primitive villages of dun mud huts, to see the Great Wall, the Ming Tombs, the Temples of the Western Hills. Regrets that I am not a travel-writer, that even when gazing enthralled at the glories that Imperial days bequeathed and the present Government has restored, I want to know what is happening to the peasants in the fields and villages.

In the ancient city and the new that is springing up outside its walls, I visit kindergartens, primary schools, secondary schools, technical colleges, universities.

An official of the Ministry of Education tells me: "In 1949 eighty-five per cent of China's population was illiterate. Now ninety per cent of the children, girls as well as boys, are receiving education. Each year the number of women teaching in schools, colleges, and universities increases. In 1957 three women were among the scientists honoured for outstanding achievements."

Hospitals for children, general hospitals, hospitals for Western medicine, hospitals for traditional Chinese medicine. All of them up-to-date, efficient.

As I collect statistics on public health and declining endemic and epidemic diseases, I understand why, when the Chinese Embassy in London issued my visa, I was told it was not necessary to have the inoculations and injections for smallpox, typhus, cholera, and typhoid usually considered necessary for Eastern travel.

I visit the largest and most modern cotton-mill I have ever seen, with 96,000 spindles, 5460 employees, innumerable women "model workers", and a woman director!

I learn that women comprise 22·5 per cent of the deputies elected to local and provincial congresses.

I meet women in charge of schools and hospitals, women judges and aviators and professors. Everywhere women in high and responsible positions.

When I comment on this to Miss Wang, gentle and charming and very feminine, the international editor of the *People's Daily*, she says, "We don't think about sex when it comes to a job. It's a question of who can do it best."

Professor Li of the Peking Union Medical College, a vital, slender woman who may be in her sixties but has the vivacity of twenty, tells me that today forty per cent of the students in medical colleges are women.

Sun Tse-chio, national secretary of the All-China Women's

Federation, tells me: "In 1950 the New Marriage Law abolished the feudal marriage system which was based on the idea of the superiority of men over women. Now women have the same rights as men—legally, politically and economically."

I read the New Marriage Law. What could throw a clearer light on the position of women in Old China than the customs it considered necessary to prohibit—forced marriage, bigamy, concubinage, child-betrothal, interference with the remarriage of widows, infanticide by drowning and "similar criminal acts"? A lawyer tells me that previously the law did not require more than a mere statement of the death of a child under the age of three to obtain a permit for burial.

I visit a court where a divorce case is being heard by three judges —*two* of them women. (The husband won!)

"In Old China divorce was a one-sided affair," the vice-director of the court tells me. "Confucius enumerated seven reasons for which a man could divorce his wife: if she disobeyed her parents-in-law, was sterile, talkative, jealous, a leper, a thief, or committed adultery. Up till Liberation," she continued, "there was only a slight penalty for the murder of an erring wife, but a husband's adultery was not even an offence. Provisions for divorce introduced by the Kuomintang had so many conditions attached that, in fact very few women benefited from them. After the promulgation of the New Marriage Law, for several years the greater number of civil cases were concerned with marital disputes."

Each time I visit a school, a hospital, a factory, a court, a State farm, I take voluminous notes. Each time I meet an outstanding woman, I question her closely.

But what is it like behind what the tourist sees? I ask myself.

How has the revolution affected women in general, the non-political, home-staying women, the ignorant, the passive, the oppressed women?

What is their role? Is it still passive and oppressed in a different way, as an English journalist tells me? Or have they, too "stood up"?

I resolved to find out. My brief experience has taught me that language is no barrier. Minds leap to each other with instinctive sympathy. The ancient Chinese reticence about women and home life has gone. Today, Chinese women can speak for themselves while efficient interpreters convey their meaning accurately.

CHAPTER III

The Empress Dowager's Lady-in-Waiting

THE last person I expected to meet in China was one of the Empress Dowager's ladies-in-waiting. But then, if I had thought about it, I would not have expected to be attending the production of *The Doll's House* in Chinese and with a Chinese cast, at which I met her. A moving and stimulating performance—but this is getting away from the Princess.

In the first interval I talked with my neighbour, who mistook me for a Frenchwoman she had met. To my good fortune, because from the moment she came in with her husband, I had been fascinated by her. Slender, fragile, elegant in a plain black *chi-pao*, with long jade ear-rings, waved grey hair, patrician face the texture of old ivory, small proud mouth, eyebrows like a moth's antennae above narrow jet eyes. Beautiful by any standard, at any age.

"I saw *The Doll's House* in Paris at the beginning of the century," she told me in her excellent French. "I would have liked to play Nora myself. You see, I studied with Sarah Bernhardt."

She smiled across the slow, graceful movements of her gold-embossed fan, the jade ear-rings catching the light.

"Were you on the stage?" I asked.

"Oh, no!" She gave a laugh like a girl's. "My father was very angry when I wanted to be an actress, though he had let me study with Sarah Bernhardt to improve my education. He was very progressive for his day—I'm seventy-four." Impossible to believe it! "But to let his daughter go on the stage! La, la! He brought me home to cure me of those ideas.

"But we love Paris." She included her husband in the "we" with a smile of such warmth and tenderness that an answering smile creased his round, plump face under iron-grey hair. "My husband was at St Cyr. He was five years in Paris. Have you been there lately?"

But the curtain rose on the second act.

At the next interval friends claimed me. Over iced drinks—it was a stifling June night—a Frenchwoman who had been some time in Peking said, "I see you are sitting near *la Générale?*"

"*La Générale?*"

"Yes. Her husband was in the Imperial Guards. Didn't you know? She is a Manchu princess and was lady-in-waiting to the Empress Dowager."

What a story! I panted back to my seat, but the last act commenced. By the time the applause had died away it was late. I had only time to say good night. And then to my enchantment she said, in English as good as her French, "Perhaps you would come and take tea with us one day?"

It was months before I could accept that invitation. Months spent travelling from one end of China to the other: to Canton in the tropical south and Harbin on the fringes of Siberia, Wuhan six hundred miles up the Yangtze, Shanghai and Nanking and Shenyang that we in the West recognize more easily as Mukden. I had seen for myself China "stand up"!

Winter had come on bitter winds out of Siberia and with it Peking's first snow. The car swept through streets where cone-shaped heaps in the gutters glittered like piles of salt on the salt-pans.

The triple roofs of the Imperial watch-towers hold the snow in their eaves like the curving branches of fir-trees as we creep through the narrow hutungs to the east of the Forbidden City. (Hutungs are mainly residential, and range from paved thorough-fares to alley-ways large enough only for a pedi-cab.)

I have the address and the driver knows approximately that it is near the East Flowery Gate of the Palace. But we crawl up endless hutungs and back down them again in a flurry of powdery snow.

At last a group of small boys pilot us up the narrowest of all till we reach a point where the walls converge and the car can go no farther. The driver goes to explore and comes back to say he's found the number at last, and I go skidding and sliding on foot the last fifty yards.

The gate-keeper leads me under a high tiled gateway, through courtyards where snow lies heavy on the fir-trees. Curious eyes peep from latticed windows as we pass through moon-gates and past a snow-man with persimmon seeds for eyes, sunflower seeds for nostrils, a padded cap with ear-flaps on his head and a paper nose!

In the last court the General stands at his door to welcome me, wearing a padded brown silk jacket and padded shoes, while

Madame waits inside and takes my hand in her two fine delicate ones. She is still slender and graceful in her high-necked jacket of black silk which she wears above silk padded trousers.

The door opens directly into a pleasant room, at present dominated by a large stove in the centre.

"You will find Chinese houses cold after your hotel. Our houses were never heated as you heat yours. I remember once in the Palace, when I was quite a young girl, it was so cold that I dropped my rice-bowl. The Palace was freezing in winter. Only small coal stoves in those big draughty rooms! The Dowager didn't notice the cold but the rest of us would be shivering, though our clothes were fur-lined. It was awful, particularly after Paris with its central heating."

I prick my ears at the mention of the Palace and would like to plunge straight into questions about that incredible woman the Empress Dowager.

"But all that is past," she says as she waves me to a chair. "I prefer to live in the present; it is much more interesting."

She is pressing delicious cream cakes on me, and a special variety called Manchu cakes, and strange and delicious sweets. The General, with his amiable smile, is making and serving tea in delicate white-and-gold cups.

"He is very good in the house," she says, a hand on his arm. "Though we have household help, he looks after the stove in the morning and I look after it in the evening. He owes that to my age—he is only seventy-two. Sometimes I have to warn him to show more respect for his elders, but not often."

They exchange the same warm smile I had seen the first night I met them.

From my seat I can see the whole room, long and narrow, a high roof, light-coloured furniture, a tall chest of some rich, dark wood with heavily worked bronze hinges and locks. Carpets on the floor, poinsettias blooming in pots, their stems trained in an intricate pattern.

On a wall there are portraits, among them one of an exquisite girl dancing, her diaphanous blue veils floating like mist. The General takes it down and hands it to me.

"My wife at sixteen," he says with obvious pride.

"Isadora Duncan taught me dancing. She was a most interesting woman."

I am in a whirl at this world opening up for me as the conversation shuttles between English and French. The General speaks only French, though Madame says that he understands English.

"He is really lazy," she says. "I tell him he should take it up again. We need people with foreign languages today."

Again she gives her light young laugh as she slaps his hand in mock reproof. Clearly the General finds all she says and does wonderful.

"I wonder if you could help me with a knitting pattern," she says, picking up a half-knitted cardigan. "I'm knitting a cardigan for my husband and I'm afraid the pattern is wrong."

But, alas, I am less versatile than the Princess and can give no advice.

"Tell us about Paris," she coaxes. "Is it very different today? Who are the couturiers now? I used to buy my clothes from Lanvin. And what are the latest styles?"

I do my best, then ask if this is their original home. She shakes her head.

"When we sold my house—it was quite up to date—we took this wing because it had a bathroom." The wing consists of ten rooms. "Most Chinese houses haven't and they keep quite clean without them. But I was spoilt very early in those things. When we were at the Palace I used to sneak home to have a bath. The Palace was most uncomfortable, even in the summer. In winter it was torture. A eunuch would bring a tub to your room and then fill it with hot water but it was such a lengthy process it was cold before you got in.

"I am Manchu, you know, though my husband is Chinese. I was the first of the Manchu nobility to marry a Chinese. It was forbidden under the Empire. But I knew him before. He was in the Imperial Guards. Actually I knew him when I was a child. I slapped him once or twice, didn't I?"

The General shakes his head vehemently.

She laughs. "There you are! He never will admit it."

She takes another cigarette. "I've just finished a book myself. The Academy of Culture and History, where we both work, asked me to write my memoirs as a lady-in-waiting. Many years ago my sister wrote a book about it, and there are many things in it that are not correct, since she wrote it to please a foreign publisher."

"I read a book years ago, *Two Years in the Forbidden City* by a Manchu princess—I've forgotten her name."

"Der Ling," she supplies. "My sister!"

"Then you are—?"

"Roungling. Yü Roungling—my family name was Yü, and you probably know that in China we put the surname first. Some of the mischievous young things where I work call me the Princess Roungling to tease me. They are really very kind. They say, 'You are of advanced age, you must not work too long', and if I look tired they make me come home. People are much kinder today than they used to be."

She lifts her long ivory cigarette holder and draws in the smoke. Under her padded jacket I glimpse the wrist-band of an underjacket of rose brocade.

"Strange, isn't it? For nearly sixty years I have wanted to go on the stage and only now does there seem to be a chance of achieving my ambition, but in a different way—as an adviser. They are producing a play about the famous Pearl Concubine, the favourite of the Emperor Kuang Hsu, and I am teaching them how to walk, to stand, to kotow—all the intricate court etiquette of our day. You can't imagine how picturesque it all was. An endless procession of richly dressed people. Unless you saw them you could not visualize the richness of the robes. Satins and silks in all the colours of the rainbow, embroidered in gold and silver and finest silks: our everyday wear of those times is today the glory of museums. The Dowager's sedan chair with the phoenix surmounting it. Guardsmen and eunuchs on horseback. I can remember swinging along the road to the Summer Palace through the steamy summer heat, the sweat pouring down the faces of the coolies who carried us."

She opens her eyes and frowns as she knocks the ash from her cigarette.

"It's better today. It makes me happy to see people so happy, particularly women.

"Young Chinese girls had no position in their own families or their husband's. They were taught to be obedient to their fathers and husbands and sons. They had no education, for it was thought that ignorance was a virtue. But Manchu girls held a high position in the family. Parents in upper-class families engaged tutors for their daughters as well as their sons. I began studying the classics so early I can't remember my first lessons! We were trained to be hostesses and something of feminine diplomats. Even before marriage girls did not kotow to their parents when boys did. When a girl was married and came home to her family she took the most honoured seat—higher even than her parents! That's probably one of the reasons that it was possible for the Empress Dowager to hold supreme power for so long, even though custom and convention were strong enough to forbid her to sit on the Imperial Throne.

"But mind you, a Chinese woman had her own place and dignity when she was old and the mother of sons. When the Lao Tai-tai went out all the household—sons and daughters-in-law and relatives and servants assembled in the courtyard to see her go and rushed out to welcome her when she returned. In many ways, if she was a strong woman—and most Chinese women were!—she became a real matriarch. Lao Tai-tai means much more than its literal translation of 'Old Lady'. It was a term of honour that every woman hoped to hear addressed to her on her fortieth birthday! Dignity increased with age. I'm reaching the age where my birthday is really an important fête!"

It is time for me to go. I take the plunge. "Madame, I would very much like to include your story in my book about Chinese women."

"Mine?" she says with surprise. "But why mine when there are so many interesting women in China today?"

"Because you link the old China and the new as no one else does."

She looks at me quizzically.

The gate-keeper's face appears at the window and I hear him say my car has come. There is time only to fix a date for them to come and dine with me.

Putting a long beige padded silk robe over his indoor clothes, a fur cap on his grey head, the General escorts me through the courtyards where the snow is falling like a swarm of white moths in the dusk.

A few days later my phone rings and Madame's voice says, "If you're not too busy I would like to drop in and see you for a moment this afternoon—I shall be lunching near the hotel."

She comes, her eyes as brilliant as ever under the fur cap with the ear-flaps that can be lowered; she has the air of irrepressible gaiety I came to associate with her. When I tell her so she smiles.

"My father said to me not long before he died—that was in 1906 when the Emperor was still on the throne—'Roungling, my dear child'—we loved each other very much—'Roungling, great and terrible changes are coming to China. I'm not afraid for you. Your adaptability will help you to make the best of every world and your *joie de vivre* will last you through everything.' He was right. I have seen the fall of our dynasty, two revolutions, too many war-lords to mention, civil war, occupation and liberation!

"*Et me voilà!* I take the new life very easily and I'm awfully happy in a different way. Why should one cry and say it's not what one was used to? Nothing in life is what one was used to: one's face changes, one's body changes, one's mind changes. I'm happier today than I ever was working at the Court. Court etiquette was so strict you scarcely dared breathe. Everything is so much freer today."

She hands me a small sheet of paper with ten lines typed on it! "But I just dropped in to give you my biography since you are interested in it. I won't stay. Forgive my typing it," she adds, "but it's so much more legible than my writing. I'm translating my memoirs into English now and typing them myself. I'll do the French later."

I beg her to stay. I may never find her in such an expansive mood again. A woman who is capable of writing her memoirs (in three languages!) and yet can sum up a life like hers in one hundred words must be taken as the mood takes her.

She stays and begins taking off her various coats. She is the only person I know who can look elegant in spite of the padded jackets and heavy fur coats needed to combat the cold of Peking winter.

As finally revealed, in her brown trousers, her brown satin jacket with a pearl-and-diamond clip at the throat and ear-rings to match, a sleeveless over-jacket of brown wool, she is the picture of elegance. I repeat the word because it is a quality one meets so rarely anywhere.

I compliment her, sincerely.

"Ah! that reminds me of France! When we used to go shopping in the Galeries la Fayette, buying the most enchanting French clothes, people used to turn and look at me and say, '*Qu'elle est gentille cette petite chinoise!* ' "

She giggles at the sixty-year-old memory. "They never said it of my sister and she used to get awfully angry. Once she slapped my face! My sister was a strange girl. She married an American." She pauses. "She is dead now. . . . Today, I sometimes wonder. . . ."

"Did you go direct from China to Paris?" I ask, urging her gently as she shows signs of going off at a tangent.

"Oh, no, we had been in Japan for some years. My father went there as Ambassador after the Sino-Japanese War of 1894. He was one of the Liberals of that time who realized that unless the Dowager Empress agreed to reforms the dynasty was doomed. They were constitutional monarchists in a system of absolute monarchy. Before going to Japan he was Minister for Foreign Affairs. There were thirteen Ministers and he was so 'foreignized' that he had caught the Western superstition about thirteen and said nothing good could come of it, so decided to ask for another post.

"He was right, but I don't really think it had anything to do with number thirteen. News of the failure of the coup d'état in 1898, when the young Emperor Kuang Hsu tried to introduce reforms and failed, shook my father very much. Those of his friends who did not succeed in escaping into exile were arrested and executed." (History says by being cut in half at the waist!)

"I was too young to be interested in politics. I was studying Japanese and English—and dancing! Japanese dancing is fascinating. Only once did I touch the political world and then I didn't really understand what it was about.

"After Sun Yat-sen had led a rising that failed in Canton, protesting against the humiliations heaped on China, he fled to Japan. My father received orders from the Court to arrest him and send him back to China to be executed. What a position to be in! He thought Sun Yat-sen was a good man, a patriotic Chinese who wanted only the welfare of his country. And his duty was to have him killed! He decided to warn the young revolutionary. But how? He had only a vague idea where he was. He dared not trust anyone on his staff—they were all Manchus.

"So I was sent—I looked just like a little Japanese girl since I loved their clothes and I spoke Japanese—to see the house where he was supposed to be hiding. I couldn't go directly to it so I went to the one next door and asked if someone or other lived there. I knew they didn't! Of course they said no, so I said, 'Perhaps she lives next door. I shall go and see.' And the woman said, 'Don't go there. There's a young Chinese there, only just arrived, and they wouldn't like it!' I took the news back to my father and in some way or other Sun Yat-sen got a warning and left Japan!

"We went to Paris in 1899 and came back in 1903. There we studied French and English and dancing. But I told you about that. And, French cooking! My father was very progressive."

She is silent, lighting another cigarette.

"*Eh bien!*" she says at last. "My parents weren't at all pleased with me when I wanted to go on the stage. Indeed, progressive as they were, they were horrified and back to China we came. In winter! And my sister and I went directly to the Palace as ladies-in-waiting to the late Empress Dowager, T'zu Hsi. It was only a short time after what you call the Boxer Rising, after which Peking was looted by foreign troops.

"By now the Palace had been restored though many rare and lovely things taken to foreign museums were irreplaceable.

"After years abroad the Court dazzled us with its richness and splendour. It was a constant spectacle, far more wonderful than the most gorgeous theatrical show. From what I have seen and read of it, I think not even Versailles could ever have been so glorious. Versailles had not the colour, and even in museums I have never seen robes so rich.

"By then the Empress Dowager was in sole control, poor Kwang Hsu having been put under house-arrest in a pavilion in the Sea Palace. I can still see her being carried from her quarters in a golden chair under a golden canopy by sixteen eunuchs in richly embroidered robes. All the men wore queues in those days. It was the Manchus' style which they had imposed on the Chinese when they overthrew the Ming Dynasty. It was a sign of allegiance to the throne.

"There were about three thousand eunuchs—you could hear their high-pitched chatter everywhere—from 'little' eunuchs to the Chief Eunuch Li Lien-yang, who taught me everything I should know about court etiquette. There were rumours that he was not really a eunuch, but that's not true. There was no possibility of entering the Palace Service unless they were really eunuchs. The entrance examination was too strict. After nightfall no man but the Emperor could remain in the Palace.

"With my adaptability I didn't find the court life difficult, though the etiquette was so terribly strict. We dare not go out of the women's quarters. To go to the Emperor's Palace would have brought punishment undreamt of."

"Who were 'we'?" I ask.

"There was the Empress Dowager, the Young Empress, the Favourite, and five ladies—my sister, myself, and three others."

"By the 'favourite' do you mean the Chief Concubine?"

Madame corrects me. "She was called the Favourite. Actually she was a secondary wife. She was the sister of the Pearl Concubine. *She* was beautiful, they said. I never knew her. Kwang Hsu loved her very much, but her sister was fat and dull. I couldn't see how she could be anyone's favourite.

"There were rumours that the Dowager had the Pearl Concubine thrown down the well near the Tunghuamen when the Court was fleeing during the Boxer Revolt, but I don't believe it.

"The Favourite—like the Empress—was chosen from among girls of the high Manchu nobility. I could have been a Favourite." She chuckles. "I was always glad I wasn't. All the poor girls I saw had a terrible life. The first thing you knew about the honour thrust on you was when several eunuchs appeared with an

Imperial Decree on a slip of yellow paper and in a yellow silk envelope summoning you to Court.

"The Empress Dowager had been a Favourite when she first came to Court nearly fifty years before. My mother used to tell us how she was chosen. When after five years the Empress of Hsien Feng had not borne a son, nor had any of his concubines, the Emperor decided to take a secondary wife. The Imperial Command was sent out to seventeen noble Manchu maidens and they all went together in great splendour to the Palace for him to make his choice. He chose her—she was seventeen, very beautiful, and intelligent and accomplished as well.

"She bore him a son and when he died she became Regent to her infant son. He died of smallpox at eighteen and she chose her husband's nephew, Kwang Hsu, as Emperor.

"She was a great woman. She liked to be compared with the Empress Wu of the Tang Dynasty. She had been a concubine, and eventually she became the only woman in all Chinese history to occupy the Dragon Throne—something the Dowager dreamed of doing but never achieved. Don't let anyone tell you Chinese women were the spineless creatures Westerners like to believe.

"The Empress—and indeed any woman in those days—had to be very unselfish. It was the custom that the Favourite was installed in the Emperor's quarters the night before the Emperor's wedding."

She laughs. "I sometimes say to my husband now, 'I don't know why you didn't buy a concubine when I wanted you to—' we had no children—'then I would have someone to help me in the kitchen now.' 'Nonsense,' he says. 'You'd have three to cook for instead of two!' "

She pauses, sipping her tea. "If you could have seen the Palace in those days—the courtyards with the white marble bridges, the enormous gilded bowls, the great state-rooms with their lacquer-red pillars, the ceilings of green and gold and blue, the gardens beautiful beyond words. The aroma of the best food in China rising from the kitchens! All of it living, not a museum as it is today, with an endless procession of eunuchs and serving-maids, dressmakers and artisans and gardeners, ladies-in-waiting, court ladies.

"When there was a banquet the thousands of flickering candles cast a strange light over it all and the lamps picked up the glitter of gold and silver and the flashing of jewels. Such jewels the Dowager had! I remember particularly—it was the most magnificent and costly thing I ever saw—a cape made of more than three thousand pearls, all perfectly matched and each the size of a canary's egg! It was linked with two pure jade clasps. Her head-dresses and shoes were encrusted with jewels and she wore gold and jade finger-nail protectors. It was said that there was no collection of jewels in the world to equal hers. There were three thousand boxes of jewels in one room for everyday wear and many others in a safety room for special occasions. Her favourite of these was a pearl nearly as large as a hen's egg.

"Best of all I loved the Summer Palace. It was so much freer there. The pavilion where I lived was on the edge of the lake—it is a tea-house now. My father said it was only a shadow of the Palace that the foreign troops had burned in 1860 at the end of the Second Opium War. That was the eighth wonder of the world."

"What did you do with your days?" I asked, trying to bring some touch of reality to this vanished world where incredible beauty and culture went side by side with chopping liberal-minded Ministers in half at the waist, and dropping unwanted concubines down wells.

"We got up at five o'clock. At six o'clock sharp we were all ready lined up in the antechamber to the Dowager's bedroom: the Young Empress, the Favourite, the ladies-in-waiting—seven of us altogether. The princesses outside came only on fête days. We helped the Empress to dress. She had thousands of beautifully embroidered robes.

"At eight o'clock the Dowager appeared in the Audience Chamber and we made our kotow—on our knees, touching the floor with our foreheads. Then she sat on her throne and the First Eunuch would appear with a box of documents. I would kneel and he, also on his knees, would hand each document to me. I would hand it to the Dowager and she would read it, and remember it. She had an amazing memory! When she had finished it, she would hand it to the Emperor, who would hand it back to me when he had read it, and I would hand it to the Chief Eunuch.

"In the afternoons there would be plays and operas. The Dowager loved music. All the parts were played by eunuchs—'home-actors' as they were called. Some of them were very good. Any who showed a capacity for music were specially taught. The Dowager encouraged them.

"Then there would be public receptions. After the Boxer Rising the Dowager was more inclined to receive foreigners. Those receptions were *awful*. Some of the foreign ladies behaved as they would never have dared behave in their own countries. Not all of them, of course. There were *real* ladies among them. Some behaved as if they were at a circus.

"I suppose it sounds a strange world to you, but I took it very much for granted and the Dowager was always so kind to me, though I was very young and did many things not strictly according to her rigid ideas of court etiquette, I'm afraid.

"In the Palace we were not permitted to laugh aloud, but at the Summer Palace rules were slightly relaxed. One day we were sitting in the garden outside the Dowager's room and I laughed outright. The Dowager called, 'Who is that laughing?' A lady-in-waiting who didn't like me rushed in and said, 'It was Princess Roungling.' And the Dowager, instead of scolding me, said, 'Let the child have her fun.'

"There were always quarrels among the eunuchs. One day at dinner one threw a rice-bowl at the other and cut his head! Eunuchs are strange people—bad-tempered and vindictive. Yet, funnily enough, all of them seemed to love their mothers, and it was strange and rather horrible that many of them had sweethearts among the maids and later, often they left the Court and married them. They bought children and so had sons to perform the sacrifices for them. The maids evidently thought the comfort and luxury eunuchs could give them out of the wealth they amassed at Court compensated! Eunuchs had many opportunities for bribery from people who wanted to obtain favours from the Court."

She lights another cigarette and sits gazing at the smoke, seeing I know not what vanished splendours in a world that seems as fabulous to me as the Arabian Nights.

"We were at the Palace two years," she says at last. "We left because my father was dying. Mourning was very strict. At the end of a year the Dowager asked me to come back, but I couldn't bear the thought of palace life with my heart still grieving for my father. So I never saw her again. But I shall always remember her. She was a remarkable woman, as everybody knows—probably no woman has ever had so many books written about her, the majority of them by people who never even saw her!"

"Is it true, as they say, that she had the Emperor Kuang Hsu poisoned before she died?" I ask cautiously.

"No. Certainly not." She looks forbidding, so I drop the subject. (Historians are less kind to the Old Buddha, whom they accuse of having had her nephew murdered when she felt her own death approaching.)

"She was not only a great woman," she says, still looking away into the past, "she was like a mother to me and I loved her."

On one of those days of blue sky, brilliant sunshine, and intense cold, typical of Peking's winter, I see from my window Madame descending from a pedi-cab, pausing to chat a moment with the driver, then, straight-backed, slender even in her brown fur coat, mounting the steps with her indescribable grace. She is overflowing with life, as ever.

"My husband is late," she apologizes. "There's always such a crowd on Sundays and he could not get a pedi-cab. I always have the same man. I am adaptable to any changes, but one thing I cannot do and that is go out on the street and hail a pedi-cab! He lives near us—such a nice man. He's like one of the family. I'm very democratic and do like to hear about people's lives."

She touches her cheeks with powder and renews her lip-stick.

"One thing I cannot get," she says, examining her hair critically in the mirror, "is a really good hair-set."

The General arrives, red of face and panting, having had to walk the mile to my hotel.

I have told the head-waiter I have special guests for lunch and he has added some "frills" to my table, as he always does on such occasions. But I'm not prepared for his excitement when we arrive.

Madame and the General and he greet each other like old friends. Rapid Chinese flows over my head. I am forgotten. They are back in a world to which I have no key.

At last the head-waiter turns to me. "I knew Madame and the Master many years ago and used to wait on them at official functions. Oh, twenty, thirty years ago." He looks at her critically and says with the engaging Chinese frankness about age, so devastating to the Westerner, "You must be very old now. You must be eighty."

"I am not," says Madame indignantly, more Western than Chinese at this unwanted honour. "I am seventy-four."

"Madame was a great lady in those days," he begins. "But what you want to eat? I remember you like . . . "

The head-waiter hovers round our table. He and the General have a long and animated discussion in which I have no share and which ends in a burst of laughter.

"They tell you about what they do when the Japanese come?"

I shake my head.

"You make them," he says, confident in my ability to extract anyone's life story. By then, between my practising Chinese and their practising English, I knew the story of every service boy and girl who came to my table!

"Don't worry," the Princess says, smiling, "she will!"

But it wasn't as easy as that. Today she was interested only in Today.

Eventually, back in my room, she yielded gracefully. "After the fall of the Manchu Dynasty in 1911 I married my husband and I wanted to live a domestic life and not be anything official any more. But the second President asked me to be Mistress of Ceremonies and I held that position till 1927, when Chiang Kai-shek moved the Government to Nanking. They wanted me to go, but I said, 'No, I have my home in Peking.' Wasn't I lucky I didn't?" She and the General exchange smiles.

"Being Mistress of Ceremonies wasn't easy with changing warlords, increasing Japanese pressure, and widening contacts with the West. The President and the President's lady had more and more to conform to Western ideas of etiquette—not easy for women trained in the seclusion of Chinese homes, for whom the social intercourse you take for granted was painful in the extreme.

"I shall never forget the first time the American Ambassador's wife invited some of the Manchu princesses to visit her! You see, though China was a republic the Emperor still lived in the Imperial City. He had no power and the Court was a shadow, but I find that people who talk a lot about democracy always adore to meet princesses!"

"What happened to the Manchu nobility?" I inquired.

"They did pretty well," the General replied, with an amused glance at his wife, "The Chinese have a way of dealing kindly with deposed dynasties, so the Manchus kept their personal property and the princes and dukes who had squandered their wealth were provided with enough to live on. They were exempt from military service, but since I am Chinese, not Manchu, I was made a general, though I had served in the Imperial Guards."

"They were exciting days, but terrible," said Madame. "We knew every move behind the scenes.

"From 1936 to 1937 I was social secretary to General Sung Chi-yuan who at that time was Chairman of the Political Council and in charge of Peking. It was so humiliating to see your country bowed in the dust on all sides that we decided that we would leave it and go to live in France. I was invited to go to dance at the Exhibition in Paris. During all these years I had never given up my dancing. When Douglas Fairbanks visited China he asked me to go to Hollywood."

"But," the General adds, "in July 1937 the Japanese took Peking."

They are both silent. At last she looks back at me and says, lifting her shoulders in a gesture too slight to be a shrug. "So we stayed. During the eight years of the Japanese Occupation we were so poor we had practically nothing to eat. We ate coarse grains. Once I succeeded in buying a bag of rice, but I made my husband eat it. 'I am a Northerner,' I said. 'I don't like rice.'

"We could have been well off. The Japanese tried to get my husband to work for them. He was frantic and said he would kill himself first. So I said, 'Pretend to be *dérangé*!' " She looks at him and laughs gently. "Poor man, he is no actor, but for eight years he pretended to be—how do you say it?—off his head. He played the part very well."

The General looks sheepish at this tribute to his histrionic abilities.

"I remember once I was at one of the embassies at a dinner and a high-ranking Japanese officer kept flattering me and talking about Japan till at last I said, 'When are you going back to Japan?'

" 'Madame,' he said bowing and smiling, 'I love China so much that I am going to stay here for ever.'

" 'How strange!' I said. 'That's how I feel about Japan! One day I will go there and stay there for ever.'

"My friends of the embassy were quite pale and my hostess pretended to call me away for something. 'Please be careful,' she begged me. '*C'est dangereux!*' "

"Was every one in Peking so badly off?" I inquired.

Madame's face hardens. Her eyes glitter.

"Anyone who was well off in Peking during the Occupation was a traitor. All the traitors' wives made a monopoly of something: for one it was vaseline, for another something else. When they played mah-jongg at parties their hand-bags were full of money. Dirty money!" Her mouth curls in inexpressible scorn.

"I wrote a book about the traitors in Peking, but when the Japanese were defeated and the Kuomintang returned they behaved so badly that I destroyed most of it, terrified at what the traitors would do to me if they found out.

"You must meet our friend Prince Tsai Tao. He would tell you some stories about those days. He is a member of the National Congress now, a close friend of Chairman Mao Tse-tung.

"You cannot wonder that we welcomed the new Government. China is so much improved since the Liberation. The poor people so much better off, and everyone so much happier. There is a kindliness there never was before. It warmed my heart when I was in a shop yesterday to see a notice: 'Don't get bored when people ask you questions.' And they don't. Not even with an old lady like me!

"To see the clean streets—they used to be so filthy. No more beggars—the city swarmed with them. All the new buildings going up. It makes me happy to see my country stand up at last. My dream! My father's dream!"

CONCUBINES OF YESTERDAY

Spring Festival and spring
is truly in the air; by the winding stream
the lovely ladies walk, looking
proudly ahead, then exchanging
sweet and charming smiles with
each other; faces so beautiful,
perfect figures showing through silk
draperies embroidered with
golden peacocks or silver unicorns;
their heads dressed in kingfisher
colours, with hanging pendants of
cut jade; on their backs little
over-garments studded with pearls;
amongst the galaxy the sisters
of Yang Kwei Fei, bearing great titles;
dishes served include the purple meat
of camel's hump, white slices of raw
fish on crystal plates; yet these
hardly satisfy jaded tastes; all that
has taken so much thought and work
to prepare, left, hardly touched;
palace servants ride carefully bringing
new dishes from the Imperial kitchens;
the orchestra gives such music that
even the hearts of devils are moved.

—TU FU (Tang Dynasty).
Translated by REWI ALLEY.

CHAPTER IV

The Big Family

SUNDAY morning in Peking. I drive through busy streets, with long queues at the bus stops waiting to go to distant beauty spots and crowds pouring into parks, fathers carrying babies and holding toddlers by the hand.

The first autumn winds are blowing out of Mongolia and the toddlers wear ankle-length, bell-shaped, cotton-padded capes with hoods, mainly in scarlet with attractive floral designs on them. Babes in arms are still more glorious. The little faces peer out from satin hoods edged with white fur and their satin padded capes glow with all the richest shades of crimson and petunia and rose and a strange almost indescribable colour that looks like a ripe persimmon.

Adults, on the other hand, are for the most part more soberly clad than I have seen them for months. They are wearing cotton-padded coats, almost uniformly blue for the young people and black for the old.

We turn off the busy main street, down a quiet hutung. The graceful curved ridge-poles of the houses show between the drooping dusty gold of the acacia-trees. Each house a world in itself. A world from which, in the old days, the women rarely emerged.

The car stops.

The gateway to the Ma household is imposing with its curved eaves and a brass-studded doorway. Two men come down the steps to greet me, both wearing navy gaberdine suits with the tunic-type coat buttoned to the neck that is almost a uniform in China, with a ten-year-old boy wearing the scarlet Pioneer scarf and a smiling young girl in her teens. They are Ma Senior, a well-preserved man in his sixties, his son, tall and handsome, whom I take to be in his thirties, his daughter and his grandson.

Theirs is a typical old Peking house with connecting court-yards, "designed to accommodate the expanding family and achieve the Confucian ideal of five generations in one house", Mr Ma explains.

"My family has lived here for a hundred years," he adds as we go through the entrance courtyard, which, in the old days, was reserved for the gate-keeper and servants of the family, but today, under the pressure of a severe housing problem, has been let to outsiders. Through a moon-gate we pass into a second court filled with flowers and covered with trellised vines whose leaves are now bronze and gold.

Grey single-storeyed buildings surround the courtyard, their curved grey tiles in corrugated rows coming down to low eaves that shade the rooms from the blazing sun in summer when the courtyards are covered with woven grass matting for coolness. With their windows and doors all opening on the courts, there could have been no privacy in these old Chinese houses. When I comment on this Mr Ma smiles. "Chinese do not value privacy as you do in the West. It was not the personal life that counted, but the family."

On the south side of the third courtyard I am ushered into what we would call the reception room—a pleasant room, with long, low windows, their middle panes glass and the side ones intricate open woodwork that in summer is left uncovered and in winter covered with fine rice-paper. Its wide, half-glassed doors open on the courtyard where tawny chrysanthemums in pots are beginning to unfold. The sun shines in on the flagged floor, smooth with much wear and polishing. The inner walls of the room are finely carved woodwork with pictured panels. On the wide window-sill beside me is a tiny landscape garden in a celadon bowl.

Everything bespeaks taste. Nothing is ostentatious. The furniture is the deep-red wood for which there is no parallel in the Western world, glossy with generations of polishing. Finely lettered scrolls hang on the walls. Delicate carved lamps swing from the ceiling, exquisite bowls and vases and small carved statues are on side stands and shelves beside splendid lacquered chests, large and small, with brass locks and bindings; on the table translucent jade screens about nine inches high are set on carved wooden stands.

The daughter disappears through a doorway covered by a fine bamboo curtain, and reappears leading a little white-haired old lady in black trousers and tunic. She is Mr Ma's eighty-six-year-old mother and I am presented to her as to a queen.

She takes my hand in her two withered ones, soft as old silk. Then she points to her ear and I understand that she is hard of hearing. She waves me to a large chair and her granddaughter and grandson help her to a similar one on the other side of the solid carved table, where she sits enthroned.

Seeing her with her family round her deferring to her every

gesture, for the first time I realize in all its fullness the role of the Lao Tai-tai in a Chinese family. Here is the First Wife and Illustrious Mother of the Family, whom custom decreed should receive high honours from husband, sons, and all female members of the family, whether secondary wives or the daughters of sons. She might be displaced in her husband's heart but not in her family role. For she alone could wear the red skirt of the First Wife, she was the official mother of all sons born to her husband. Upon her fell the responsibility for strict observance of family etiquette—a responsibility so grave that in ancient days a woman might be condemned to death, with or without torture, for some violation of the usages.

She turns towards me, silver pins glinting in her hair, peering at me out of cloudy eyes. The fine wrinkles deepen as she smiles. Most Chinese women, it seems, remain unwrinkled till their sixties and then wither like a rose-leaf. She says something in a soft, whispering voice, her grandson bending close to listen. He explains with slight embarrassment that she is saying that this is the first time a foreigner has been in their house, if you don't count the time it was looted by foreign troops in the Boxer Rising and the family was thrown out into the street! She was expecting a baby at the time.

As though sensing that what she has said was not the polite thing, Grandma leans across the table and puts her hand on mine. We are at ease again.

"In a way, our family covers all the changes in the last hundred years of Chinese history," Mr Ma goes on. "My mother came from Nanking and her father often talked about the days of the Taiping Rebellion and told her about the Government that the rebels set up there. My father used to tell how after the Second Opium War for a month the western sky was full of smoke from the burning Summer Palace. And I remember well the establishment of the First Republic in 1911."

Jasmine tea is served in tiny fragile bowls set in black-lacquer boat-shaped saucers, with one end higher than the other. Through the doorway into an inner room I can see an old-fashioned *kang* —the brick platform of North China, sometimes covered with wood, with a hole in the centre front in which a fire is placed to heat the brick in winter time. During the day a low-legged table is placed on it, so that it is bed, settee, and heating unit all in one. Even the Imperial Palace had its kangs.

As a guest privileged to ask questions, I ask how, in addition, they heat the home in winter, and they show me a small coal-burning stove, explaining that in addition everyone puts on extra clothes. Grandma, for instance, during the Big Cold sometimes wears two or three fur-lined robes, which were the usual wear in the old days, and the others have padded jackets and trousers with long knitted underwear, and everyone wears padded shoes.

By now the room is crowded with representatives of all four generations, sons and grandsons and their wives, great-grand-children, cousins and their wives and children. Mr Ma Senior apologizes because it has not been possible to get all the family together since some are working and others had important engage-ments they could not break.

On Sunday everyone who is free comes home to see Grandma and at the Moon Festival and the New Year everybody turns up.

I am bewildered by the introductions, and ask how many there are in the family.

"Thirty-five," says Mr Ma. " 'The family' in China has a sense much wider than yours. By 'members of the family' is understood the parents, the sons, then the grandparents, great-uncles, and cousins. Daughters were not included in the old days. We count as our family all the living members of all generations. Actually, my mother had three sons and one daughter. In the old days, of course, we should all have lived together still. The system of *all* members of the family living together was made a law in the tenth century by the first Sung Emperor and this law was in force till Liberation, though, of course, not always enforced. When my brothers and I were married—and we are now in our sixties—all the daughters-in-law came to live in the house. Today it is reversed. My younger daughter is married and she and her husband live here."

She is pointed out to me—the laughing, bright-eyed girl who greeted me and whom at first glance I took to be a schoolgirl!

"Daughters were not considered part of the family in the old days," he goes on. "They belonged to their future husband's family. Because of this they were less valued than sons, but not, I think, less loved.

"The basic cause of the position of Chinese women through the ages lay in the fact that only a man could perform the rites of the Ancestral Cult. The West has throughout history shown this preference for sons, but it was based on more materialist con-cepts—such as property inheritance—than ours.

"Our Ancestral Cult was based in the belief in the Yin or Shadow World, where ghosts have the same needs as in the Yang or Light World. The woman represented Yin, the man Yang. They are complementary. Yang expresses all that is powerful, active, bright; Yin all that is weak, passive, dark. It was on this that Confucius based his concept of the role of woman—a concept and a role inherent in all the religions of two thousand years ago.

"The Sacred Commands of the Emperor K'anghsi, which contain the quintessence of Confucianism, said that according to Chinese moralists a wife must always come after his parents and brothers in a husband's estimation. There was an old saying: 'A wife is like your clothes but brothers are like your hands and feet.'

"In the old days, among the upper classes, a man referred to his wife as *nei-jen* (the person inside) ; she referred to him as *wai-tse* (the man outside). The common people usually spoke of 'Little Mao's Pa' or 'Ma', Little Mao usually being a boy. Since Liberation *ai-jen* (the beloved person) is used for both husband and wife. Formerly the wife was responsible for the running of the household but knew nothing of 'outside' affairs. On matters so close to her as the marriage of her son or daughter she was frequently not even consulted.

"The head of the family was responsible for all the expenses of the whole household, which encouraged idleness on the part of those so inclined, and was a great source of discord in some families, though we had no difficulties. Now things are different. Only eleven members of the family live here. Some of the others have gone to other cities and more and more the young people are tending to live in the apartments in the building provided by the establishments in which they work, like my son here."

Ma Junior apologizes for his wife's absence. She is working today and very much regrets that she cannot be here to meet me. A number of other members of the family have also sent their apologies. I can't really regret it for I don't know how I'm ever going to sort out the group sitting round the room, though if I'm ever to understand the working of a traditional Chinese household I must endeavour to do so.

Mr Ma Senior guides me through the ramification of the family, saying as he does so, "The importance of order of seniority in a Chinese family must be stressed. Members took precedence by age, the younger owing almost unquestioning obedience to the elder. The father's power was absolute, filial piety the law. Respect for age kept the family together."

"It was sometimes a tyranny," Ma Junior adds and Ma Senior nods.

"There were different terms for certain relatives, according to whether they were older or younger than you."

He begins to present the gathering to me.

I find that these are Elder Brothers, Younger Brothers, Elder Sisters, Younger Sisters, Cousin-sisters. "Sister" seems to cover an infinite variety of relationships, while "Younger Brother" apparently applies to anything up to eighth cousin! The daughter of Grandma's cousin and her husband live here. Also their daughter, Yen-li, who makes a brilliant spot in her red woollen overalls, two long plaits tied with red ribbon. And the eldest great-grandson in the Pioneer scarf who at the moment is busily occupied preventing the toddler, his younger brother, from hurting the cat and the cat from hurting him. Then there is the daughter of Ma Senior's third brother, who is in the North-east, and her husband and small daughter. There is a constant flow of children I never sort out.

At this stage I am foolish enough to ask the toddler's name as, tiring of the cat, he comes to inspect me.

Mr Ma smiles. "His name now is Little Peace. That is what we call his milk-name, and is used only by his parents and elder brother. To others he will be Second Brother. When he goes to school he will be given his book or student name. At fifteen or sixteen he will be given his official or distinctive name."

I decide that, for the sake of my whirling brain, I can skip names, so I ask how old Little Yen-li is. "Eight," I am told. "In your country that would be seven. In China a child is considered to be a year old at birth! New Year was everyone's legal birthday, so if a child was born a short time before New Year he would be reckoned as two years old on that day!"

Little Peace clamours to be lifted up, calling, "Pa-pa, Pa-pa!" As his father takes him on his knee he says, "Ma-ma?" and shakes his head. There is something deeply moving in this language so strange to me to hear a child using the words a child uses the world over.

Ma Senior goes on explaining the family to me.

"My father was an office employee under the Manchu Government. He brought my mother who came here when she was married."

"A traditional marriage?" I interrupt, unnecessarily, but I want to hear what Grandma has to say.

Her grandson, who is sitting beside her tenderly anticipating her needs, shouts the question to her. She nods, her face lighting.

"Weddings were really exciting then," she says, with animation. "My family were advanced and did not bind my feet, but they believed in choosing the husband for their children. I never saw my husband till I stepped into this house. Of course I accepted this. Indeed, there was no thought in most minds that it would ever change. We chose my son's wife for him in his turn."

I then discover that the quiet older woman who has not spoken a word, but sits withdrawn in the background, knitting, is the wife of Mr Ma Senior, prototype of the older Chinese woman who officially had no rights but only obediences and still bears the marks of her training on her.

I look from her to her laughing daughter; physically they are alike but there it ends. The daughter, with a laughing, candid face, swinging bobbed hair, graceful athletic stride in skirt and bright sweater; the mother, moving with a restrained gait in cotton-soled shoes, a knee-length dark-blue three-quarter knitted jacket above dark-blue cotton trousers, and with the firm grave mouth, the withdrawn expression, the high forehead rising to a hair-line deliberately squared an inch above the normal hair-line. (In the olden days a high forehead was considered not only beautiful but lucky, and on marriage a woman plucked out the hairs so that the hair-line was the equivalent of a wedding-ring in the West.)

Grandma smiles in the direction of her daughter-in-law, who is bent over her knitting.

"And a very good daughter-in-law she has been. She never disobeyed me, never quarrelled with her brother-in-law's wives. No one could have chosen better. Even today she is responsible for all the shopping and cooking for this big house."

A faint smile touches Mrs Ma Senior's face.

"Now things are different," I detect a note of regret in Grandma's voice.

Grandson laughs. "Yes. I was just in time to make my own choice. My wife and I both work."

Grandma pats the toddler's head as he leans against her.

"The happiest thing in my life was in counting my big family, and although I have moved with the times and have given up all my old ideas, and agree with girls choosing their own husbands, I regret the fact that they now no longer all live under the same roof. Think how nice it would be to have all my sons' children and their children's children round me all the time."

"How many children have you?" I ask Mrs Ma Senior, hoping to bring her into the conversation. She gives me a faint, warm smile and looks at her husband, obviously expecting him to reply.

"Seven," he says, "five sons and two daughters."

My head reels at the thought of adding them to the problems of identification.

"My sister lectures at Peking University and one of my brothers is associate professor in the Institute of National Minorities. My mother was very sad when my brothers and their families had to leave home on account of their jobs."

I ask how Grandma has liked the changes in the lives of women. Her grandson replies to my question.

"She was more sympathetic than most old ladies." He presses her hand affectionately. "In this district the problems raised by the New Marriage Law took a lot of solving. The women were mainly middle-class women who, although they were very backward socially and educationally, had not suffered the hardships of poor women in the towns or villages. But she has welcomed all the changes—except when she thinks it is breaking up the family, but, as you can see, we are a long way from Western attitudes in that."

"Could your grandmother read and write?" I ask, wondering whether in this family of progressives the women were advanced.

"Grandma was illiterate and still is. Confucius said that ignorance is a virtue in women. She was too old to begin learning, but since Liberation one of her grandsons has taught my mother to read and write. We are very proud of her. She is a good student."

His mother's pale face colours slightly at the praise and she looks across at him with eyes that smile.

"The younger women, of course, are educated. They are all working, though it wasn't until after Liberation that my wife learnt to read and write. And she still continues her studies at spare-time school at night. That is why our children go to boarding-school during the week. Grandmother didn't like the idea at first, but now she sees how happy the children are and the progress they are making, she has come to the conclusion that it is probably better than the old days when they just stayed round the house learning nothing."

"Would you like to see the rest of the house?" Ma Senior asks. I assure him I would and we go out into the sunny courtyard with the clan following, Grandma alone remaining enthroned.

We go through the court, the rooms of the various members being pointed out in passing, into the centre court, where Ma Senior and his wife live in the south wing. It is the same type of long narrow room with carved wood partitions that divide bedroom and reception room that is also a study, judging by the number of books that overflow the shelves. On the wall are innumerable photographs and snapshots and I am taken through the whole pictured clan from Grandfather in his long, fur-lined Manchu robe and domed satin cap through Ma Senior's sons in army uniform, his daughter who is studying at Moscow University, down to a delightful poster for which ten-year-old great-grandson served as model several years ago.

I say I would like to see the kitchen.

Mrs Ma Senior is too polite to refuse, but I detect the reluctance that any housewife would feel about taking a stranger into a kitchen when Sunday dinner for a clan is in preparation. The kitchen is in the opposite corner of the courtyard—a small room where two small cylindrical stoves provide the cooking equipment. From our point of view there are no conveniences, and I marvel once again how Chinese women manage to turn out such varied and delicious meals with such meagre equipment.

Small narrow tables take up two sides of the walls, several of them equipped with chopping boards, for the great art of Chinese food is in the preparation. Generally everything—meat, chicken, fish, vegetables—is chopped to varying degrees of fineness before cooking. Mr Ma lifts the lid of a wide deep pan that stands on one of the stoves. It is filled with steaming rice. He lifts the lid of another. A rich dark sauce sends out a tantalizing smell, in which I detect ginger and garlic. Under covers on the table are the chopped vegetables and meat ready for last-minute cooking. Mrs Ma is obviously as competent as she looks.

Back in the courtyard, Ma Senior sums up the family.

"Our family is just an ordinary family. We were never really rich nor really poor. My father never owned anything beyond this house and what is in it. He would have said he was non-political, but during the Japanese Occupation we were so badly off that we had to let the front courtyard, and when he found later that he really let it to the headquarters of the underground Resistance he was very frightened, but because he was a patriotic Chinese he did all he could to cover up their activities. When the Japanese were defeated in 1945 the underground workers had trouble with the Kuomintang and moved away, and although the K.M.T. suspected that my father knew about it they decided to do nothing, since he was an old man, very highly respected, and had actually never been active in politics."

"Our family history can really be divided into two, like that of all the rest of China," Ma Junior adds, "before Liberation and after. Even though my father's life and my grandfather's had been very comfortable, we were really poorly off when I was a boy. Once the Japanese invaded the country there was no security

for us. Living itself was difficult. There did not seem to be any
future. Food was extremely difficult to get and what there was
was inferior. My mother had to stand in queues for hours, which
she felt bitterly because up till then she had rarely put her foot
outside the house. It was during those years that my brothers and
I learnt our nationalism. We began to realize that there could
be no freedom for China and no happiness for any one of us till
all the aggressors were driven out and we ruled ourselves.

"Then, when the Japanese were driven out, the corruption of
the Kuomintang and the inflation again made it difficult to live
because money lost its value progressively. I can remember that,
when the question of buying a new suit came up, it was discussed
for weeks on end."

Smallest great-grandson has wearied of chasing the cat and
staggers back to grip his father's legs, crying, "Papa!"

Ma Junior stoops and picks him up. Elder great-grandson
stands gazing up at his father with bright, proud eyes.

"Now, how different it all is!" He puts a hand on his son's head.
"Now we can do the work we like doing. Wages are steady. We
can eat well. Our children can go to school. We have enough
money for pleasure. But above all we have the knowledge that
at last it is our China."

It is twelve o'clock. Remembering the pan of steaming rice
and knowing that Chinese families dine at midday, I decided,
reluctantly, that I must go.

Back to the reception room to say my farewells to Grandma,
who rises from her chair with the help of her son and grandson.
She takes my hand in her two soft, wrinkled ones, gazes at me with
her cloudy eyes and says in English, to everyone's astonishment,
"Good-bye"—out of the recesses of some ancient memory to which
no one has the clue.

Postscript. My friend with whom I lunched—an American woman
married to a Chinese—laughed when I told her of my confusion
at the Chinese family relationships.

"You should meet my friend Lucy," she said. "She belonged to
the family of a Manchu official who had several secondary wives
and several concubines. The difference was that the latter were
bought, not married, but they all seem to have been treated alike
as far as I can see.

"My friend was the daughter of the youngest concubine. She
never had any name except 'Little Slave' till I called her Lucy.

In that family, you would have had to distinguish between the Principal Wife, the Second and Third Wives, and the First and Second Concubines."

I remark that I'm glad I didn't try to investigate Chinese home life in the old days.

"Don't worry," she says. "You'd never have got your nose inside the door! But if by any miracle you had, you'd have gone crazy in that kind of household where, in addition to all Papa's harem, there were several married sons who also owned concubines. This wasn't exceptional and it was very complicated. For instance, the third concubine of the fourth son would be called . . ."

But I refuse to listen.

Oh, blessed Confucian ideal! Four generations under one roof in *harmony*!

BITTER FATE

Most bitter thing it is
to be born a woman; pushed so low
we cannot speak; a child
who is a boy, commands all
from the time he is born
      but should the baby be
just a daughter, no notice
is taken of her; growing up with but
little love spared for her; when grown,
imprisoned in the depths of the house,
ever taught to hide her face
from people: then married off
and leaving her home for a strange one
not knowing a single person in it,
                    ever
lowering her head, watching
the faces of others to see how
to act; young and pretty still,
always bowing and kneeling,
looking at the master's concubines
as honoured guests; should she
be lucky enough to be loved
by her husband, they may be as happy
as spring flowers getting rain
from heaven; but should the two

not care for each other, then are they
as fire and water; all kinds of evil
attributed to her. Then with age
her beauty goes; and her husband
seeks newer, prettier faces. . . .

     —FU HSIEN (Third Century).
     Translated by REWI ALLEY.

CHAPTER V

A Model Wife for a Model Worker

Lou Yu-ling greets me at the entrance porch to the courtyard of the old Peking house where he and his wife live. He ushers me in, speaking rapidly all the time, giving me no time to examine a notice on the wall of the porch about which he seems slightly embarrassed. A dominant young man, I decide.

Before I've crossed the courtyard on which their room opens I learn that he is a mechanic in Peking Number One Motor Lorry Repair Workshop, has been decorated as a model worker, and earns 84 yuan a month.

His wife Lei Su-chin is waiting for me at the door of their flatlet. Bright-faced, short, two small plaits tied with red ribbon, she has made no effort to beautify herself and wears a faded blue tunic and trousers, while her husband's blue pants are spanking new and he has a smart high-necked fawn pull-over. But the room, I feel, has been polished until everything shines for my reception.

I pass the little recess in which the cylindrical cooking stove is burning with all the neat cooking utensils ranged in a cupboard beside it and covered with a curtain. Lei Su-chin should be classed as a model housewife, since she has made their one room attractive with every inch of space used to advantage. The walls are freshly whitewashed, and many pictures of Peking Opera decorate the walls. The flagged floor shines. The bed has a pleasant floral cover over it and there is a pile of newly made padded quilts against the wall. I sit on the bed which serves also for a settee, beside a little lacquered table about six inches high with tea-cups set out and cigarettes.

The long window overlooks the courtyard where the morning sunshine lights up tall red dahlias. Obviously, like so many homes in Peking, this has once been a single family house and across the court is a wide arched doorway leading to a spacious room now occupied by another family. Above the doorway are four characters moulded on hexagonal plaques that read: Happiness, Good Luck, Tranquillity, Beauty.

On a side cupboard are two of the most beautiful bouquets of porcelain flowers that I have ever seen, carefully protected by glass covers, a large elaborate clock also in a glass case, and a three-foot-tall vase of fine shape and design. Seeing my admiration, Lou Yu-ling explains that both he and his wife belonged to merchant families and although they were hopelessly impoverished by the time Liberation came there were still a few beautiful things left in the family. By the way they sparkle I can see that Lei Su-chin treasures them.

On the table is a modern radio (radios here are dearer than in the West).

Yu-ling has taken charge of the conversation and tells me that he was born in Tientsin and when his father died during the early days of the Japanese Occupation he had to go to work in a factory at the age of eight (he is now twenty-eight) to help his mother. He opens the packet of cigarettes and offers them to me. In the meantime his wife serves me with tea—very good tea. The teapot is an unusual shape with a pleasing design: another family heirloom.

She stands beside me to see I lack for nothing, and at last I beg her to sit down.

She sits reluctantly, looking adoringly and a little anxiously at her husband. It is easy to see that though she is only twenty-eight she is something of the traditional Chinese housewife and, New Marriage Law or not, this is something of the traditional household not limited only to China.

She is shy, though her small slit eyes radiate her pleasure at my presence. It is with difficulty I can persuade her to speak.

Her story? "I have no story to tell you," she says, surprised that I should want to know about her as well as her wonderful husband. "I'm just a housewife. When I was a girl I didn't go to school. I just helped to look after the house."

She stops. I persist. "Go on!"

"I was married in 1949 and since then I've looked after my husband and my little boy."

She drops her eyes and a faint flush stains her sallow face.

Her husband hastens to tell me that their second child died and her health has not been very good since then.

I acknowledge the interruption and turn again to her, feeling that this is a chance to find out something of the problem of women with babies.

"I went to the maternity hospital to have both my babies and I was there ten days the first time and twenty days the second, because the second time was bad."

I ask what it costs to go to hospital.

Her husband breaks in. "I get free medical service as a worker and I pay half the usual fees for her. It cost about forty yuan the last time."

I ask where the little boy is.

"He's living with his grandma," he replies. "You see, the housing isn't very good yet and we're very crowded here. We'll have him with us when my factory builds blocks of flats for the workers."

He is rather impatient, I feel, as though he thinks that things are not going fast enough. I suppress a smile when I think of the number of workers who have told me how, in the past, they lived seven and eight in a room no bigger than this.

Mrs Lou is never still. (It is incorrect for me to call her Mrs Lou, but here it is simpler. By the Constitution a Chinese woman retains her own name and the children take the name of either the mother or the father; generally the girls take the mother's name and the boys the father's.) She goes backwards and forwards to the stove where she keeps a long narrow saucepan at boiling point to supply me with endless cups of fresh tea. She is diffident yet welcoming.

A book is open on the table—an exercise book, and I ask, "Are you studying?"

Her husband answers for her. "She's learnt to read a little since Liberation, but she can't write. Of course I learnt to read and write before the Liberation, because my father had a tutor for me when I was very young and even when I was working in the factory my mother had a little bit of property that was sufficient to pay for lessons for me."

I think of widowed mothers I have known in the West who gave everything for their sons, content to adore them. I think of women I know, too, who are content to adore their husbands. Mr Lou, I think, has been accustomed all his life to be adored by his women-folk and takes it rather for granted.

"What do you do with your day?" I ask Mrs Lou.

She looks at her husband, and he nods.

"I get up at six o'clock and after I've washed and dressed I get breakfast for my husband."

"What does he have?"

"Eggs and also bean milk. Then I prepare his lunch."

"And what does his lunch consist of?"

Mr Lou goes to the kitchen and takes down an aluminium billy-can.

"I take rice in this," he explains. "I have stomach trouble, and the food in the factory canteen is not to my taste. I take my own, which I put in an oven there to keep warm."

I look back to Mrs Lou; with some hesitation she starts again.

"When my husband has gone I wash up and do any washing that has to be done, clean the house, and about nine o'clock I go out and do the shopping. And at four o'clock in the afternoon I go out again, because my husband likes everything fresh. I get everything at the co-operative store up the street because it's not only cheaper but more hygienic than the street markets. I get the evening meal ready about six o'clock, or later if my husband is going to be late."

"I go to night class at the Factory School every Wednesday night," he adds. "I'm weak in maths because in my schooling as a child I learnt only classical Chinese."

There is something touching in this confident young man's frankness about his weakness as well as his strength. Something touching, too, about the picture his words evoke. Occupied Tientsin. War raging everywhere. The tired boy coming home from the factory to the poor home where the impoverished widow, out of her scanty store, paid some doubtless equally impoverished scholar to teach her son classical Chinese, a dead language even then!

I come back to the present and Mrs Lou's housekeeping problems by asking, "And what do you cook?"

"Rice, meat dumplings, steamed bread, vegetables, sometimes meat, and sometimes fish. My husband particularly likes fish." She gets up and uncovers an enamel basin near the door. "See, I bought this fellow this morning at the market for our dinner." "This fellow" is a fish at least a pound in weight with large scales, green and brown. "He was alive when I bought him. It is dearer that way, but my husband likes everything fresh."

I look from the fish to Mrs Lou and then to her husband.

"It's obvious that to become a model worker one needs to have a model wife."

Mrs Lou blushes deeply. Mr Lou looks momentarily surprised at a point of view that has never occurred to him, but follows his own train of thought.

"We're very well off. We can have meat and vegetables practically every meal. And in the week-end it's 'high tide' and we buy more fish and meat."

"How much do you spend on food each week?"

Mrs Lou begins to speak, but her husband interrupts. "I'll get the account-book."

He takes down a book from the shelf but can't find what he's looking for. He looks at his wife and nods for her to go on.

"We spend about fifteen to twenty yuan a month for food for each of us," she says. "That is flour, rice, vegetables, fruit, oil, tea, meat, fish, and sometimes chicken."

Mr Lou breaks in. "In all, with rent and electricity and food and entertainment and everything else, we spend about fifty yuan a month. I estimate that we have an average thirty yuan left over either to put in the bank or for clothing. We go dancing on Saturday evening and on Sunday I take the wife and the boy out to the Park or one or other of the beauty spots outside Peking."

"Do you make your own clothes?" I give Mrs Lou a smile of encouragement.

"I make my own, but I buy my husband's at the co-op, all except his shirts, which I make myself. Sometimes I do some piece-work at home and make extra money that way."

She shows me a pile of soles for cotton-padded shoes that she has been making.

Her husband has launched into an account of his work which, being full of technical details about motor engines, does not convey anything to me.

When he finishes I thank him and go back to Mrs Lou. "And what else do you do with your day?" I persist.

She grows animated and this time answers without looking at her husband. "I'm on the Street Committee," she says. "My special job is to look after the hygiene of our area—how to keep the court-yards clean and get rid of the rubbish and make sure that all the rubbish boxes are put out every evening to be collected by the carts that go round. Then we have to see that the place is kept clear of rats and flies and mosquitoes and we take it in turn to go up and down the street at certain hours of the day to see that there is no filth anywhere."

I look at her with new respect, realizing that, like many of her sisters elsewhere in the world, Mrs Lou has no idea of how important a part she plays.

"Sanitation problems in Peking—as everywhere else in China —were acute at the time of Liberation," Mr Lou tells me. "But now the whole of the old drainage system has been overhauled and made to work again and everywhere you go you can see new drains being put in. Of course, only new buildings have water-closets, but the new interest in hygiene sees that the latrines are kept clean and closed sewage carts collect the night-soil once a day. Practically all the streets now have piped water."

I nod my appreciation of his information, which makes me
understand this new Peking much better, and turn back to Mrs
Lou, who has been listening with sparkling eyes.

"What else does the Street Committee do?" I ask. Mention of
the Street Committee transforms her. I'm sorry I can't see her in
action. I have an idea she is much more competent and assured
than I thought.

"We deal with all sorts of problems. Training children not to
play on the streets and how to behave in traffic. Fire-prevention."

Mr Lou explains. "There is always a danger that our portable
stoves will be knocked over, particularly when there are a lot of
children about."

"We tell people what to do in case of emergency," Mrs Lou
rushes on. "And also we warn them how to take measures against
thieves and reactionaries."

"You see," Mr Lou explains hastily, "although we are a new
society there are still bad people about and it's very necessary
that honest folk should be warned against them. That's why we
have the notice at the front entrance about closing the outer gate
at eight so that no thieves can get in, and taking in any clothing
you've left out to dry or air, and locking up bicycles and being
careful of your money when you go to the co-op *and warning
children not to talk to bad people.*"

It comes out in a rush. Honest Mr Lou is obviously guilty about
hurrying me past that notice, but also worried least I get the
wrong impression of his quarter and of Chinese behaviour generally. I hasten to set his mind at rest by saying that in our countries
we have to take even greater precautions. He looks relieved and
explains that in the old days there was so much poverty and so
many people were beggars and vagabonds that they got bad habits
and it is difficult to re-educate them.

I say, "You can't change people overnight and there are perhaps
people you can never change."

"Oh no!" Mr Lou shakes his head vigorously. "If you explain
to people patiently and show them how they can play their part
in the new society, there is no one you can't change."

I look at his earnest strong face and I am touched by so much
faith in human nature. I decide that, after all, I like Mr Lou.

Mrs Lou says a few words and he looks at her, surprised, smiles
and nods. The smile does not leave his face as he watches her get
up quickly and go to one of the large black-lacquer chests piled
one above the other.

Her face is flushed and her eyes moist when she comes back to me, holding two strips of white satin carefully folded in her two hands: the ultimate in old Chinese courtesy is to offer a thing with both hands.

She stands before me and makes as though to speak, but words don't come easily to Mrs Lou. She looks at her husband appealingly.

"My wife says your visit today has made her so happy that she would like to give you a little gift."

She places the strips of satin on my hands with graciousness that transforms her dumpy little figure and her sallow face. Then she unfolds them. The ivory silk is embroidered in intricate red designs each set within a gold or silver circle or half-circle. These are the treasures she embroidered for her wedding day and each of the designs has its own symbolism. I recognize some of them—Happiness and Fertility. Red, the wedding colour. The circles with their supplementary circle the Yang and the Yin, male and female, the complement of each other. The embroidery is exquisite. But it is the gesture that moves me. It is as though a woman in our country had taken out her long-treasured wedding veil and given it to me. Lei Su-chin and I stand speechless clasping each other's hands. She begins to speak haltingly. "I am not clever and I cannot find words to say what is in my heart but I want to tell you .that I shall never forget today."

Suddenly we embrace in the Chinese way, cheek to cheek. Mr Lou looms over us, at once proud and solicitous.

"I shall never forget it either," he assures me, shaking my hand in both of his and, for the first time in his life I'm sure, echoing his wife. We go out hand in hand, Mrs Lou's wide smile rivals the sunshine. I think perhaps it is the first time she has felt important. Mr Lou has on his face the look of a man who has just realized that he has a remarkable wife.

"I shall never forget today either," I say, as I bid them good-bye. And I see them still, standing in the arched doorway, his arm across her shoulder protectingly, waving me good-bye.

CHAPTER VI

Yesterday and Today in the Village

Out through the suburbs beyond the Wall on a brilliant September morning, through the "new" Peking that is growing with extraordinary rapidity. Only a few years ago it was farmland and even now mud huts stand incongruously beside the five- and six-storey modern buildings that stretch for miles on all sides. Fields with ripening crops form little islands in the earth that is being torn by bulldozers for new construction sites.

Beside enormous earth-shifting machines, a long file of workers with two baskets dangling from shoulder poles trot up and down, carrying the soil away with that loose-kneed gait that seems to ease the strain of the shoulder pole and its heavy load. Yesterday and today meet in Peking. Nothing that can serve the work of construction is too old—or too new!

The Western Hills are a misty blue against a clear sky. Cocoa-coloured, the fields stretch away punctuated with frail young trees. In Peking alone in the past few years over 2,700,000 trees have been planted. "Soon all Peking will be a garden," my guide says with pardonable pride.

Fields of cotton are topped with white bolls; kaoliang (sorghum) waves browning tassels; in paddy-fields long stalks of rice are drying.

Everywhere peasants in working clothes, white towels, typical of Northern China, tied round their heads. Here the prevailing colour, as in Italy, is black, though the younger girls are defying tradition and make spots of bright colour among the green.

Blindfolded donkeys turn water-mills. On a bare earth threshing-floor the grain is being threshed by hand; the flails rise and fall rhythmically and the dust of the winnowing hangs in a powdery pall. I am reminded of the book of illustrated Bible stories I had when I was a child.

Beyond, a tractor attached to a harrow, and a crowd of women and girls as well as men standing round it fascinated. A young girl about twelve climbs into the driver's seat and goes through the motions of driving it while everybody laughs. The ambition of every village girl in modern China, it seems, is to become a tractor driver!

Flocks of white ducks float on a willow-shadowed pool. They will make the famous "Peking Duck"; fortunately they don't know it!

We slow down slightly to pass a string of Bactrian camels coming from Mongolia. Mysterious saddle-bags lie between their double humps. The thick brown hair on neck and hump and legs swings in their easy plodding gait as they go by with the air of ineffable contempt common to camels everywhere.

Past a fallow field giving off a revolting smell of compost.

Off the main road onto an earth-track that winds through mud-walled villages where the houses seem to have risen out of the soil: cocoa-coloured huts, their ridge-poles slightly concave, gourd-vines rioting over them.

Over roads rutted by the iron-rimmed and studded wheels of farm carts of a model as old as the history of China. I have a stone-rubbing from a Han Dynasty carving over two thousand years old that shows just such wheels as those we pass on a cart drawn by a horse and a donkey. Wider ruts show where the large motor lorries have passed.

Families sit outside their huts eating from bowls with fast-moving chopsticks. It is half past nine and they have been in the fields since before dawn. Stalls before the little shops are piled with fruit, pears and grapes and apples and watermelons and tomatoes, and a variety of vegetables, the vivid red of the chillies, the orange of carrots, the pale yellow of corn-cobs, the light green of Chinese cabbage, spinach and marrows and cucumbers and a host of others I don't know. Old men with meagre beards sit smoking long thin pipes with a thimble-sized bowl. Old women with bound feet in dusty black are feeding the fowls. A young woman in a brilliant blue tunic waves as we pass. Past a rough clay statue like a snowman-in-mud at the cross-roads—the local god still guards the fields.

(Lao Sheh, author of *Rickshaw Boy*, once told me how in a village he knew, in the old days, the villagers, infuriated when their sacrifices to the Temple God didn't bring the wanted rain, took him out and left him unprotected for a couple of days to teach him what it was like to sweat under the blistering sun. It worked, they boasted! The rain came two days later. I told him about the Sicilian peasant I knew who in similar circumstances took the wax statue of the Virgin out into the parched fields with disastrous results to her—she melted. But in this case, it didn't work!)

We bounce along the unmade road, past that ingenious vehicle with a large wheel in the centre and the carrying baskets on each side, and with two legs near the handles so that it can stand. Often its load is so large that it obscures peasant and barrow alike.

Through narrow lanes between high mud walls and into the village itself, primitive by any standards, with the air of poverty long endured upon it that I have seen only in some Southern Italian and Spanish villages. But the peasants who stop to wave as I pass are adequately clothed and clearly adequately fed. There is laughter even in the faces seamed by ancient misery. There is no hint of the despair to which I grew accustomed but never inured in Southern Italy and Spain. There you felt decline and decay. Here, it is clearly all better than it was. We drive along the main street of the village and up to the brick building that is the headquarters of the Jinkuang Agricultural Producers' Co-operative.

Yang Wang-jing, vice-director of the co-operative, wearing a wine-checked tunic over blue trousers, is waiting for me. She is a brown-skinned, strong-faced woman who shows stained, irregular teeth when she smiles. I had expected someone older in such a responsible position but she looks quite young, two long plaits adding to her air of youth.

She leads me into a long, low room, its walls hung with many banners and portraits of Chinese national leaders. A blue table-cloth on the long table at which the co-op holds its meetings adds a further touch of colour. A solid brick traditional building this, with curved eaves and the convex grey tiles. It used to be the local headquarters of the Kuomintang.

Wang Sui-lei, with oblique eyes and lustrous, very long plaits, wearing a pale-blue shirt and trousers, serves us with tea. She is pretty enough for the National Dance Ensemble I saw the night before. She is, in fact, the kindergarten teacher, just nineteen years old.

Yang Wang-jing is very proud of her village. She grows animated as she tells me, in her deep, rather guttural voice, of the changes she has seen in those nine years. Her hands as she takes and lights a cigarette are the hands of a field worker.

"The seven years difference between Wang Sui-lei's age and mine mean a whole world of difference," she says. "She studied up to lower middle school while I was completely illiterate. She chose her own husband while my marriage was arranged for me.

I came to the village nine years ago when I was only seventeen, having never seen my husband before, though I lived in a village only two miles away.

"It was to a bitter life. My husband was the son of poor peasants with very little land, so that we were obliged to work for the landlord for very little pay. My mother-in-law gave me a very bad time. In the winter she would send me out to gather fuel in the hills near by, clad only in thin cotton. When she beat me my husband had also to beat me to show he was a filial son, even though he didn't like doing it. In those days we accepted everything without question because we thought it was our fate and you can do nothing against Fate. Now we know better. . . ." She smiles at Sui-lei.

"Yes, I've seen a lot of changes in those nine years. When I came here it was a miserable poverty-stricken place. There were two thousand people in the village and twenty-six landlords owned more than half the land."

"Where are they now?" I ask with stories of landlord extermination I had read abroad flashing into my mind.

"They all joined the co-operative when land was pooled. Of course they got their fair share of land, like everybody else, including the women. Everybody except seven rich peasants joined the co-op. They said they can make more money working on their own. 'When the co-op members make more than we do we'll join,' they say. Of course, they join in all the other village activities and come to meetings when agricultural experts come to teach us better methods."

It seems to me that these seven rich peasants are making the best of two worlds, so I inquire, "Why don't you force them to join?"

Mrs Yang looks shocked and Sui-lei who has surreptitiously been stalking a fly round the room, stops and looks at me as though I had committed blasphemy.

"It's against our principles to force them. They must join voluntarily or not at all. Besides, what use is an unwilling worker to any co-operative? They'll come when the co-op member's share is more than they make, and that won't be long the way we're going. The standard of living has risen for everyone—except the landlords and rich peasants.

"In the old days we lived on the coarsest grains. In bad seasons sometimes we had only grasses and wild vegetables to eat. We had very poor clothing, really nothing but rags and in the coldest winter weather—Peking's temperature descends to twenty degrees below freezing point—we couldn't afford padded cotton clothing. The year after Liberation was the first time in my life I ever had a summer dress and proper padded clothing, and it was the same for most of us. Now everybody eats well and, in addition to many draught animals, we own sixty-four milking cows. And we have bought a truck."

The pride with which this last is stated! But the pride is easy to understand when one realizes that only a few years ago the village ploughed with single-bladed wooden ploughs and used implements whose counterparts have been found in graves two thousand years old.

"Now production is mainly concentrated on vegetables and grapes. In addition we have a mill where we grind green beans to make noodles. We also have two brick kilns, and four hundred new brick houses have been built by our own hands where previously we had only mud huts. Before, only the landlords could afford bricks.

"We have two nurseries where babies can be left while the mothers work in the field, a kindergarten, two primary schools, and also a middle school with two classes. Two things completely transformed the lives of women in the village. First, our old dependence went when we were given our own land. Secondly, the New Marriage Law. . . .

"But here comes Feng-yuan. She will tell you about the work. Though she's only twenty, she's head of a production team."

Shaking back a heavy bob, Feng-yuan greets me warmly. An attractive girl, though film scouts might find the chin a little too determined. Her striped tunic and blue trousers are neat and well fitting and show off her slender figure.

That chin isn't deceptive, I find. Laughing, she says, "I have an easy job now. Every day I must contact the co-op's council to find out what work is required and where. After receiving the directions I take them to the various groups. I am really liaison officer between the council and the villagers—an easy job since we've developed into the highest form of co-operative.

"In the early days after Liberation the production team had to work very hard to break down the old prejudices among the women as well as the men, who looked down on them as useless creatures who couldn't earn a living. We had a busy time persuading the women that it was necessary for them to come out of their homes and work together to improve their standard of living. Women here were very backward. Previously they had to stay in the house and it wasn't considered proper for them to do anything but household work, even when there was little to do.

"When they saw how much better things were when they could earn work-points for themselves either in the fields or in lighter work like seed-sorting or handicrafts if they were physically weak or old, they began to co-operate, even though it was against everything they had been taught to believe. You'd have to be very stupid to remain backward when not only did the new life give you a better living but greater dignity. Now their husbands couldn't jeer at them for their dependence. They couldn't beat them, either, or they'd find themselves up before the village head!" She gives a peal of laughter and her eyes flash.

While she has been talking Sui-lei has continued to stalk the fly. Mrs Yang's eyes try not to follow her, but her face pales as the fly swoops and hovers over my tea-glass.

"And how did people like the change?" I ask. Mrs Yang plunges in: I think it is her favourite subject.

"The change didn't come easily, because when the New Marriage Law was introduced many of the older people opposed it. I never could understand why women who had suffered so much in the old days should cling to their past. It was as though not only their feet but their minds had been bound. But then, in my mother's generation, she told me that women were the worst at insisting on binding their daughter's feet. She was considered a very odd woman because she wouldn't allow mine to be bound.

"One of the most difficult things to break down was the system of arranged marriages. We had a battle about that very early in the piece. One young couple, Tsao Fu-yin and Pi Po-lin, wanted to get married but the parents of both opposed it as they had betrothed them when they were children to people in other villages. That was a real fight." She grows animated. "Finally, after haggling for weeks to persuade the parents—it was considered better to get them to agree if possible—and getting nowhere, the young couple, supported by the village organization, decided to go ahead, which was very important, as it gave a lead to the whole village. The parents were most dissatisfied right up to the day of the ceremony, but tried to put a good face on when they realized that nothing could be done and the whole village was celebrating with drums, cymbals and all the gaiety associated with village weddings. Indeed, this wedding was very important, because in the old days the wedding ceremony used to cost so much that more often than not the parents got so heavily in debt that they found themselves bound to the landlords at extortionate interest for the rest of their lives and often lost their land.

"When we were married, though my husband's family was very poor, they borrowed money to hire the sedan chair and the candlesticks and goblets and all the other things considered necessary for a wedding. Even my wedding dress and veil were hired. My mother-in-law never forgave me for the money I cost them. They were in debt to the landlord, at such an interest that the debt grew instead of being reduced, until Liberation, when all debts were remitted.

"Now a wedding is a simple ceremony. After the marriage has been officially registered the young couple just buy some cakes and sweets and have a simple feast and a party in the school hall or in one of the homes where all their friends gather. Very different from mine." She gives her deep laugh that has always a hint of pain in it.

"Of course the change in women's conditions has gone along parallel with the whole improvement in village life," Mrs Yang says. "But I think you'll understand that better if you come and see it for yourself."

I nearly leap out of my chair at a terrific bang behind me. Sui-lei has caught the fly!

Out in the village street peasants pass us coming and going with well-kept donkeys and horses. It is a primitive place to the eye, with its rough roads and its mud walls, but Mrs Yang and Sui-lei look at it proudly.

"See how clean it is," Sui-lei remarks. "We have a special group that looks after the sanitation and hygiene of the village and we have built several lots of public brick lavatories." They are clean, too.

Corn husks are piled high in the courtyards of the houses we pass. "We use them for fuel," Mrs Yang explains. The houses run to a pattern, mud walls forming a courtyard with single-storey wings on three sides. We pass high brick walls and glimpse through the open gate a larger, solider house of brick.

"That is an ex-landlord's house," Mrs Yang says when we have gone beyond it. Always curious, I go back to have another peep and meet the ex-landlord at the gate doing exactly the same thing! We both save face by pretending we meant this to happen. A plump man in his fifties, he shakes hands with me—they are soft, boneless hands that have never done any work, before or after Liberation, I'm sure. His tunic and trousers are of silk.

Women are washing in the little stream that flows through the village as I have often seen them washing in Southern Europe. An old bound-foot woman with a baby grandson on her back comes up and peers at me out of half-blind eyes. She smiles a wide, toothless smile. Incredibly old! I think she must be nearly ninety. I find that she is only in her sixties. Life in the old days was hard.

The village is picturesque in its own way with the willow-trees drooping over the water and a curved arch-stone bridge. But its new brick constructions stand out against the low mud huts they will gradually replace. A poor village, though I would not dare to say so to my two friends, whose faces are alight with pride as they show me the miracles wrought in the past few years. We pass the new brick granary that has been built to house the food supply for the winter.

"In the past five years there has been no shortage of food and each year it gets better," Mrs Yang tells me. "Now we have rice and wheat, and even meat several times a week. Most of us never tasted meat in our lives in the old days. As a result a doctor from Peking told us that children now weigh more and are taller than they were twenty years ago. I can remember once when I was a child we had to eat the bark of trees."

Women are round a well letting down the clanking buckets and drawing them up hand over hand. The strain shows on their faces. Free of the well, they attach the buckets to a carrying pole and move off bowed beneath the weight. A primitive and backbreaking way to draw water, I say to myself. Why not a windlass? But before I can voice the words I am told: "We are never short of water now. The co-operative has put down many new wells and the water is free for all. I remember in my old village a landlord would not let us touch a well we dug ourselves because he said it was on his land. Things like that often happened. We were illiterate and if a landlord made a claim we had no means of knowing whether it was right or wrong. At Liberation it was found that sometimes peasants had been paying taxes the landlords should have paid and they were said to have debts they didn't have at all."

We follow the powdery earth road till it reaches a playing-field equipped with basketball goals and other playing equipment and then into the primary school, a one-storeyed brick building built round the typical courtyard, where the headmaster welcomes me.

The yards are clean and shadowed by trees. The simple buildings have their own charm with their curved grey roof-tiles. One end is well equipped with parallel bars and swings. A singing class fills the morning with a song I've heard on the radio.

In another class a reading lesson is in progress and boys and girls bend over their books, too interested even to look up at the advent of a visitor.

"In the old days only the children of landlords and rich peasants went to school," the headmaster tells me. "Now all the children above eight in the village can go, and not only to primary school. There are a hundred pupils from here in the near-by middle school."

I peep through the window at a drawing class, depressingly like drawing classes I've seen in many Western schools with its copying of an uninteresting formal design on the blackboard. The class is as bored as are similar classes everywhere, and my face at the window is a happy diversion which sends many of them into fits of giggles. One small boy stealthily begins to draw a picture of me with a nose of proportions that would have suited Cyrano de Bergerac. The little girl beside him suggests improvements and hastily covers it with her hand when she catches me looking.

The class-room blackboards have each its own decorations in coloured chalks, charming and full of life. The teachers nod smilingly as I pass, but there's no time to waste on visitors. And I have a feeling that the headmaster, pleasant and welcoming though he is, heaves a sigh of relief when I depart.

Outside I meet the kindergarten out for its morning walk. Two by two, hand in hand, a boy and a girl. They are like a flock of brilliant birds in their gay cotton split pants and aprons. They set up a cry of "*Ai-yi! Ai-yi!*" ("Aunty! Aunty!") as I appear. I shake hands with the leaders and then they refuse to move on till I shake hands with all, the line having broken and clustered around me. Shaking hands is a foreign custom they find most entertaining.

They re-form and go off under the willows on the bank of the stream, gay and chattering like parrots and turning to wave till I pass out of sight into the co-operative store.

Mid-morning and the co-op is crowded. It is a pleasant, well-lighted brick building, built only recently, with a book counter and a counter for writing materials and another for electric torches and thermos flasks, mostly of large size and covered in woven cane or with metal covers printed with brilliant designs. The proudest possessions of every Chinese peasant today are the ball-point pen, the vacuum-flask, and the electric torch, all made in China! An old woman with bound feet is trying pen after pen, advised by a teen-age grandson.

"He's going to teach her at home," Sui-lei whispers. "She's too shy to go to the classes." When I leave she is still trying pens.

"Vacuum-flasks have changed our lives," Mrs Yang says. "Now we can take hot water with us when we go to the fields." Tea is much dearer in China than in the West—far too expensive a drink for peasants yet! "The torch makes it possible for us to see our way home from meetings or picture-shows at night." Considering the state of the village roads, I think it must save a lot of accidents.

Sui-lei laughs. "And the pen means that the Revolution brought not only light to our eyes but to our minds. For girls of seventeen and eighteen there is a special spare-time class so that they can go on with their education even though they are working in the fields or elsewhere, and three hundred and seventy-five are studying. There is also a literacy class for older people. The short-term class has been so effective that after the two years' course they reach fourth class in the primary school.

"In springtime, when they are very busy in the fields, the teacher comes to the fields and gives lessons during their midday break for the men and women who are studying."

The drapery counter is piled with dress materials of bright-coloured prints and others with large patterns more suitable for the cotton-padded quilts which the housewives are beginning to make for the winter. There is a pile of cotton padding in the corner and an assistant is weighing and parcelling it.

"A village housewife is kept busy," I remark.

Mrs Yang smiles. "We don't mind that. In the old days they would never have dreamt of buying things like these."

The food counters are clean, with glass cases for the perishables and mosquito netting covering other foodstuffs. The assistant at the counter is in white and does not handle the food but picks it up with metal tongs. Four-foot jars, like stage props for Ali Baba and the Forty Thieves, contain oil, vinegar, soya sauce, and bi-jou, a potent spirit. There are several bins with different varieties of flour, more bins for several varieties of rice. Sections of the shelves contain dried mushrooms, ginger-root, peppers, sesame seeds, melon seeds, sunflower seeds, and numerous seasonings to which I can give no name and which baffle the interpreter, Young Chen.

A dog pokes the screen door with his nose, looks in and is shushed away by attendants and customers alike. He looks at us pathetically as we go out as if he was not in accord with all this passion for hygiene which makes his life a dog's life indeed!

We follow an uneven, dusty road with deep cart-ruts to the Maternity Clinic, a lime-washed building erected only three years ago. Nurse Lei, young and smiling, in her clean white overall, comes to greet me. She has been trained at the school of maternity nurses in Peking.

The room is light and airy, hung with hygiene posters. I drink tea on a stool that faces large posters which show all the stages of pregnancy and the proper means of delivery. Excellently designed posters that I wish could be shown to many women I know in presumably advanced countries, who are completely ignorant of the processes their own body undergoes.

There are two beds where women can be kept for observation. They are canopied with thick fly-proof netting and, though the floor is of stamped earth, everything is immaculate.

"My particular job is to attend to the pre-natal health of the mothers and the delivery of children," Nurse Lei tells me. "If the mothers are too busy to come to me I go to them, but, in the main, pregnant women come to me here for check-up. I also act as midwife. In the cases of complicated birth they go to the hospital. We have a general clinic and one for women and children in addition to this, which is really only for checking up. I also give young mothers talks on how to bring up their babies.

"In the old days, all kinds of superstitions surrounded birth and the child was usually delivered by one of the older women who had had no training and who knew nothing about asepsis, and who, too often, was chosen because she had had a lot of children, most of whom had died at childbirth. Since Liberation many of these women have had courses to teach them modern methods and consequently they are able to do their work today in a proper manner with no danger to mother or child.

"One of the tasks of the clinic is to educate mothers in general hygiene. The result of this campaign has been that the mortality rate has dropped extraordinarily—not only for children but for women. There used to be many deaths from puerperal fever and tetanus.

"It wasn't easy going at first. When health exhibitions were first organized in the village women refused to attend them. Then we opened a maternity clinic and families kept expectant mothers out of sight!"

The arrival of a young woman carrying a plump baby blowing bubbles with great satisfaction puts an end to our talk. To judge by the village's junior population the mothers have learnt their lessons well!

We go down the road past fruit and vegetable shops where two old men are sitting, gossiping in the sun. They nod and wave their long pipes. What has happened to the conservative Chinese peasant of story?

Hanging from a tree is an ancient bell with a finely moulded dragon round the top. It came from an old temple in the village that fell into ruin thirty years ago. Now it is sounded for work or for special meetings, being struck, as all Chinese bells are struck, with a wooden bar or mallet.

Over a stone bridge with carved railings, relics of the distant past. Past an inquisitive grey piglet that is tethered to a tree and comes inquiringly to sniff at my legs. If I tickle his side, Young Chen tells me, he will go to sleep. I tickle his side. His eyes close sleepily and with a long sigh he stretches himself on his side and goes to sleep. The villagers all around burst out laughing.

Past a crop of aubergines heavy with purple fruit. Yellow gourds hang over a wall. Through a clean courtyard equipped with playing-pens and home-made playing equipment, into the nursery where a brick kang runs along the wall of the main room, and the sixty-seven babies who come to the nursery sleep side by side, each covered with its own cotton-padded quilt.

"The loveliest sight in the world," Sui-lei assures me. "You should see how wonderful they are when those who are old enough are playing in the yard. We are very proud of our nursery, for we women organized it ourselves so that women who work in the fields would know their babes were well cared for while they were working. In the old days women stayed at home, wasting their time and earning nothing. Indeed, often they did nothing but quarrel.

"One of the guarantees of the co-operative is to look after old people and they are guaranteed food and clothing and help with their housework if they need it—old people can't draw water, for instance, and we also guarantee to give them a decent funeral—something very important in China."

Along the road that leads back to the co-op headquarters we stop for a moment to see the cultural centre. Here are stands full of pictorial illustrated books—China's method of providing for a populace emerging from illiteracy. There are over two thousand books in the library, and many newspapers and magazines. A whole new world they never dreamt of is opening up for villagers and their thirst for learning is insatiable. Reading groups have been formed in private houses and even work-teams borrow books or papers to take to the fields. These are read to the others by someone with more education during the meal-break. There is also a radio with a loud-speaker, to which the whole village listens.

On our way again, we meet a group of young men admiring the latest purchase, a shining bicycle; one of them has just ridden it back from Peking.

Sui-lei tells me that lots of the young people now earn enough to buy bicycles, which are dearer than in the West.

Symbol of the new days that have come to the village, the co-op's motor-truck hoots loudly as it slows down to let pass the school children running home for dinner.

"And now we have the truck, groups of us go into Peking in the week-end if there is anything we want to see."

"Not that we need to," Mrs Yang insists, "but it makes a change. We have lantern-slide showings four times a month and film shows. They are held in the square in front of the village school and practically everyone turns up to see them. In the old days nobody but the landlords ever saw a film or a play."

"Now sometimes opera troupes come from Peking," Sui-lei breaks in, her eyes dancing at the thought, "and we also have our own spare-time drama and opera troupes."

"It wasn't all easy going at the beginning," Mrs Yang adds. "Old people objected to women going on the stage. The mother-in-law of one girl who played the heroine in *The Women's Representative*—a play that mirrored many of our own problems—used to carry on frightfully about it, nagging her and sometimes even refusing to give her anything to eat. In fact, she was just like the mother-in-law in the play. But the girl continued and the play was a great success. And the mother-in-law was quite changed after it, for she thought the author was showing her up in the play!

"Then there was the problem of parts. Young girls were frightened of being ridiculed if they played married women's parts, and men and women players didn't dare so much as shake hands on the stage or the old feudal-minded people would be down on them like a ton of bricks! Now all that is past. The village is proud of its drama group and even approves of players shaking or holding hands. You must come back and see us put on a show."

"There's nothing I'd like better," I tell them as I begin to leave.

All the village is going home for dinner as the car moves slowly through the main street and they stop to wave and call the Chinese good-bye: "*Tsai-chien, Tsai-chien!*"

I went back at the Chinese New Year, the traditional lunar festival. The fields slept under snow, but the village was enjoying its three-day holiday to the full. Drums and cymbals and one-stringed fiddles announced the beginning of the theatrical performance. It was a modern opera based on the story of an eighteen-year-old girl who was forced to marry a ten-year-old boy, a situation not uncommon in the old days. When at last the District Head righted the wrong and she married the young man of her choice the applause was tumultuous.

Postscript. A cutting from a newspaper of 1935 reported that in a village twenty miles east of Peking a Miss Liang became engaged to a Mr Wang. Since the young couple were modern, it was a "free-choice" engagement, and though their parents were conservative farmers, they approved.

However, Miss Liang got extravagant ideas. She cut her hair, wore bright dresses revealing her legs, refused to stay at home as a "nice girl" should. She even talked to young men! The village was shocked.

Wang Senior and Liang Senior were most upset by the gossip. But Miss Liang was impervious to their reproofs. The honour of two families was threatened, so the cutting reads:

> Miss Liang was taken to a quiet spot outside the village by the outraged father and future father-in-law and there buried alive.
>
> Hearing about it next morning, young Wang was frantic. His love for Miss Liang and his grief at her murder were so strong that he proceeded at once to the District Government, where he lodged a formal accusation against his father and Mr Liang.
>
> Although, according to the old laws and according to custom, parents were entitled to do away with daughters who bring dishonour to the family name, the new laws are different. It is recalled that some months ago a man and his wife in Tientsin were sentenced to life imprisonment for a similar offence. It is not known, however, what action will be taken in the present case.

CHAPTER VII

Lady of the Roses

WHEN I first saw Tsiang En-tien (or Mrs Chen Yi, as she learnt to call herself in America) she was in the large garden of her bungalow in Tientsin, "putting up" her roses for the winter. In Tientsin's winter you dare not leave a precious rose unprotected and all Tsiang En-tien's three hundred roses are precious. Lovingly she wrapped the stems of the standards in paper and straw. The hybrid tea-roses were heaped with earth a foot high to protect the root and stems.

She worked quickly, her small fine hands wrapping the delicate branches deftly. They were scratched, but she preferred to work without gloves.

Behind her modish glasses her big brown eyes sparkled as she told me in her quaint English the story of her rose-growing.

"I have about a hundred different varieties. Generally I work by myself, but sometimes I need help," she said in her soft, sweet voice. "Rose-culturing is my hobby. I foresee that some day my country people like to have more and more flowers, so I try to propagate more and more varieties. I experiment with cuttings and try to cross them to have new types. Lots of families of roses come from China for more than two hundred years. In 1705 the English named one they imported the 'tea-rose'. I like to work in this line and also find history of rose and find a very good meaning in growing better roses to make more beautiful world."

Expressed so earnestly in her own phrases it seemed to carry added meaning.

"When I started my garden I think perhaps people will think I am not doing something useful, but the Government has helped and encouraged me in many ways. This year I have already sent to the Botanic Gardens in Peking two hundred and forty-five small plants and five hundred cuttings. In the old days people were jealous and critical, but now everyone helps you and encourages you."

She stopped to untangle her hair and as she raised her arm the sleeve of her fawn cardigan caught on the thorns, and when she moved another snagged her gardening slacks. She gave a soft, deprecatory laugh.

A charming woman, Mrs Chen Yi, with the same absorbed expression on her face I have seen on the faces of my rose-loving friends all over the world.

"I would like to exchange cuttings with someone in your country," she said. "Do you think you could find someone for me who would like to?

"You must come back and see my garden in the summer. It is so beautiful. My husband is still manager of the factory of which he is the main shareholder. He has the same salary as before and we have a stable income and nothing worried. Now they have a new plan for a big new factory building.

"My children—I am sorry you cannot meet my children—I have a daughter seventeen and a boy fifteen. My daughter is a student of music at the university and my son is in the higher middle school.

"Since I am very busy with my garden I have one maid to help me. Capitalists' wives have a much more interesting time than in the old days when they just sat round idle or went to the tea-parties and mah-jongg parties, smoking all night. Many of them smoked opium. And many of them were also worried because their husbands were always wanting to buy concubines. There was no real security in the home.

"Many capitalists had much money, but their wives were not regarded as human beings—I was lucky, it was different in our family. But women had no independence and a husband could take as many concubines as he liked and a woman had no redress. I could introduce you to many women like that in Tientsin. Now, of course, the New Marriage Law protects them and their children.

"In the old days husbands didn't worry about the children, and there were so many temptations for young men with money—brothels everywhere and prostitutes soliciting on every street corner—every mother lived in terror of her son being corrupted and catching a disease that would ruin his life. Now women are relieved of all these distresses. Their husbands have changed with the changes in society and their children have free and healthy and happy useful lives before them.

"And women are learning to play their part in new society. Some are helping with nurseries, many on their Street Committees, all are learning new things.

"When I went to Peking this year to the conference of capitalists' wives I felt so proud, and I also felt that I had wasted **too** much of my time. I am educated, I said, I can use my knowledge in a bright and broad way. I felt ashamed when I came back from abroad and saw everybody in such plain clothes, working so hard —such selfless people, and I did nothing for my country but worked only for myself.

"So I said to my mind, I will grow roses and each year I will translate one hundred thousand words from an American or English book into Chinese. Perhaps you would let me translate your book? One day I will be coming to Peking and I visit you and we will talk about it. . . . "

I knew Tsiang En-tien's voice at once when she telephoned one day in Peking to say she was coming to see me. But I scarcely recognized the elegant woman who came in, a thick fur coat over her *chi-pao* of fine blue wool and a diamond-and-pearl clip at the throat and matching ear-rings, high-heeled toe-peeper suede shoes, hair well dressed. Only the gleaming eyes behind her glasses were unmistakable, and her laugh.

We have more to talk about than translations, for the American friend, Betty Chang, who had introduced us had said, "You should ask En-tien to tell you her story. It's interesting."

En-tien demurred when I asked her. "My story is a very common one. There is not anything remarkable about it you would like hearing."

I persisted, and gradually it unfolded, accompanied by expressive gestures of her small hands; on her wrist was a tiny exquisite watch.

"My father was a primary-school teacher in Kiangsu Province. My mother died thirty years ago. As a child I saw people suffering all round me, beggars, starving peasants, and I asked myself why people suffered.

"Usually girls did not go to school, but my father taught me reading and writing. My father remarried a woman who had no education and she wanted me to help keep the family because we were not rich, but I wanted to go to school so I can have independent life. I cried and cried for three days and at last my father let me go. When I was sixteen I went to Suchow Middle School, a private mission school where there was a much admired principal, Miss Wang, a returned student from the U.S.A. She didn't marry because she dedicated her life to the education of girls. She gave up everything to Chinese girls.

"I began to learn English then and graduated in 1929 and went to Chinghua University in Peking. Miss Wang and her friends helped me to come.

"For the first two years I study very hard. English literature was my main subject. Then in 1931 the Japanese invade the Northeast. I joined the Student Movement against Japanese aggression. I was elected Chairman of the Movement and I was sent to Nanking, the Kuomintang headquarters, asking the Government to fight Japan to free China. I failed. The Kuomintang was corrupt. So after graduation in 1933 I went to Inner Mongolia to teach. It was strange for a Southerner to go to the Far North, but I wanted to teach there to help students understand Japanese aggression and help women advance.

"I stayed there for two years. It was so beautiful and I was so happy. I travelled all around to get to know my country better and met so many people from distant provinces.

"Then after two years I came back to be Assistant in Department of Literature. Then in 1937 I married Chen Yi. He had also been a student at Chinghua, now a banker. We married in Maytime when all the flowers were coming out.

"Chinghua students liked to go to the U.S.A. to do more studies so we decided to go. We went as far as Hong Kong but war broke out against the Japanese. We thought it wrong to go to U.S.A. when our country was suffering: we must share our country's fate, so we came back to Peking which was already occupied by the Japanese. My husband went back to be the manager of his bank again.

"I had nothing to do and was unhappy shut up in the home so I tried to translate *Emma* into Chinese. We lived in the big house of my husband's parents, though they had died. My two children were born there.

"When the American-Japanese War began in 1941, the Japanese arrested my husband. I suffer. Terrible things happened in Japanese prisons. I said to myself, 'I have no country, no protection, but if anything happens to my husband I know what I do to avenge him.'"

Her eyes filled with tears at the memory of those days.

"When my husband was released I didn't want to stay in Peking any longer. I cannot bear to suffer it, no freedom. Anything can happen to my husband, so we decided to go to the freeland and leave secretly for Szechuan.

"It was a terrible journey. My daughter was five and my son three. We had lots of troubles. Getting away without Japanese knowing where we were going. But the policemen were Chinese and they took care of us and helped us.

"It's a long, long story to tell. Too long. Sometimes we went by train and when there was no train we went on foot, my husband holding our son on his shoulder. Sometimes we hired a cart. Sometimes a boat. And the country and the people so poor, poor! And so miserable. At last by all kinds of transport we come to the free country. I still remember the first time I step on land and I say, 'This is free country.'

"I think it is not sufficiently appreciated what part the Anti-Japanese War played in breaking down the old family system in China. People in the West speak as though it all happened over-night in 1949. It's true that although there was a percentage of women like me, up till the Anti-Japanese War most women led the traditional life in their homes. But war changed that for too many people. There were over fifty million refugees, and in the awful conditions of continual bombing and shortage of food and accommodation it was not possible for families to stay together.

"When all these refugees got into the liberated areas it became necessary for women to work as well as men. Even in the cities where people were not driven out of their homes they could no longer live the same way. Women, unless they were rich, had to seek work and once that happened the old family system was gone —for ever.

"The Kuomintang was in control in Szechuan and we got a shock, because the first thing we see was a man shot dead on the road before us and no one knowing why. The city was not under good government. But at least there were no Japanese.

"My husband found a job and I taught in the school and looked after my children.

"When victory comes in 1945 we were so excited! I start to write pamphlets. Since 1933 I wrote pamphlets and essays to newspapers. So excited we were! Now China can be a country, we say.

"In 1946 we came back to Peking. My husband goes back to his bank. We begin to look for a house. We thought that now the Japanese had gone that China would begin to recover and we would live again. The people had suffered so long. But Peking was horrible. Filled with beggars and prostitutes, and poor unemployed workers who could find nothing to do. Prices were jumping. The inflation was so bad even professional people suffered and the students were so poor—so poor.

"This was the time of the Kuomintang and Communist struggle. The K.M.T. were rotten, no good men. Nothing but squeeze and corruption. They don't know how to rule. They do nothing for the people, only for themselves. We were capitalist, but I was patriotic. I loved my own country. Chinese people suffered so long. So long! All I wanted was a good government, whether Communist or Kuomintang didn't matter. China mattered.

"We could not bear it. In 1948 we all went to the United States. We lived in Berkeley, San Francisco. I took courses in the university because I like to learn more.

"I liked American people. So young, so nice, but I don't like their education. No rules. Children do not obey. Comics and race prejudice I do not like.

"Though people were so kind to me I hated to think that those 'Four Families' who really owned the Kuomintang had so little national pride that they ask America for aid to keep Chinese fighting Chinese. I was also ashamed to know from my husband's banking friends that they were taking so many millions of the moneys they stole from China and investing it in the United States.

"I felt Chinese people had suffered so much and I'm so proud of my country and I hoped it would one day be a strong and good country. I did not like Americans thinking money could buy China. In some way I don't like the United States. Money is too important. There are more important things than that. Chinese capitalists know that.

"Soon all China was free of the Kuomintang and we were so happy there was peace, but we were wondering what the new Government was like. So I wrote to my friends and when they wrote back I felt a new light like a sun come out in early morning. So in 1949 we decided to come back.

"So we plan to take a trip round the world to England, France, Switzerland, and Italy, and come back to Peking. At that time I joined the Y.W.C.A. and was a member of the board. The Y.W.C.A. play very important part educating Chinese women. Now there is a branch in every big city and we have a conference with more than two thousand women coming. Never before so big in China. I also start to learn Leninism-Marxism so I can understand the new philosophy.

"I felt strange at first back from foreign countries. Gradually I began to like it. All round us we could feel our country growing better and better and we felt we should be taking part in the work of construction. So my husband left the bank and put all our money into a factory. So in 1953 we moved to Tientsin and now I look after my family and my garden.

"It is only seven years since Liberation and China has done so much. It is such a big country with so many people, many things so backward.

"Friends write to me from other countries and ask me, 'Have you freedom?'

"And I write back and tell them, 'We are not free to be bad. But we are free to do good things. Give us time and peace and we shall build a great country.' And that, I think, is all!"

She turns her soft mild eyes on me and gives a little deprecatory laugh. "I'm sorry it was not more interesting, but as I told you my story is not a remarkable one."

It is clear she means it!

CHAPTER VIII

Peking-Nanking

FIVE O'CLOCK on a hot summer afternoon, and from the appearance of the railway station I would say half the city is migrating. The usual crowd is swollen by the hundreds of students who are going home for the long summer vacation. Swollen it is! It looks like the Bank Holiday crowds at Victoria, London. Hundreds of would-be travellers for the night train reposing on their bedding outside the station; long queues before the barriers headed by harassed mothers with babies on their backs—mothers with babies go to the head of the queue—young girls and boys, men and women, carrying enormous string-bags, enamelled washbasin, a drinking mug, a towel, a washer, a toothbrush, neatly folded clothes, and frequently a rolled padded quilt on the shoulder, for in China you carry your own bedding.

Sometimes a swag of things in a matting cover and, as everywhere else in the world, odd-shaped last-minute parcels wrapped in newspaper. Piles of luggage beside the train, woven rush suitcases, neat cloth-covered suitcases. Students going home, workers going to the new constructions in the North-east and North-west.

My friend introduces me to two railway apprentices, young girls in neat blue tunics and trousers piped with red, tight plaits tied with red ribbon bobbing beside smiling faces. When they have completed their apprenticeship, which teaches them the general set-up of a train and how to serve passengers, they will join a train crew. They forget their official dignity a moment to wave to me as my train moves out.

Through the crowded suburbs of Peking where brick gives way to mud houses, and then suddenly we are in open fields, though in the background rise huge new factories and enormous groups of residential and office buildings. To the west the Marco Polo Bridge (the Lukouchiao) with its graceful marble spans each topped by a pillar on which sits a marble lion, no two of them alike. Eight hundred years ago Marco Polo crossed it and in 1937 the Anti-Japanese War broke out with the Lukouchiao Incident.

Scarcely has the train moved than the routine of Chinese trains began, a routine that resembles nothing I have experienced anywhere in the world. Sunk back in the corner of our comfortable sleeper, we listened to the train director welcoming us over the loud-speaker that is in every carriage. An important person, the director; all the train crew is under his or her supervision and his or her job is to see to the comfort of train passengers. The announcer is responsible for seeing that everyone is on the right train, that anyone sick obtains proper attention from the Red Cross worker every train carries, that no one is overcarried. After the welcome, he gives advice to the passengers, particularly those who have never travelled before. To so many travel is a new luxury.

While we are listening to the radio admonitions the attendant in charge of the security of the train goes through, very smart in his white coat and blue trousers, with a revolver in the holster at his waist and a round brown merry face looking most incongruous under his peaked cap. It is not so long ago that acts of sabotage were committed on trains by Chiang Kai-shek's agents. He is followed by the tea-boy, spick and span in white, who carries a large brass kettle of boiling water. He opens tiny packets and shakes the large green tea-leaves into the lidded glasses on our tables. Then he lifts up the glass and, holding it in mid-air, pours in the boiling water. His fingers must be made of asbestos. We feel sure he or we shall be scalded. The tea costs ten cents; tea is dear. Refills of hot water cost nothing, since it is the opinion of the Government that it is healthy to drink much hot tea on a train journey. I share its opinion.

The vast, intensively cultivated plain of North China glides by, and the announcer tells us its history, past and present. Blindfolded donkeys tread patiently their worn circles as they turn the primitive water-wheels that dot the fields. Grave mounds like giant ant-hills cluster together in corners of fields. Sometimes a single one stands solitary in the spot the soothsayer has chosen. According to immemorial belief, *feng-shui* (the elements of wind and water) made some spots auspicious for the living as well as the dead, for if the dead rested happily it brought luck to their descendants. In the old days no one would dream of touching a grave, and today the Government will not allow them to be touched unless the peasants themselves so decide.

Not half an hour after our departure, a service boy arrives with a wet mop, looks at us with what we think is an accusing glance, mops the compartment floor, dusts the table and every bit of wood. Why, it isn't clear, since everything is immaculate.

I have reduced the tea in my glass by one inch when the tea-boy reappears and refills it. Again no casualties.

The radio is playing an excerpt from a Peking opera I saw last week: the *Mu Ku-chai*, in which a woman bandit overcomes all the generals sent against her, including the Marshal and the Marshal's son, whom she "persuades" by rather unfeminine methods to marry her. Why is it that Chinese opera is full of tales of heroic women of a stature one never finds in Western literature of a similar period? Did Chinese men subconsciously prefer something less docile than the creature they were supposed to idealize?

The radio breaks off to advise passengers that we shall soon be at the next station. Don't leave anything behind, have your ticket ready, don't get off while the train is moving. Don't spit!

(There is a nation-wide campaign against spitting, China's most unlovely habit. That it is only partially successful as yet, the presence almost everywhere of spittoons and ubiquitous ear-shattering throat-clearings testify.)

The station is clean, freshly watered. Fruit-stalls with water-melons, and yellow melons, peaches and plums. Cake-stalls with sesame cakes, soya-bean biscuits. Rice wrapped into triangular shapes made with banana leaves.

Twenty-three centuries ago the poet Chu Yuan drowned himself because of grief at the corruption of the Court. The people knew that Chu Yuan, in a way, died for their cause, and the boats went to seek his body. Each year on the date of his death the Dragon Boat Races take place and glutinous rice, wrapped in bamboo leaves is eaten in his honour. Two thousand three hundred years ago! Not many poets have so perennial a memorial.

Green and flat, the country stretches interminably with occasional trees to hills that are only a cloud on the horizon. The radio plays "Vienna Woods".

More tea. Another mop. Another dusting.

Past a river with fawn-coloured clay dykes—the rivers are silted and flood easily.

The fields are coloured patchwork. Red ploughed fields, the tender green veil of young wheat, the yellow-ochre of ripe crops. Harvesting is in full swing.

Beyond it a tractor is bumping its way home across a ploughed field. Beside it a donkey drags a single-bladed plough.

More tea. Another mopping. We look guiltily at our shoes this time. But since the whole corridor is mopped we realize it's not us but routine.

With its intensive cultivation, its streams of peasants, nothing

could be less like the vast, empty spaces of my own country, yet
its very vastness gives me a pang of homesickness.

The radio has broken into my favourite minority song and its
poignant melody harmonizes with the darkening landscape, the
long files of wide-hatted peasants silhouetted against the low
light as, hoe across shoulders, they make their way home.

What looks like a Mongol encampment turns out to be round
haystacks covered with new rush matting of a pale amber colour
that rise in regular peaks. Smokestacks of a large new factory
pierce the jade sky. A train of oil trucks rumbles beside the
express. Endless new factories and workshops. A forest of radio
masts—Tientsin!

Night: a comfortable bunk; gay flowered-cotton quilts. A good
sleep, broken only by a pig train stopping beside us and a nightmare din of protesting pigs. To sleep again. Six a.m. A loud-
speaker at a station gives what I presume to be advice to early
travellers in an irritatingly hearty voice following with a tune
I've heard used for morning physical jerks. I burrow into my
enormous, wonderfully soft pillow and go to sleep again. Seven
a.m. The train radio begins activities with my favourite minority
song and then announces the news. I give up.

We have passed out of the dry North China Plain, and I breakfast in the comfortable dining car looking over endless irrigated
rice-fields. Brilliant arsenical green, yellow-green, chrome live as
flames. The rain sweeps in glistening swathes over the drowned
land. Men in straw capes looking like hedgehogs. Men in high
rubber boots and yellow mackintoshes. One in scarlet shorts and
bright blue shirt, a Van Gogh dream against the yellow rice. Four
fishermen jogging down to the river with long poles on their
shoulders and five cormorants sitting on them with a faintly par-
sonical air.

A train laden with motor trucks passes.

Across the fields goes a red sedan chair inscribed with the golden
double character for happiness, carrying a bride to her new home.
A traditional Chinese marriage. Probably compromise, my companion, Lao Chang, says. Parents say, "All right. You can marry
the husband of your choice. But you must have a sedan chair."
Compromise, compromise. The art of Chinese government.

Flooded fields. The Hwai River has extended like a great lake
of clay-coloured water for miles and miles alongside the railway.
A village of mud huts on higher ground looks as though it may
disintegrate at any moment into the clay-coloured water.

Once this was a terrible flood area, with many deaths and

much damage every year. Today flood-detention, huge dams, and hydro-electric schemes are controlling it to a great extent. Soon it will be controlled completely.

Peasants with baskets on poles trotting along a submerged path to the village.

A small boy has fallen in the mud and gets up plastered and howling.

A mud house is canting perilously, submerged to the roof.

Four small boys are paddling in a pool. Mother, water up to her ankles, is obviously scolding them.

Chickens sit on a ridge-pole gazing with doubtful expressions into the water.

Boys are cleaning ditches to divert the flood-water.

Now only the presence of boats distinguishes river from fields.

The first water-buffaloes under grey lowering skies; boys, in hedgehog capes bestride the lumbering beasts in driving rain.

Long lines of workers go by under red oiled-paper umbrellas, carrying picks and shovels.

We are leaving the flood area. The rice-fields glitter black under a brazen sun; teams of peasants stoop in the back-breaking labour of planting rice seedlings.

Luncheon, and the restaurant staff beams as the waiter carries to us with infinite care a bowl of soup with large white characters floating on the top, each sprinkled with green and red and black. I recognize them from seeing them so often: *"Ho-ping wan sui"*— literally, "Peace ten thousand years!" I raise my glass of iced shandy. There is no toast to which I drink more readily. *Kan-pei!*

Twenty-four hours' travelling. The radio warns us that we are approaching Nanking. Alas, I get my first glimpse of the Yangtze through the haze of a streaming cold in the head. It establishes a legend of my fragility that is to follow me throughout China.

CHAPTER IX

The Resurrection of Happy Village

IT was a lucky cold after all. Without it I might never have met Loo Ta-ma. By the next evening I was in a more presentable state, but still unfit for a second banquet. The very word nauseated me. It was still very hot.

Late in the evening the door opens and Loo Ta-ma is announced. A small woman in blue slacks and a pale-green seersucker tunic comes in like a whirlwind, face full of sympathy, arms outstretched. I may not understand what she's saying, but I know what it means without translation. She bends and embraces me, small strong arms round my shoulder, bright eyes gleaming in a nut-brown face, under a broad high brow, thick black bobbed hair swinging. If it wasn't for the wrinkles at the corner of her eyes, the lines graven at the corner of her mouth, I would wonder at the "Ta-ma", title of dignity for an older woman.

Holding my sticky hands in her strong, hard ones, she explains that, hearing at the banquet that I was sick, she had insisted on coming to ask me to come and see her district when I am better.

I jump at the chance, assure her I am already better, and ask her about herself.

She smiles at me, displaying all her small white teeth under a tiny upturned nose, but shakes her head. She will tell me later when I am stronger.

I insist.

"All right, I'll tell you about the later part of my life," she concedes.

"At the time of Liberation we were living among the poorest and most despised people in the district that was considered the filthiest in Nanking. We had expected nothing when the Liberation armies came, neither better nor worse. In the old days everyone had oppressed us. War-lords and Kuomintang and Japanese alike. We were so low we could be pushed no lower, so poor nothing could be taken from us except our lives, and they were so hopeless that we scarcely cared whether we lived or died.

"We had survived the Japanese invasion in 1937 when tens of thousands of their drunken troops just went mad in the city for weeks. Any female creature they came upon—girl, old woman, or young woman—was raped, and often bayoneted when they'd finished with her. They murdered men and women and children indiscriminately. They bayoneted and beheaded babies as though it was sport. There was no horror they didn't commit. We were too poor and miserable for them to bother entering our quarter because we had nothing they could rob or pillage and I kept my daughters out of sight. But all round us there were massacres and looting and rape.

"Then, when the Japanese were defeated, we had the Kuomin-tang troops who went mad in another way, slaughtering everyone they suspected of being Communists or Communist supporters, as they used to do in the days before the Japanese came. It didn't matter whether you'd never heard anything about the Com-munists. You had only to be suspected and you were beaten or shot.

"So you see for the greater part of our lives we had nothing but war and destruction all round us and the town buzzed with frightening rumours before the Liberation Army came.

"But when we watched the troops enter the city in their poor clothes and worn shoes we thought, 'These aren't like the K.M.T. or the Japs. These are different.' And when I saw that not only did they not pillage and beat and shoot the citizens but helped them and gave them food, I decided that maybe there was some hope for my family after all. For the first time in our lives soldiers stopped to speak to me and my husband and asked if they could help us as though we were human beings instead of despised animals in the gutter. So we encouraged our three sons to join the army to fight in defence of thousands of mothers and fathers like us.

"And when the Government called on us all to stand up, because of the help given and the different treatment we received we began to feel that we, too, should do something for ourselves. I and my two daughters took part in the campaign to improve the district.

"It was difficult at first, not because people were opposed to the new Government but because they didn't believe in anything. In the old days it was said that your troubles were all due to your fate and you could do nothing about them. If you were poor, or your husband beat you, or some other trouble befell you, it was all due to your 'star'.

"The first thing to break down was this idea and show people that they could do things for themselves. When you come to our district you can see for yourself what we did.

"Now I'll tell you only my part in it. At first the hardest thing was to explain the Government's policy on sanitation to the people. No one had ever taught us before the link of disease with dirt. We began with rats. It was very difficult. The old people, especially the women, were not only very conservative, but very careless. They were also very sceptical. Rats there always had been and rats there always would be. And didn't everyone know that rats, and particularly the rats in their filthy area, were too cunning ever to be trapped? Indeed, some of them boasted about the cunning of the rats that had infested their houses for years.

"However, I thought up ways to convince them that even the most cunning rat could be trapped. When a few veterans whom popular opinion regarded with almost superstitious awe were taken in the traps their attitude changed. The women of the district were mobilized and the campaign spread from this district throughout Nanking City.

"Simultaneously we launched a campaign against flies and mosquitoes. Once the enthusiasm of the people was aroused the campaign gathered force, for other people, like myself, had only to compare their past lives with their present to work with enthusiasm.

"Because of my work in 1952 I was classed as a First-class Model Worker. When a national conference on sanitation workers was held in Peking I was awarded the honour of a First-class National Worker and also given a present of three hundred yuan." (This would be about £45.) "Never in all my life had I seen so much money! I did not want to spend it on myself, but it was decided that I must equip myself with things I needed. Up to then we had been living in a broken-down shack, sleeping on the floor. I spent some of my reward fixing the house and buying a bed and a table and some chairs. Now for the first time in my life I sleep on a bed, I eat from a table and sit on chairs. I spent the greater part buying hygienic equipment for the district.

"In 1953 we built a beautiful new house." (A " beautiful new house" for Loo Ta-ma meant two lath-and-plaster rooms with a mud-floor and a lean-to kitchen.) Her face saddens. "My husband died in 1953, at the age of seventy-three. He died happy, for he had seen the change that had come and at last brought the security that had been denied us all our lives. If he had died before Liberation he would have been buried in a pauper's grave. Now he was buried in a proper coffin donated by the people of the district and everybody went to his funeral. He had a beautiful funeral," she says, with the same wistful pride I have heard all over the world in the voices of poor women who have put themselves into debt for years to give their loved ones a fitting farewell.

She sits silent a moment, gazing abstractedly out of the window where a full moon silvers the garden, seeing perhaps the one moment of glory in a life that had apparently known nothing but poverty.

I am more than ever anxious to know about the life that lies behind her.

"You said that when Liberation came you could be pushed no lower. Would you tell me about those days? I would like to know."

Her brow wrinkles. The lines at the corner of her mouth deepen. Without her smile she is all her forty-nine years. I recognize in her pale skin the tautness that long malnutrition leaves and that nothing can ever remove. She demurs.

"Tomorrow. . . ." Tomorrow it is.

Next day, bit by bit, the story comes as I question her. Reluctantly at first, then rapidly, her face reflecting every aspect of her history.

"My real name is Loo Tsang-lan," she begins. "I was born the daughter of poor peasants in North Kiangsu Province. At that time my father owned nothing, but worked land that belonged to the landlord. Indeed, everything belonged to the landlord. When I was only ten—I am forty-nine now—we had to leave the countryside. We came to Nanking, begging our way along the roadside. Sometimes we were given rotten sour rice, sometimes people only jeered at us. Dogs were loosed on us, stones thrown at us. We were so hungry, we devoured anything. People laughed to see us pick up decaying cabbage-leaves. Our stomachs swelled, we were so often ill from the rotten food.

"After eating rotten rice for weeks we became so ill we had to lie in a deserted broken-down temple for three days thinking we were going to die. We had vomited all we had taken and lay in a stupor, unable to move. When we got to Nanking we had no money for a house and lived in a stable, our food discarded vegetables and grass. For months we had no rice, oil, or salt. My father found it impossible to get work and my mother kept the family alive on her meagre earnings by mending clothes. The only rice we had in these days was the rice strained from the pig-swill.

"From ten to twelve years I begged throughout Nanking, trying to bring something back to the family. At twelve I was old enough to start heavy work and I worked at any odd job I could get, beaten by my employers, always underfed, always hungry, always in rags. My parents had to sell my sister when she was less than ten. We never heard of her again.

"At twenty-three I married a poor peasant twenty-four years older than I was. To help us to live I worked as a maidservant for rich families, doing the washing and cleaning. When I became pregnant I still had to work until the day my child was born."

Her voice has throaty notes in it. It deepens as she tells the story of her marriage, and her work-worn, expressive hands, emphasize points with an uplifted forefinger.

"Only that my husband was a kind and good man, my life would have been utterly unbearable. But he suffered many illnesses and consequently could not earn much, so all of us led a life lower than that of animals.

"We were so despised that no one would speak to us and no one cared whether we lived or died. My children were born on the floor of the dilapidated hut in which we lived and I attended to everything myself, wrapping the baby in rags. We had only one rag-cover, under which we all slept in the cold weather. So poor were we that we had no warm clothes or coverings, and when the bitter winter came and the icy winds blew through the cracks of the hut we all huddled together for warmth.

"I had ten children altogether. Two sons died because we couldn't afford a doctor. Another child was born prematurely and died. Five days after I had to go to work. Another boy was given away because we had no way whatever of keeping him. He would be twenty years old now. I don't know where he is now, although I've made many inquiries.

"When the Japanese came things got even worse. Often there was no food at all. My husband was too sick to work, but he never complained. He was a very kind and lovely person and when there was no food to eat he just sat in the corner, tightened his belt, and starved. I would not let him go out because if the Japanese saw a sick man they just took him and threw him in a common grave outside the city.

"Five of my brothers were carpenters and they helped us when they could. One day one of them was at the hut trying to mend the broken wall when the Kuomintang police took him for no reason at all and hurried him off to the Japanese. Terrified at what might happen to him, I rushed after him. When I finally got to the Japanese base I found that they had literally torn him to pieces." Her voice breaks and the tears run down her cheeks and she is shaken by hard sobs.

"I was filled with such horror at the sight that I collapsed and had a serious illness. After my brother's death I still had six children dependent on me. I worked as a laundress as well as doing any kind of manual work. Indeed, all the family as they grew to labouring age did the lowest kind of work, the despised work.

"At eleven my eldest son was apprenticed to a small maker of glass but he learnt very little, being regarded as an odd-job boy to be beaten whenever it suited his master.

"That was our life. Our main food was the residue of bean-curd. We lived in houses that other families had deserted because they were uninhabitable. We wore what other people threw away. We were outcasts whom everyone despised.

"In the past one could see people lying dead in the streets of Nanking in winter; on the roads outside the city there were always dead bodies of those who died of cold and hunger. Indeed, if it had not been for Liberation and the People's Government probably all my family would have died, because by then we had reached a stage where we had suffered so much that we had neither hope nor ambition.

"Then everything changed." Her voice is scarcely audible, a faint smile plays round her lips as she speaks.

"Today all my sons are working at good jobs. One is an electrical worker, and is also studying in a short-term middle school. My second son is now demobilized, and works in the District Government in Nanking. He became a commanding officer in the Liberation Army, and is now on the reserve." Her face lights with pride at this honour to the son of a beggar.

"The third works in a glass factory in Nanking. My eldest daughter-in-law has a son to look after but she also does welfare work in her district. My second daughter-in-law has no children and is studying at the university. My third daughter-in-law does some work on the Street Committee.

"My eldest daughter is married to a railway worker, the second one to a man who was a pedi-cab driver but who now has a good job, filling pillows in a factory. My youngest daughter, eleven, is still at school, and she hopes to go on to the university. She is very clever.

"In the old days I was always sick, but now that my life is different and I always have sufficient food, I am very well. We are all well. And well dressed," she adds, smoothing the sleeve of her green seersucker tunic with a touch of vanity I like.

"Before Liberation I would never have dreamt—" she emphasizes the "dreamt"—"of putting on this tunic!

"I was illiterate, but I found with all the new things I have to do I just must learn, because without knowing the characters I could not make notes and had to store everything in my head. So now I am studying in a group, three times a week, and already I know many characters.

"Because I thought always of my sons in the army I spent time visiting servicemen's families. For this work I was again given the honour of First-class Model Worker. Greatest honour of all, I was elected deputy to the Kiangsu People's Congress in 1954, but what I feel is equally important is that the people of my district love and respect me, and they all call me Loo Ta-ma, a term of honour as well as of affection."

Her face is radiant as she speaks of her new life and she says, with a proud lift of her head, "Once we were the most despised of people. Now we and other people like us can attain any heights we wish. Like China, the Loos have stood up."

On a sweltering afternoon we speed along the wide streets of Nanking, lined with trees and large European-type houses. Past the Monument to Martyrs, erected to those who died in the struggle for China's freedom. Past a line of boys and girls with the red scarves of Pioneers round their necks; past horse-drawn vehicles; past a husband and wife drawing a heavily laden cart, ropes taut from their shoulders, the sweat glistening on their faces; past endless shabby pedi-cabs, modern cars, American, Czech, Polish, Russian; past huge hygiene posters, illustrating in vivid colours the war against rats and flies and mosquitoes.

Then the car slows as it turns into a narrow side-street that leads to the Wu Lu district where Loo Ta-ma mobilized the people to wipe out the foulest blot in the city.

The street is so narrow that we crawl along between the crowded, open-fronted shops where the metal-workers bend over primitive iron stands on which they beat out the vessels they are making; where traders and workers of all descriptions carry on their activities on the footpath. A crowd of lightly clad children follows the car's progress, laughing and waving. Men look up from their work. Women run to the doors and smile. It is obvious that here a motor-car is an event. There are smiles and hand-waving and an occasional clap. We skirt a watermelon stall, almost taking it with us. A fat baby decides to cross in front of the car and is pursued by a bound-foot grandma, hobbling on her tiny deformed feet. The sun beats down. The temperature is in the nineties. Pools of water still lie from the overnight storm.

As we reduce our speed to a still slower crawl a waft of hotter air brings us a tantalizing smell of cakes and large wheaten pancakes cooking on an outdoor stove.

Down a narrower metalled side-street. Mothers and grand-mothers and grandfathers and children of all ages clap as we make our way down the road. Hands are outstretched in greeting. An old, toothless, bound-foot woman puts out a clawlike hand and we shake. Grandfathers with straggly beards wave their long pipes. Naked children crawl between the legs of the crowding adults to get a better look.

The children are plump and healthy by any standard, though the older people bear ineradicable marks of poverty and malnu-trition. Everyone is adequately clothed.

The houses are of mud-brick and wood, some of only matting. The doors are open and I can see into the rooms. It is very hot. Not a fly or a mosquito and no smells. I am aware only of the scent of a flowering tree.

There are young trees everywhere, lining the road, overtopping the fences. We stop at a whitewashed building with wide windows, headquarters of the Street Committee of Wu Lu District, which comprises three hundred and seventy families and more than nine hundred and eighty persons, most of them tradesmen and unskilled labourers.

Four women greet me, members of the committee.

We sit on hard chairs in the large, cheerful room. Scarlet banners with brilliant gold characters decorate the walls, recog-nition of their achievements in their fight for the better sanitation of their district.

The walls are hung with numerous photographs showing Champion Fly-catchers with the special nets they invented, Spider Eradicators at work with long poles in the eaves of mud-brick houses, Champion Rat-catchers with the equipment they devised, Champion Mosquito-catchers—all with their neatly lettered ac-count of their achievements in the great hygiene campaign.

They tell me in the old days this room was just a filthy shed, but the men lime-washed the walls and put in windows and made the furniture and turned it into this meeting-place of which they are clearly very proud.

Lidded glasses are set out on the long table and hot water flavoured with ginger is poured for us.

My hostesses are responsible for the health, housing, education, welfare, security, and conciliation affairs covered by the Women's Federation of the area.

The chairwoman, Cheng Wen, is a married woman in her twenties. Two short plaits with curled ends frame a round, laughing face. She wears a green-flowered tunic over her light-grey slacks. Wang Wen-chen, an older woman, tells me that she has three children, sixteen, ten, and three years old. Then there are Shu Che-feng, slender and middle-aged, and Wu Hsiao-ling, who looks fourteen but tells me she is twenty with a shy smile that compensates for her reserve.

I ask them how they manage to combine the exacting duties of the Street Committee with their housekeeping, and they laugh, saying they are so well off now compared with their old life that they don't find anything too hard! "Besides we don't want to return to old conditions, and we know that it is only by working together that we shall maintain and still further improve our new life."

I think it is better to let them tell their own story, each interposing at some stage to contribute an item.

Mrs Cheng begins: "Looking after our district is part of the work of the country as a whole, for husbands can work without worrying, knowing that their wives and families are well looked after and freed from the dangers of pestilence that once hung perpetually over Wu Lu.

"The very name of our district illustrates the changes that have come. Long ago when it was a village and not part of the City of Nanking it had been called Wu Lu—that was 'The Village of The Five Old Men'. But as Nanking grew and it became a living sore on the edge of the city people called it simply 'Wu' or 'Very Poor'. Now it is called 'The Happy Village'."

Mrs Wang takes up the story: "In the old days three-quarters of the area was swampy, since it is low-lying. During the rainy days most of the houses were flooded. We had no way of cooking since the water flowed into the clay stoves. So we had to improvise and cook on the table. We had to raise the beds on clay platforms. Dirty stagnant water was always lying round."

"The rest of the city used the area as a garbage tip," Mrs Shu explains, "and therefore, on hot days, nauseating smells arose from it. Flies and mosquitoes bred in millions. During the summer and autumn there were always epidemics. A common phrase was that 'you prepared to be sick in those seasons'. People lived terrible lives, many unemployed, all poverty-stricken, most of them suffering from malaria, with periodical outbreaks of typhoid and cholera and other epidemics that wiped out many victims. We got no help from the Municipal Council or National Government."

Mrs Cheng's face grows brighter as she tells me, "Nanking was liberated in 1949. Immediately the People's Government drained the stagnant water, built a new road—our lovely metal road outside—and put in new street lamps. This was the first improvement and it made us realize that it was possible to do something to alleviate our misery and improve our surroundings.

"When the sanitation campaign of 1952 began the first thing we tackled was a filthy ditch which ran from one end of the district to the other, which the Government estimated would cost six thousand yuan to fill in. It was a plague spot. Children fell into it. Old people and blind were sometimes drowned in it. Despairing mothers threw their unwanted babies—unwanted because they knew they could not feed them—into the ditch. Dead cats and dogs floated there, and it was the receptacle for rotten and decaying vegetables. Now everyone set to work. Even old women with bound feet came with baskets and primitive spades to help fill it. We completed it in eighteen days and converted it into a nice park."

"You know," Mrs Shu explains, "it was the filling in of the ditch that really roused the enthusiasm of the women and made us realize that we had a part to play in improving our own lives."

"In 1953 two classes were opened by the Women's Committee," Mrs Cheng goes on, "one on sanitation and one on first aid, under the leadership of the Chinese Red Cross. Because we now have a knowledge of the causes of epidemic diseases we can control them. In 1945 there were twenty-six cases of cholera here; in 1951 only two and from 1952 to 1957, none. Eighty per cent of the inhabitants were diseased in some way or other when examined in 1950, and many suffered from malaria, which has been wiped out.

"Slogans for the prevention of diseases are put up everywhere saying: 'Kill it early. Kill it small. Kill it thoroughly.' Because of the excellent work of prevention there now are no recurrent epidemics. The general health standard has risen because of the better general level of life. People have even saved a little money and can make a better life for their children and themselves.

"Very few women could read or write and when we started a campaign to eliminate illiteracy one hundred and fifty-two came to attend the class. We found we had to use different methods to suit people's needs and wishes. A woman can attend a spare-time school or join a team. In other cases, the husband or children guarantee to teach her, or a literate neighbour takes care of her teaching. But you tell her about it, Wu Hsiao-ling, you're the expert."

Little Miss Wu blushes and begins: "Small teams have proved more popular. They work for one hour a day. The teachers are all voluntary. Where women are too occupied by children to leave them, we organize groups of children in a house with an old woman to mind them. These old women do this as their contribution to improving the village. Starting from January this year we have finished three books. And we plan this year to 'take off the hat of illiteracy'."

Mrs Wang laughs. "We found that one thing led to another. We wanted to go to literacy classes, but we found that unless we could solve the problem of the children we could not find time. So it was decided that we had to have a kindergarten. We selected as director Ching-fung, who was literate but who told us in despair that she could not come and join in the activities because she had too many children to look after. We thought that as director of the kindergarten she could look after other people's children as well as her own and she was most enthusiastic about the idea.

"First big difficulty was teachers. We had no money to pay them, so the youth of the village voluntarily came as teachers.

"Then the workers gave ten cents each so that the children could have boiled water and we could buy cheap beans and candies."

"It really was beginning from nothing," Mrs Shu says. "When we started the kindergarten we had no place to house it, so we taught in the open street. Afterwards we used the literacy classroom. Then we rented a room."

Little Miss Wu grows excited. "After the kindergarten was organized, the other people in the district, hearing that we had a kindergarten, came over and contributed so that we then could buy towels, basins, and first-aid equipment. More and more people heard of what we had done and gave something towards the school. As a result of all these efforts the village was given the honour of being a Model Village."

"The Vice-Mayor of the City Council offered money to repair the house in which the kindergarten was, but the Government decided to build a new one," Mrs Cheng says. "The estimate was fourteen thousand yuan—such a big sum that the people thought they must do something to save the Government money, so everybody helped. The men worked on their days off to erect the building and make furniture and we saved the Government seven thousand yuan. Now the kindergarten has been raised to the level of a municipal kindergarten, but it's still under the direction of the Street Committee. There are small fees." (I found that these fees run from threepence-halfpenny to fivepence a week.) "Part of the fees goes to the teachers, part for meals for the children. We have full-time teachers now. At lunch-time the children have beds to sleep on and there is regular health inspection. We started with forty children. Now we have one hundred and forty. We're going to take you to see them."

Out into the glaring sunshine, that beats down on the road that was the first gift of the Government to Wu Lu Village. Past the crowd of grandmothers and grandfathers and mothers and fathers and babies, followed by a growing tail of excited curious children.

A gaily painted archway bearing "Happy Village" in large characters spans the beginning of the roadway that leads to the kindergarten. A hundred yards of uneven metalled surface where three years ago was a quagmire.

"It is called the Women's Road, because three years ago when the first conference of the Women of Nanking was held, the women of Happy Village banded together to make it," Mrs Shu says. "We made it with our own hands, levelling the earth, carrying the stone in shoulder-baskets, two women to each pole, breaking the stone, smoothing the surface."

Saplings lined the road. I forgot how many trees the inhabitants of Happy Village have set. Enough, I can see, to justify their boast that when I come back in five years it will be like a park.

The familiar noises of any kindergarten—with some local trimmings fill the air.

I am greeted by the smiling, plump director, and led on to the veranda of a weatherboard building, partitioned into three moderate-sized rooms.

As I entered the first room the three-to-four-year-olds greeted me with an ear-splitting yell of "Welcome, Aunty!", and the clanging of cymbals.

I shake hands with the teacher and we exchange inaudible greetings above the din and I leave amid repeated shouts of, "Good-bye, Aunty!"

The five-year-olds are singing a song of welcome. Their shrill voices rise as I enter and their cheeks grow pink as they give full force to it. A small girl bobs and shakes hands to welcome me. I'm introduced to the teacher. Our mouths move but we hear nothing. The song swells as I leave and pursues me to the next room where the six-to-seven-year-olds are in a state of nervous tension preparing to give me a concert. The concert is given. A song of greetings, which I hear through the noisy clashing of cymbals and beating of drums and the continuing song next door.

It is all much like home. The towels and mugs on the wall, each with their little picture to indicate the owner, the posters, the illustrated stories. Only the roll of mats on the corner of the veranda is different. For at lunch-time these will be unrolled in traditional Chinese fashion and the children will sleep on them.

All the one hundred and forty are well cared for and the clothes are clean and neat with every variety of style and colour from short pants and tunics on boys and girls alike to frilled cotton dresses that might be seen on any children's playground anywhere in the world.

When the concert finishes the class spokesman in a loud shrill voice, asks me for my criticisms so they can improve their work! It is laughable and at the same time so moving that I have a lump in my throat. What can I say? I bring them greetings from little boys and girls all over the world. They look at me with small grave faces, intent eyes, and as my message is translated the smiles flash, the eyes dance.

"Tell them to come and see us," the spokesman says and the class claps enthusiastically.

I promise and leave one hundred and forty pairs of black eyes and a chorus of voices follow me, calling, "Good-bye Aunty!"

Happy Village comes in full strength to see me off. One by one I shake hands.

Cheng Wen smiles her warm smile and takes my hand in both of hers.

"Come back again when we have done more towards making Happy Village beautiful. The revolution has only begun here."

I look over the garden that was a swamp, along the road that was a foul ditch; the air that was once full of pestilence blows warm and scented over a flowering shrub. I feel beneath my feet the solid road that was a quagmire. I see the bright faces round me, their clean neat clothes. I think of Loo Ta-ma, and the poverty, the misery, the degradation of her life; of the poverty and misery and degradation that all these people have known.

No, Cheng Wen, revolution is too simple a term for what is happening here. It is resurrection.

CHAPTER X

Nanking-Shanghai

SUCH strange things happen to me that I find nothing odd, on my last evening in Nanking, in standing with a Chinese professor on top of the hill called "Raining Flowers Mountain" and discussing in French the surf at Bondi and how well Australorps, an Australian breed of fowls, do in China.

We stand awhile looking at the city of Nanking below, within its walls that are thirty miles in extent.

"A hundred years ago this was the capital of the Taiping Revolution. I think we have never properly assessed the influence of the Taiping Revolution on the emancipation of Chinese women. Women must have played a big part in it, since the Taiping Government, which ruled for twelve years, gave them freedom as complete as they have today and much wider than they had in many parts of Europe a hundred years ago."

I was shaken out of my Western complacency by learning that on 20th March 1912 a group of Chinese suffragettes broke in on a meeting of the New Senate convened in Nanking and, following the example of their English sisters, began to break the windows! What force made these middle-class Chinese women so forget their upbringing that they fought with the police when an attempt was made to restrain them?

Why this outburst of feminine anger when the Revolution of 1911 had overthrown a social form that had lasted for three thousand years and already profoundly transformed the conditions of women's lives—in theory at least?

But although Sun Yat-sen was sympathetic to the women's movement and was prepared to listen to their claims for the right to participate in politics, equality of educational opportunities, equality of marriage laws and the abolition of concubinage, the New Government did not grant their claims and the provisory Constitution of 1912 contained no explicit statement on the question of the equality of the sexes, so the Chinese suffragettes, like their English sisters, demonstrated.

A humid summer morning when the train pulls out of Nanking

Station at eight o'clock. A crowded train. Peasants and business-men and mothers with babies on their backs, and soldiers.

A suburban-type carriage with sets of double seats facing each other. Our seats are apart, but a soldier gets up and offers us his so that we can sit together.

An old peasant couple goes by through the train, he with his sparse beard quivering in the vibration, a domed bamboo hat on his head, two woven bamboo baskets in his hand. She, timorous, with bound feet and thin grey hair scraped back into a chignon, a basket full of fruit, a bundle tied in a bright cloth. He tells us excitedly that this is the first time they have been in a train and they are going to Shanghai to visit their son who is in charge of an electrical plant!

A little girl comes up and leans on the arm-rest of my seat, chattering away and showing me her loose tooth. Her name is Little Third Sister. Second Brother has his nose glued to the window.

Little Third Sister's mother tells me that the last time she travelled Second Brother was a baby and the Kuomintang sol-diers crowded onto the train and forced the passengers off and threw their luggage after them.

The train service boy comes along distributing miniature chess-boards, magazines, and story-books which are mainly pictures—and very good pictures—with a minimum of script. These serve both children and a population whose older people are just emerg-ing from illiteracy. Little Third Sister takes me through a tale about a fairy princess who leaves heaven to marry a mortal—but, alas, the gods force her to return. Second Brother settles down with a book about aeroplanes.

It is very hot. The young soldier opposite reads a newspaper, and graciously offers me his fan.

A service boy comes through mopping the floor, sweeping up invisible rubbish, dusting the table where I can see no dust.

The train radio is giving advice to new passengers. Opposite, four soldiers argue passionately over a card game. It sounds (as in Italy) as though it will end in murder. But they dissolve in gales of laughter, throwing their narrow cards on the table and starting again.

Outside water-buffaloes plod stolidly over the paddy-fields, draw-ing a primitive plough through the water. Two men almost hid-den under wide latticed-bamboo hats pedal rhythmically, turning a long ratcheted wheel that pumps the water from one level to another. Water-wheels everywhere. Two men, two women. Brown legs treading tirelessly. One machine pump could release them all. The roofs here are more deeply curved with sharper eaves. The burnt-orange roof of a new State farm blazes against the lime green of ripening rice. A flock of white ducks half runs, half flies down the banks and into a sheltered creek.

Two men under glistening amber-yellow hexagonal hats tow a junk along a canal, a woman in bright-blue tunic and trousers poling to keep it clear of the red-ochre banks.

Advice from the radio to people getting off the train.

Wu-hsi! A heterogeneous crowd getting on. Indignation loudly expressed by new-comers because the train has pulled up too far along and they must walk through our compartment to reach theirs—"the hard"—farther along. There'll be some stinging criticism of the train crew about this! The train starts. Terrific commotion. A woman bursts into loud wailing. Some of her baggage has been left behind. Where is my London acquaintance who always talks about the impassive Chinese? She is comforted only when the train director promises to wire back from the next station!

Our soldier hops on at the last moment and comes back beaming and presents us with a basket of peaches. He introduces himself. Wang Kei-fang, son of a peasant family from the North-east. He is tall, with a long brown face, strong white teeth. When he hears I am a writer he takes out his pen and prints in neat characters on the margin of the newspaper he is reading.

Alas, I must have it translated!

"You are the engineer of the human spirit," he has written. "You must use your pen to appeal for peace, to save mankind and civilization, to abolish war."

I am so moved I ask him to inscribe it in my diary. Where else in the world, I wonder, would a young peasant-soldier do this?

Will I please tell everyone in my book, he says earnestly, that though he is an army man he hates war? After all, he and his family have suffered from war, they want only peace. When he has finished his service he wants to go back to the farm and grow things.

We eat his peaches. It grows hotter, steamier. A water-buffalo turns a water-wheel protected by a palm-leaf shelter. Under the blazing sun the brown backs of a rice-weeding group glisten with sweat. They move with measured strides through the water, their arms swinging in unison.

A heat-haze shimmers over the fields. Windmills with curved white cloth sails move intermittently in the faint breeze.

Slogans on the walls of houses. Exhortations to work well for the Motherland.

The model-tea-pourer refuels us.

The carriage is mopped and dusted again.

The radio is playing what is steadily ceasing to be my favourite minority song.

Wang Kei-fang disappears as the train pulls into Soochow. One of the beauty spots of China, the radio tells us, centre of the silk industry.

Just as the whistle blows Wang Kei-fang returns, smiling more widely than ever, with a basket of better and bigger peaches. We demur. A soldier's pay doesn't run to providing peaches for foreign writers. He insists. They are delicious peaches, too. He beams as the juice drips down our chins.

Off through the same unbelievably green countryside, with its innumerable peasants working under an infinite variety of curved and domed and conical hats. Camel-bridges curve gracefully above little streams. Everywhere rising like green sugar loaves, the ancestral graves. Marble memorial arches to some forgotten dignitary or faithful widow.

The outskirts of Shanghai, factory chimneys—and Shanghai, where I descend to a welcoming group carrying the rest of the good peaches that generous Wang Kei-fang has insisted on my taking with me.

CHAPTER XI

Capitalist Family

SHANGHAI sizzles in the heat of a midsummer day as our car toots its way through the crowded streets.

Yen Ching-hung is taking me to visit a capitalist's family. She is dressed in a cool cotton *chi-pao*; through the side-split her bare leg is visible above the knee; her arms are bare, but the high tight collar hides her throat completely!

A capitalist's family in Shanghai will be up to date, I imagine. After all, Shanghai has been open to foreign trade and settlement since the Treaty of 1843 which followed the First Opium War. And their lives in old Shanghai must have been comfortable, to say the least.

Tooting his way through an apparently inextricable mass of pedi-cabs and handcarts and perambulators and pedlars with baskets dangling from shoulder poles, the chauffeur turns into a narrow lane, leaning out like any taxi-driver anywhere in the world to express his opinion of a pedi-cab that pulls up without warning. The pedi-cab driver shouts a withering retort. A policeman rebukes them both, mildly. Swearing is frowned on in modern China, and I am told the old picturesque oaths are rarely heard.

Each side of the street, high walls, some topped by broken glass, others with barbed wire, relics of old Shanghai.

The car stops at a big forbidding-looking gate. A wicket door opens to our knock. The big gate is opened and we enter. It closes behind us and we crawl along a drive onto which face a group of identical three-storeyed brick houses in a walled compound.

A tall man I take to be in his early forties, in a well-cut Western suit, is waiting to receive me, accompanied by two women.

He is the eldest Chi son, he explains after he has greeted me and introduced me to his wife and his sister-in-law. As head of the family, his mother has asked him to welcome me. His wife, in a *chi-pao* of soft grey material, shakes hands with me gravely. She has a reserved manner, full of a quiet dignity. Glasses make her look still more grave. Her sister-in-law's face breaks into a smile of great sweetness. On the pocket of her black *chi-pao* is a white enamel badge inscribed with red characters. Both the women have fashionably permed hair, though everything else about them bespeaks the "old" Chinese life, from their embroidered satin slipper-shoes to the air of dignified reserve that is so unmistakably a sign of the old régime. Second shock: three of the houses are occupied by sons of the family and their families! Here, in its modern form, is the perpetuation of the ancient Chinese ideal: all the generations living together under one roof!

A smiling, bound-foot old amah in white tunic and black trousers, a small child in her arms, bows to me as we enter.

The sitting-room is cool after the blistering heat of the street, with a large ceiling fan that keeps the air circulating. Wide windows look on a walled garden. It might be a room in any Western house, with its comfortable blue lounge suite. But the windows are barred with curved iron bars that are singularly decorative against the brilliant light without, and if the furniture is Western, the picture-scrolls and the character-scrolls that cover the walls are Chinese. So is the large brass spittoon!

We exchange comments on the weather.

Conversation lapses. There is a feeling of expectancy in the air.

Mrs Chi Senior makes her entrance.

She is slender as a girl in her black silk *chi-pao*, and her face, with its old-ivory skin and oblique eyes, is oddly like the famous head of Nephretete. Only for the smooth glossy hair drawn back to the nape of her neck, I might have been looking at the Egyptian Queen of three thousand years ago. Her face is proud and aloof, her manner imperious. But when she smiles—a wide smile of extraordinary charm—her whole face changes.

She welcomes me graciously. I am the first foreign guest who has ever been in her home.

She sits beside me, fanning herself with a sandalwood fan, offers me a cigarette from a carved lacquer-box, and with supple thin fingers fits a cigarette into a long ivory holder, questioning me rapidly as she does so.

"Is it true that women are so free in your country?"

I assure her it is. She looks at me directly. "How many women have you in Parliament?" I am saved from revealing my national shame by the arrival of the old servant with a tea-tray. She skitters with astonishing speed on her bound feet.

The strong black tea is almost cold. I am astonished. It is utterly unlike tea that most Chinese drink. Then I realize from the fact that nobody else does more than sip their cup that this brew has been specially made for me, someone having told them that this is the way foreigners like their tea and politeness demanding that they drink the same. Over the untouched tea the story of the Chi family is unfolded.

"We are a traditional family," Mrs Chi says. "We kept our sons at home and the daughters-in-law came to live with us. But now we are changing with the times, and only three of my sons and their families live here. Five of the others live in Shanghai and my two daughters also, while my youngest son is working in Shansi Province.

"Things have changed a great deal since I was a girl—I'm sixty-three—but it's only in the last six years that I have realized the changes. You see, I was reared in the old-fashioned way to concern myself only with the affairs of the house and the family. A generation later my two daughters-in-law here were brought up in the same way."

I mention the suffragettes of Nanking.

Mrs Chi and her daughters-in-law smile. "Laws about women's rights did not affect our homes. My eldest daughter-in-law here, who was married to my son in 1935, never saw her husband before her marriage. Indeed, all my four elder children had traditional marriages."

The eldest daughter-in-law gives her faint, reserved smile and lowers her eyes.

"And you, too?" I ask the younger daughter-in-law.

A flush sweeps over her face as she says, "I came just in time to be allowed to see my husband."

Mrs Chi goes on, "I came from an old-style, large family, wealthy and with much prestige. That hasn't meant that my life has been an easy one. When my husband and I were first married he had a small hosiery factory in Soochow, a few hours' run from Shanghai. But my son will tell you about that."

Mr Chi inclines his head. Throughout his mother's story he has watched her with an expression of respect that deepens at times to reverence. Now he takes over.

"My father used to tell us of his difficulties in those early days. Soochow had few cotton industries and those there were experiencing great difficulty in getting the necessary material to carry on. Between that and the competition from Japanese goods which were being dumped in great quantities he was forced to close down in 1920. The family came to Shanghai and my father set up the Pa Ta Underwear Factory. It was a great struggle because we had to depend on foreign countries for machines as well as raw cotton."

"It was a terrible time," Mrs Chi adds. "Not that I had much time to worry about the factory, because I had ten children, seven sons and three daughters, and that kept me busy. But I did worry about my husband. Those were bad days in Shanghai that got steadily worse as the years went on. Between the worries of my family and the worries of something happening to my husband I worried day and night. He was constantly followed by gangsters who threatened to kidnap him. I used to worry each day until he returned from the factory.

"It was just about this time that a well-known capitalist was kidnapped and the gangsters demanded an enormous ransom. It was quite a commonplace for wealthy men to have armed bodyguards. Sometimes I would take a pedi-cab and follow him to see that he got to the factory safely, but people began to say, 'How odd for the wife of the master to follow him!' So I stopped. It was not considered proper for a woman to go out alone at all.

"Every New Year my husband received blackmailing letters." She makes a gesture with her fan towards the windows. "Perhaps you are wondering why we have iron bars on the windows. Well, one New Year, before we came to live in this house, we had a large sum of money for the workers' wages. That evening ten men came in with guns. Fortunately my husband and sons were upstairs. When I saw the men coming in I rushed up and locked them in.

"The men demanded to go to the room with the safe. There was not much money in it so I showed them in and they took what there was as well as the jewellery that was there. I thought they would be satisfied. But they said, 'This isn't enough. You've got more than this. Show us the rooms upstairs.' I thought rapidly. Suppose they take all the money, how can we pay the workers? I tried to make them believe that was all the money. They said they didn't believe me and demanded to know where my husband and sons were. I said, 'At the factory.' Finally they pushed past me and went up the stairs. I rushed ahead into a front room and locked the door, but they shot the door open.

"I was afraid they would shoot me as well as my husband and sons if I did not get help, so I ran to the window and jumped from the first floor to the ground, shouting, 'Robbers! Robbers!' thinking to attract the police and save my husband and sons.

"Some of the servants rushed in and the kidnappers scattered, shooting wildly, but the only damage was to a passer-by who was shot in the leg. Then the police arrived. Miraculously I wasn't seriously injured by the fall, but all my teeth were smashed. That's why I have false ones. Next day another letter came demanding the balance of the money and threatening that if it was not paid they would throw hand-grenades. We immediately left that house and moved to this, which we have occupied ever since, buying the next-door houses as my sons married.

"During those years I suffered from constant bad health because of the continuous worry lest something should happen to my husband. And I have no doubt that what he went through hastened his early death. He died in 1943 and my three eldest sons took over the management of the factory."

But I am more interested in her than in the factory and try to lead her back to those long-ago days in Soochow. What was her life like?

She smiles. "So much has happened since that I've almost forgotten. You see, there was nothing exciting about our lives. We lived in the typical house of the wealthier type, and I lived the life of the typical well-to-do Chinese girl in a rich family. I rarely went out, staying always with my mother. If male guests came— even relations—I had to run away and hide, always to efface myself.

"A girl was really enclosed in her family. If she was seen in public people would say, 'What a disgrace! What a family!' Girls were not allowed to go to school. Even a generation later my daughters-in-law did not go to school."

The two daughters-in-law smile at my look of surprise, and nod affirmatively. One said, "Even if we had studied with a private tutor, we would have been taught only what had been taught for two thousand years, the Four Virtues and the Three Obediences."

"That is, obey your father, obey your husband, and, if a widow, obey your eldest son," Mrs Chi explains. "The Four Virtues referred first to your behaviour, which must be always morally beyond reproach. Secondly, to the correctness of your language: you must speak softly, be always conciliating to your husband and your mother-in-law. Thirdly, your clothes must be suitable to your station, elegant but not showy; and, last of all, you must be skilled in the things that were considered women's work—managing a house, looking after children, embroidery and sewing. We were trained not to turn our heads when we were talking, not to show our teeth when speaking, to keep our legs absolutely still when sitting. When I look back on it it all seems so unnecessary and unnatural."

The amah skitters in and removes the tea-cups and replaces them with bowls of delicious ice-cream. She hands me a steaming towel faintly scented with gardenia and I mop my face and hands.

Mrs Chi is reliving her past. "It was all very different from my granddaughters' lives today. From the age of seven girls were reared quite apart from their brothers. Boys were taught to say yes strongly and forcefully. Girls were trained to say it in a very humble tone. Usually girls had bound feet. My oldest sister had bound feet, but I, for some reason I'm not clear about, escaped this.

"At fifteen we were considered marriageable, though generally did not marry till some years later. But when you were fifteen there was a special ceremony called 'the putting on of the hair-pin' and you changed your manner of doing your hair. From then on you were more strictly trained in docility and obedience so that you would not disgrace your parents by being a bad daughter-in-law. My parents died when I was only sixteen. It was a terrible time. Many people died from an epidemic which swept the country. After their death I lived with my brother and sister-in-law who had a large department store in Soochow.

"At twenty-one, I married Mr Chi. I had never seen my husband, nor he me, until the day of our marriage."

I am not going to let an occasion like a Chinese wedding pass so lightly, so I ask for details.

Mrs Chi smiles. "Unless a girl was already betrothed, parents set about finding a suitable husband for her when she reached a marriageable age. For this a go-between was always considered necessary, and the first thing to be done when the parents of a young man approached a go-between to find a wife for their son was to consult their horoscopes. It was believed that an old man who lives in the moon has a big book containing the names of all those who are intended by Fate to marry and that he ties the feet of bride and groom with a red cord that can never be untied. If the horoscopes were harmonious the go-between was sent with an offer of marriage. If the girl's parents were satisfied the be-trothal contract was signed. This was really the most important ceremony.

"Then the groom's parents sent gifts—a goose and many other things. The goose was a symbol of fidelity, since the wild goose paired but once. In a fifth ceremony, the go-between asked the bride's parents to find a lucky day to 'set out the embroidered coverlet'. Last of all came the day when the bride was taken to the groom's house after spending three or four days before the marriage in strict seclusion.

"The ceremony itself was simple, but sometimes all the things connected with it put the bridegroom's family in debt for years. If you did not have a splendid reception for the bride you lost face, and sometimes people borrowed money from friends and relatives. We did not believe in this and always kept within our means.

"In our day—" Mrs Chi includes her silent daughters-in-law in the glance—"it was considered necessary that a bride should have enough clothes to last her for a year and all the boxes containing these and the bed-covers and furniture and other gifts were sent to her new home a day or so before the wedding. If a family wanted to make a great show sometimes they would hire between two and three hundred men to carry the gifts.

"On the wedding day the sedan chairs, each with eight bearers, set out from the bridegroom's house to bring the bride to her new home. The bride's chair was red, the others green. The most important person to escort the bride was the marriage dame, a relative of the bridegroom. She had to be a married woman who had a child and whose husband was alive, for widows were considered unlucky. The procession was accompanied by a band and numerous other people in festival clothes carrying banners all meant to draw attention to the magnificent bridal chair.

"When they arrived at the bride's house the marriage dame entered and covered the waiting bride's head with a veil of red embroidered silk, with red tassels and hung with many strings of pearls. The bride wore richly embroidered red silk robes."

She is silent a moment. We are all silent. I should like to ask the two older women what they felt as they stepped into the gorgeous bridal chair. Not all the custom and training in the world could make a young girl's heart less fearful as she set out on the journey to a strange house to meet the bridegroom she had never seen. But there are things one cannot ask. Things one does not need to ask.

Behind the simple narrative I see the trembling bride stand beside the husband she cannot see; see them prostrate themselves before a table on which are placed a tablet to Heaven and Earth, a pair of lighted candles and an incense burner from which rise the fragrant fumes that must almost suffocate her under her thick veil.

"They exchanged wine-cups tied by red cords," Mrs Chi goes on, "and kotowed to the ancestral tablets and the bridegroom's

parents. Then, walking backwards, the bridegroom led his wife
to the nuptial chamber where they sat together on the marriage-
bed. Then and then only the bridal-veil was lifted and for the
first time the bridegroom looked upon his bride's face.

"It was only when they had tasted the wine and made a pretence of eating the wedding-dumplings that they were considered
man and wife. But there was another ordeal for the bride. After
the bridegroom had departed to join his friends in the wedding
feast, the bride—alone in a strange house—was submitted to that
test of self-control known as 'Teasing-in-bridal-room'. Guests
inspected her, exchanged unflattering comments on her appearance, made rude jokes and teased her as much as they liked. If
by so much as a sharp intake of breath, a change of expression,
she showed her feelings, she lost face."

I begin to understand the self-control of Chinese women a little
better.

Mrs Chi comes back from the past and says to her son, "Now
you must tell our foreign friend about the business."

"Ours was only a small factory," Mr Chi says, "but what happened to us on a small scale happened to all the larger factories
in Shanghai unless they were collaborating closely with the Japanese. We had only one shareholder, the family. We had only one
hundred and thirty-seven workers.

"No question of it, they were badly off," he says, nodding his
head several times. "It was not surprising that relations between
them and us were extremely bad. They worked in conditions I
have since come to realize were disgraceful. We were not bad
people, my brothers and I, any more than my father had been.
Indeed he was always considered an honourable business-man.
But we regarded the workers as a lesser race and did not worry
about how they existed as long as they did their work.

"On the eve of Liberation we were very frightened about the
Communists. Everybody said, 'Your property will be confiscated.'"

Mrs Chi gives a little laugh. "I was even terrified that my sons
might be killed because they were capitalists."

"Yes. At first we suspected every proposal made by the new
Government. Every promise was regarded with distrust. But
gradually we came to believe what the Government said—that the
national capitalists had their destiny in their own hands. So last
year we decided to apply for joint-State ownership."

"At first all we women were opposed to it," Mrs Chi breaks in.
"So a family meeting was called and my sons explained to me and

my daughters-in-law the advantages the new system would bring, and we agreed that they should apply."

"Now, as a result of the decision, our business is prosperous and our lives free from worry," Mr Chi goes on. "Before, there was always trouble between the capitalists and workers. Now the workers co-operate with us in the management and we get on very well. We also work harmoniously with the State Representative in the factory.

"Altogether the lives of capitalists in Shanghai have improved beyond description. We can get all the raw material we need, we can buy new machines—many made in China. The big factories give help to the small. We get our salaries if we are active in the business, and the fixed five per cent on the total capital we placed in the business. And even if the enterprise makes a loss, we still get our five per cent interest."

Mrs Chi agrees. "In the old days I used to be upset and worried about my sons, because they were always so disturbed and anxious. Now they look healthy and have at last lost their worried expression. My eldest son has got rid of his stomach ulcers. And when I see the difference between my sons' lives and their father's life I am convinced that the new system is good. Indeed, I know their father would agree with them, for he originally founded the factory to give the family a good life and one free of worry. But now the young ones don't want to be capitalists at all! The youngest one has already graduated and is employed in the kind of job he always wanted to do in a big engineering factory in Shansi."

The "afternoon tea" arrives, in silver cake dishes. Mrs Chi Junior serves me with a plate piled high with heart-shaped yellow cakes with red characters on them and little brown bean-rolls.

Mrs Chi Senior apologizes because they had not had sufficient warning of my coming to prepare a proper welcome for me. With one eye on the pile of cakes I make the proper responses, knowing that this deprecatory reference is part of old-time courtesy.

We sip our pale-green tea with relief. Mrs Chi looks over her cup.

"I must tell you that during all this I have often behaved in a very 'old-minded' way. My sons were much more advanced than I. Although I had agreed to the transformation to joint-State ownership, it wasn't until last March I realized that the change that had come to China was for the benefit of everybody, women as well as men."

For the first time the two daughters-in-law show signs of animation.

"One morning, to my great astonishment, I received an invitation from the Women's Federation to visit Peking. I was stunned. Go to Peking alone! I, who in all my life had never travelled anywhere except between Soochow and Shanghai, and then only when carefully looked after by my family or maids!

"I said I couldn't go, but everyone, including my daughters-in-law, said I must go along to the Women's Federation to explain personally why I couldn't possibly go. But they were so nice to me when I got there that I decided that I would risk it and go!

"What a trip it was! I was full of fears when I got into the train. I was afraid that my luggage would be lost. But there it was in my compartment—all of it!

"Everything was perfect on the train. Beds were made up, the heating was just right. I had thought I would be most uncomfortable because I would not know anyone. But here were almost a hundred delegates, like myself, all going to Peking. They all treated me in such a friendly way, just as loving as my own family. More so!" she added as an afterthought.

"I had been afraid of being sick. But I felt very well, and went in with the other women to have meals, beautiful meals, in a wonderful dining car. I had been worried, too, about the food, for I needed a special diet." Had pre-Liberation Shanghai given *her* stomach ulcers, too?

"But there was a special diet all prepared for me!

"It was my first trip to Peking. Long lines of big motor-cars were waiting for us at the station. We were taken to a new hotel with magnificent carpets, and I had a room more comfortable than the one I have at home.

"Before I left for Peking I had made a new dress—navy blue with white spots." Mrs Chi's manner indicated that she had considered this rather modern and daring. "But what did I find? Women as old as myself in bright colours, and looking very nice, too."

The daughters-in-law are smiling now as their mother-in-law talks, sharing vicariously the marvels of the journey. The sandalwood fan flutters, her jet eyes dance, she laughs. The amah lingers in the doorway and listens to a recital she must have heard many times before.

Mrs Chi taps her fan on the arm of her chair for emphasis. "It was a most wonderful experience. We spent three days visiting all Peking's beauty spots and one night we had a wonderful party and danced together and sang songs. There were about a thousand women from all over the country.

"One day Teng Ying-chao, the Premier's wife, gave us a party and spoke to us about the future of women in New China. It was all so strange to me to think that henceforth women were as free as men and that equality meant that they, too, had a role to play in the new society. Of course, I had heard it before, but never thought it affected us. But then and there I made up my mind to find out just what it all meant and how it applied to us all. . . ." The amah nods vigorously and approvingly.

"No question of it!" Mrs Chi adds earnestly. "This year a lucky star came to our family.

"It was while I was away that I began to realize that I simply couldn't go on being illiterate any longer. Why, I even had to get other people to write letters for me to the family to tell them all the wonderful things that were happening to me! I came back determined that all the Chi family, not only the men, must be transformed. Now my grandson is teaching me to write, and all my daughters-in-law are busy with new activities."

The second daughter-in-law, who has been playing with a floral handkerchief, like a shy girl, now speaks vivaciously. Two deep dimples show in her cheeks. "All of us are studying, we read newspapers now. I work on the Street Committee in our district."

"And Mrs Chi Junior?"

A faint smile rather in her eyes than on her lips relieves her grave expression and she tells me she is a member of the Democratic Constitution Party and is busy learning about the political situation.

"What is the badge you wear?" I return to the second sister-in-law. She positively sparkles. "I am studying in a political school for families of business-men and industrialists. Altogether there are two thousand students, two hundred of whom are wives. We study political economy, so that I can explain the Government's decrees to all the others. I am just finishing my first term. It is very interesting."

"And how do you all like the New China?" I ask.

There is an animated discussion between mother and daughters-in-law.

"We like it much better than the old," they all agree, "because while retaining our same conditions of life we now have the security to enjoy it free from worry, and have interests in life we never had before."

"They look much happier," Mrs Chi says, "and are much more

interesting to live with. Our family is happier than it ever was. My eldest son was manager before. He still is manager. The two younger brothers occupy their same positions as factory directors. And now, instead of always quarrelling, everybody works together and everything is discussed with the sole object of increasing production so that everybody is better off.

"The Chis represent the old-time, thrifty capitalists and we live in just the same way, in the same house, as when we were in a small way. I go to a discussion group once a week. The group has been studying the New Marriage Law. I am entirely in favour of it. In the old days when the parents picked their children's husbands and wives there was much unhappiness. But it is surprising the number of old-fashioned people there are about still. Members of our circle still come to me and ask me to act as match-maker." She fans herself vigorously and her eyes flash. "I tell them what I think of such feudal ideas!

"In the past no Chinese girl of good family would ever have dreamed of dancing with a man, but now my granddaughters do it and never give it a thought. And why shouldn't they, after all? They all play sport, too, and I think that's good for them."

On a sudden impulse she suggests that the younger women should go and get the family album to show me and I look through the photographs that mirror the world-shaking changes that have come to Chinese women.

The return of the other men from business makes me realize how quickly the hours had passed. I get up to leave.

They press me to return, write their names and their address in Chinese characters in my note-book, Mrs Chi Senior proud and ashamed at the same time of her shaky writing.

Three generations of the Chi family, mother and sons and daughters-in-law and children of all ages, the youngest in the arms of the amah, crowd round the car and follow it to the outer gate to wave farewell to the first foreign friend who has ever crossed the Chi threshold.

CHAPTER XII

Chang Sui-ying, Textile Worker

AFTER my visit to the Chis I asked to meet a textile worker who could tell me something of her experiences in Shanghai's factories in the old days. Chang Sui-ying came to see me in my hotel.

She is a small, thin woman, very pale, with freckles on her nose and, like most Chinese, she has large, beautiful teeth. Her waved hair is less luxuriant than that of most women I have met, and in her white tunic and blue trousers, she has the body of a sixteen-year-old girl. She is so reserved and unsmiling that I wonder if I shall learn much of her story. All my efforts to put her at her ease have no effect. She has the air of the patient at the dentist's who wants only to get the ordeal over, as she sits rigidly on the edge of the chair, her small hands with filbert nails playing with the ball-point pen she keeps in her tunic pocket.

In some indefinable way she has on her the mark of the mill-worker and a hard, chronic cough shakes her at intervals.

I ask her to tell me her story in her own way and not to hurry.

Staring at her hands, she plunges into the telling. "I was born in a district of Shanghai near the North Railway Station thirty-four years ago. My father was a house-painter. We lived in a very poor house, eight persons crowded into one room with no light and no water. My father died at forty-five from painter's lead-poisoning. That also killed my elder brother. My mother had nine children, but since the family could not afford so many two of the children were given away. Three others died of illnesses. When I was twelve it was necessary for me to get some kind of job. One of my elder sisters was a textile worker, so it was decided to smuggle me into the factory to learn the trade without apprenticeship. This was often done, since you had no chance of a job if you did not already know the work.

"At first I worked in the night so as not to be caught by the foreman. Once when I was obliged to work on the day shift I was caught and ran and hid in the toilet until the foreman had forgotten.

"I worked twelve hours a day and my married sister brought a meal to the factory to keep me alive, since the family could not afford to feed me. My sister was generous, but all she could afford was second- or third-quality rice-porridge that was more water than rice. Sometimes I had salted cucumber, but I never saw meat or fish or eggs. Sometimes as a treat I had a little flour-and-salt fried in oil.

"After a year I had learnt the trade and I became a mill-worker at a wage of eighteen cents a day, from which I had to pay four cents for the ferry-boat across the river.

"I worked in the spinning department taking off bobbins. When I didn't work well enough I was beaten by the foreman—the Number One, as he was called—or beaten by other members of the staff. When I would come home and show the marks of my beatings my mother would weep and try to comfort me."

Her teeth are set as she tells her story. Sometimes her voice is harsh. I can almost follow the story by watching her face. The fingers continue to pluck the hem of the handkerchief. She seems to shrink as though the memories are all too vivid.

"The spinning room was very small, with too many machines with narrow ways between them. It was badly lit, with only single bulbs high up. There were no safety devices and workers were often injured. If one had a finger cut off she was dismissed, and had to turn to begging, since her trade was no longer any use to her. The owner of the mill had a saying, 'It is easier to find a hundred workers than a hundred dogs.'

"The room had no ventilation whatever, and there were too many workers in the room, so that there was always a horrible stench. The owner would hold his handkerchief to his nose as he passed through, commenting aloud on the stinking workers.

"In the summer temperature in the workshops would often rise to a hundred and ten degrees Fahrenheit. We perpetually had headaches and often fainted. We were left lying where we fell. The foreman would say, 'What does it matter if they die?' In winter our hands were so cold we could scarcely work.

"There was no canteen, so we carried our food box and put it by the machine. The tin was left open on the machine and we would snatch a mouthful whenever we could. By the time the food came to be eaten it was covered with cotton dust.

"There were no proper toilets, only pans which were not emptied every day, so that the stench and the flies were everywhere. If a worker stayed too long in the toilet one of the foremen would rush in and smack her face.

"If you were not well and applied for leave it would not be

granted. There were always plenty to take a vacant job. Women were so terrified of losing their job if it was known that they were pregnant that they would bind their bellies tightly and hope their condition would not be noticed. It wasn't uncommon for a woman to be taken with labour-pains in the mill and have to sneak off to the toilet and have her baby there."

Her face wrinkles with disgust and pity. "It is hard to remember when I look at my clothes today, what a miserable, dirty lot of poor creatures we were. Most of us were in rags or patched clothes, since everything earned was necessary for food.

"In the old days there was a terrible gulf between the workers and the staff. The foreman was a tyrant who browbeat the girls. He paid particular attention to beautiful girls, but usually it didn't bode any good for them. There was a particular Number One who used to favour the pretty girls and ask them to marry him, though he was already married. After a month he would desert the girl and she had no redress at all, because it was impossible for her to go to the court since she had no money and he could afford to hire a good lawyer." Her voice rises harshly with indignation.

"Before he succeeded in seducing the girl he treated her very well, but afterwards treated her worse than a dog. This was quite a common occurrence among the foremen and the girls were left in a terrible position. Some of them found they were pregnant and would have an abortion rather than have the baby, since that would destroy any hope they might have of marrying. Sometimes they would let the child be born and then kill it.

"In addition to the work at the mill, every girl was forced to do needlework or knitting in her spare time for the foreman. If you refused to do so the foreman would complain to the owner and you would be dismissed. In this way the foreman made up for his low wages.

"I married when I was twenty. My husband worked in a refrigerator factory at the time, but not long after our marriage he lost his job and remained unemployed till the Liberation. He tried to keep the family by becoming a small pedlar. I was dismissed when they knew I was pregnant. Now we had no money at all coming in, so the three of us went to my native district in the suburbs of Shanghai to plough less than one-third of a mou of land.

"Two years later, through a friend, I was able to go back to the same factory, but now my home was very far away from it and I had to ride to it on the back of my husband's bicycle. I was pregnant again. When it came I had to deliver my own child. It was born on the earth floor because I was too weak to climb on the bed. On the tenth day I had to send the baby to other people because I could not afford to keep it. Since things have improved we have tried hard to find the baby without success. Whenever I think of it I am very sad." Her face is full of sorrow but she does not weep.

"By this time I had already had four children. The first died. The third had been given away and now the second baby died from illness." Now the tears overflow and she struggles to control them.

"Several months later I got back to the factory once more through a friend. According to the custom of the factory, the worker had to give a present to the foreman. But I had no money. So the foreman gave me harder work than the others and constantly tormented me.

"I reached such a state of despair and weakness that I thought it was better to stay at home and starve than to be harassed in the factory. I went back to peddling vegetables. Ten months later Shanghai was liberated. And in October 1949 I was asked to go back to the factory and work."

Her nervousness has gone. She begins to lose her withdrawn attitude. The shadow of a smile appears.

"At present both my husband and I are working—he is in an automobile factory. Alone I earn eighty yuan a month. My health is greatly improved since at the factory I take dinner in a special room for special diets and I have not missed a single day since Liberation, because I have been given proper medical treatment and conditions in the factory are so greatly improved."

She meets my eyes and, for the first time, she smiles at me. Her fingers cease to pluck at the handkerchief and her hands open and she holds them out as though she was greeting a new life.

"Although I am working in the same factory where I worked for twenty years all is changed. There are proper safety devices, proper ventilation. Indeed, so much improved is the ventilation that in summer we now prefer to stay inside since the temperature is less inside than out, and in winter it is centrally heated. There are new women's toilet-rooms. We even have a nursery for children. There are flush toilets and proper washrooms and a canteen where we can buy our meals very cheaply.

"Under the new laws, women are entitled to the same working conditions and treatment as men. We work eight hours a day and we get equal pay and have the same rights under the Labour

Insurance Regulations. We get free medical service and, if it is necessary, free treatment in hospitals and sanatoria.

"Expenses for pre-natal check-up and child-delivery are paid by the factory management or the Government. I am an assistant in charge of a section and enjoy a happy and prosperous life I would never have dared dream of in the past.

"We are still in the same house, but more rooms have been added and we have electric light in the house and piped water. Soon we hope to be moved to one of the new housing estates. My twelve-year-old daughter, Chang Si-yuan, is now in the fifth grade and helps me to study, too. Before I was illiterate, but now I am in the fourth grade."

Her story, simple, unadorned, is finished. She has to leave because she is on the afternoon shift. We walk together to the lift.

On a sudden impulse she takes my hand in both hers and laughs outright. I scarcely recognize her for the little mouselike creature who had entered my room an hour or so earlier.

"My heart is laughing, too," she says, "because for the first time I am meeting a foreign friend. I shall call you Ta-chieh, 'Elder Sister'."

CHAPTER XIII

Housing, Old and New

THE heat beats down like a palpable thing on the narrow
stone-surfaced road through which the car can scarcely
move because of the teeming mass of people.

I am seeing the most crowded quarter of Shanghai, I am told,
with an area of 130,000 square yards. Here live 4260 families,
comprising a total population of more than 18,000, chiefly mill-
workers, pedi-cab drivers, and unskilled labourers.

Tung Hsiao-mei, president of the Women's Federation, welcomes me, wearing a green printed tunic over her blue shorts.
Her face is flat and lined, but the sweetness of her expression
makes one forget her plainness. A young woman in a plain black
chi-pao shakes my hand. They take me by the arms and pilot me
down the narrow lane, lined with unlovely grey brick two-roomed
houses interspersed with matting shelters, each with its cylindrical
cooking stove outside the entrance. My heart sinks. It is much
worse than "Happy Village", because here there is no open space
with flowers and shrubs, no feathery-leaved trees beside the road.
Everything is drab, the only colour the clothes of the women and
children.

They usher me out of the sun that turns the lane into an oven
into a simple whitewashed room about nine by fourteen with the
educational posters on the wall that I have seen everywhere.
There is a chain of bright-red fire-buckets on the wall, and I have
a moment of horror as I think how inadequate they would be in
this overcrowded quarter with its mat shelters, its thatched roofs
and flimsy walls. We sit down on hard seats at a solid table.

An old woman, thin to the point of emaciation, shoos out the
crowd of children clad in shorts, or nothing at all, that streams in
after us. Their skins are healthy and glistening, no diseases, no
sores, none of the signs of malnutrition.

Hot water in a painted glass—peanut butter jars serve for the
locals. The reception committee beams at me over fluttering fans.
Tung Hsiao-mei sits beside me and fans me rhythmically as I ask
questions and take notes. They are all most anxious to tell me

about the changes that the New China had brought to their district.

"Before Liberation ninety per cent of the houses were made of matting," Mrs Tung begins, "only ten per cent were of brick. Now, because of the improvement in the standard of living and the better wages we receive, sixty per cent are brick. In the past our streets were in a frightful condition. Only one road was surfaced, many were only running gutters and there was no drainage at all, the lower-lying areas and streets being ditches. There was a saying, 'If it rains for one day you must wear overshoes for seven days!' "

"If there was fire it swept through the place like a typhoon." The girl in black takes up the story, her words tumbling out in her enthusiasm. "There were always many deaths because the conditions of the road made it impossible for fire-brigade or ambulance to reach most of the points in the area. Now twenty-five of the roads have been surfaced, there are three fire-hydrants and five public telephones. In the old days only a few people had electric light. Now ninety per cent have electricity. In the old days there were only five public lavatories. Now there are fifteen. Only seven public garbage bins; now there are twenty-seven." (For a population of 18,000!) "There were only twelve street lamps. Now there are one hundred and two."

The figures she pours out horrify me, as much for the present as for the past. I look at their excited faces, their shining eyes as they nod proudly at her enumeration of all the "modern conveniences" that have transformed their lives. Today my imagination cannot encompass what it was yesterday.

Mrs Tung wrinkles her flat nose in disgust and goes on when the girl stops for want of breath. "The summers were terrible. The stench was frightful and there was always a plague of flies and mosquitoes. Many people died from cholera and smallpox. Now, in March, April, and May vaccinations and injections are given to the children and, as in the old days there was a fair amount of T.B., all babies are given BCG."

The window beside me is filled with the curious faces of children who have apparently legged each other up. The smaller ones crowd the door, where a young man has been put on guard. Apparently his duty is not so much to keep the children away as to roster them so that all get a look. Who in China would rob a child of its pleasure? The doorway is a screen of faces. They flow across in an apparently unending stream. Higher up the pock-marked faces of older people, old women with the square hair-line of their generation, lower down the seven- and eight-year-olds, skulls marked with the blue patches of old impetigo sores, and, at ground level, the tiny ones, some of them dexterous enough to crawl between the young man's legs. The shorts, split pants, are made of brilliant red, blue, and green in floral, striped, and spotted patterns, obviously new—and clean! A small boy, carrying a naked baby a few months old, sidles into the doorway and stares at me with round eyes.

The young woman bursts out: "In the old days, we had only one primary school in the district, which could take only two hundred pupils. Now it has been enlarged and can take a thousand. The children go to school in three shifts, but in spite of that ten per cent can't be accommodated and must still wait the building of a new school. We still have no kindergarten or nursery, but next year we plan to establish them." She says it with such certainty that I almost see them.

"About ninety per cent of the adults were illiterate," she rushes in breathlessly. "Today the majority have been through literacy classes and a thousand are still studying."

The telephone rings. The old woman answers it. She calls the president. I have time to enjoy the scene in the open doorway. A naked little boy, with a large silver ring round his neck, has infiltrated. When parents have lost several children in succession they put the silver ring on the next comer to placate the evil spirits.

The president comes back to tell me that they are expecting me at the New Housing Estate. I leave reluctantly. There is so much I would like to ask.

Out in the street it is hotter than ever. I see it all with new eyes. The neat brick houses with their clean-swept earth floors, the occasional matting shelter that houses a family—new matting, new furniture, new clothes. Orderly queues of people with buckets waiting their turn at the taps.

We pass an open-air stage erected so that people who are too old to go out of the district to a cinema or other entertainment can have it brought to them there. In a narrow side alley a very pregnant woman is unselfconsciously washing her feet in a basin, a gardenia tucked into her glossy black hair.

It is incredibly poverty-stricken by our standards, and yet so incredibly better than it was. Mrs Tung presses my arm.

"You will see some of the people who used to live here at the New Housing Estate. They were the ones who lived in such appal-

ling conditions that they simply had to be moved or they would
have died!"

Everything is relative!

Everyone, young and old, clusters round to shake hands as I
say good-bye. The car has been standing two hours in the sun
and is like a furnace. A chorus of good-byes and a thunder of clapping from young and old as we begin to crawl through the packed
street.

"Come back and see us again next year," Mrs Tung says.
"Everything will be so much better than even now that you'll
hardly recognize us."

We speed on our way to see the new settlement of Sweet Fountain
Village, part of the Council Housing project for workers.

Gone are the ugly Europeanized streets, with their Europeanized house fronts; in the suburbs a forest of young trees spring
up; cool green lawns surround block after block of two- and three-
storeyed buildings that stretch along well-made streets.

From the veranda of Sweet Fountain Village's kindergarten a
cheering horde of half-naked infants gives us a shrill welcome.

The director, a serious young man, accompanied by a young
woman, greets us and we are ushered into a very large, airy room
where electric fans cool us a little and we thirstily drink lukewarm
lemonade.

In a brief, business-like introduction the director tells us that
the money was allotted by the Council in 1951 to build this housing project. In 1953 it was finished: forty-six blocks which house
twenty thousand people. Two types of block have been erected;
one which houses ten families, one which houses six. This is one
of thirteen such settlements, and another three are in course of
construction.

Each block has electric light, running water, water-closets, and
community kitchens, each one shared by five families. A nursery,
two primary schools, a clinic and a co-operative store serve the
blocks. There are in addition three markets and three branch
co-ops, so that the housewives can be saved the inconvenience of
going long distances for their shopping. They have three public
telephones.

Ten thousand trees have been planted and eighteen lawns laid
so that it will soon be a green village. Two bus routes serve the
settlement.

Its brief history told, we follow our hosts on a tour of Sweet
Fountain Village.

The usual crowd of children precedes us across the lawn to the flats, two, more daring than the others, taking my hands.

We go first into the community kitchen. Five little cylindrical cooking stoves are ranged around the wall and on each a large flattish pan is simmering. Hot as it is outside, it is hotter inside, since the stoves burn a briquette. There is a concrete sink and running water and everything is neat and well arranged, even though several women are preparing the evening meal. I am introduced to them and they look up with the shiny hot face of housewives-over-the-stove common to every kitchen! Wang Kwei-hua, middle-aged, with a strong face on which privation and suffering have graven indelible lines, invites me to visit her flat. She precedes me up the narrow concrete stairs, my two escorts jostling for space beside me, and behind me as many other children as can squeeze in.

Mrs Wang's flat is one room which she shares with her daughter, who works in a textile mill. My hostess draws out a stool for me and herself sits on one of the beds covered with a protecting woven mat. On the wall are posters, gaily coloured pictures of flowers and the Summer Palace. She is obviously so proud of it that I feel I must know why one small room in which two people live and eat and sleep inspires such pride.

"Before," she tells me, "our whole family lived in a mat shelter in the Tu-tu district"—the very district I have just come from. "My husband was in business—he was a pedlar!—and died from illness because not only could we not afford to get medical attention for him, but when he was ill it was impossible to keep him from being soaked every time it rained and the water came through the matting. We had a saying, 'Big rain outside, small rain inside.' My one regret is that he did not live to see the wonderful day when we moved into this lovely flat. If you only knew what it means to be dry and to be able to cook in comfort!"

I see the kitchen in a new light.

"My daughter earns eighty yuan a month and we pay only two yuan sixty cents a month for the room. We are very well off. One can eat well in Shanghai for twenty yuan a month and all our medical treatment is free."

She looks down at her neat bright-blue tunic and smoothes it. "It is only in the last few years that I have had a special summer tunic at all. Before, winter and summer, we wore the same ragged clothes. Now I am making a new dress for my daughter." She shows me the attractive cotton print *chi-pao* on which she is working.

The two small children at the door are getting restive. They appear and re-appear, obviously terrified that I will go away.

"Who is this?" I ask, turning to a ten-year-old boy who is working at the table.

"He is the son of a neighbour," she explains. "A very studious boy who comes into my room to study because it is so quiet here."

"And this?" I point to the photograph of a serious young man that stands on the large chest of drawers. She takes it down and wipes imaginary dust from the glass before handing it to me.

"That is my son," she says, with the look on her face of every proud mother in the world. "He is studying geology in Peking. If only his father could have lived to see the day!"

As I say good-bye, the two small children take possession of me again. Willy-nilly I am drawn down the hallway. We burst with an excited chattering into another room where a flustered old lady looks up from a table where she is laboriously practising characters in an exercise book. She rises to greet me, walking stiffly on bound feet. She apologizes that she has been caught unprepared. Her daughter and son-in-law are at the factory. She recovers herself and welcomes me graciously, saying that all the same she is very happy to welcome the first foreign friend she has ever met.

This is a two-room apartment for which they pay ten shillings a month. Again it is very clean, with straw mats on the beds, one of which has a canopy with cheese-cloth curtains looped back. This is because her daughter has a six months' baby which she takes to the crèche at the factory and it is very necessary that no improbable infiltrating fly or mosquito should reach the precious child.

My triumphant escort with the two plaits is her granddaughter, with whom she shares a small room with two narrow bamboo beds. On the walls are educational posters, highly-coloured prints of opera favourites. The old lady turns round, eyes shining with wonder. "Never in my life would I have dared dream of ending my days in such a lovely flat with electric light!

"Before, we all shared one filthy low room with an earth floor," she says, "where the rain poured in in summer and the snow and the icy winds came through in winter and bugs infested every crack."

She points to the washing equipment. "If you only knew what it means to have running water and be able to wash yourself! Before, we used to draw filthy water from the creek."

Each room has its flowered enamel wash-basin, its individual floral washer and gay towel.

"Before," she tells me, touching a bright towel with hands like a claw, "we had only one rag for the whole family!"

Smiling toothlessly, she presses my hand in farewell.

My second escort tugs at my hand as I come out. I demur. It's no use. I am towed along the corridor. A sleepy woman with tousled hair and in singlet and shorts springs from a bed as we irrupt into the room. The child bursts into a long triumphant recital. The young woman is confused. I apologize for disturbing her.

"That's all right," she says. "I am on night-shift this week and I was just going to get up anyway to prepare dinner. My husband and I both work in a factory. We get seventy yuan a month each for we do the same job. Before—" she smiles and her hand goes out to the smooth bobbed head proudly oscillating between us— "before, we lived in a sampan on the river with my husband's parents and younger brother. Little Apple is the only child of four who survived."

I am ashamed of my intrusion and do not stay long, to the intense disappointment of Little Apple, who clearly wants me to stay to supper. We cross the lawns to the up-to-date clinic, where the medical superintendent tells us that the staff consists of five permanent doctors, seven full-time nurses, and four midwives. The special clinic for mothers has bas-reliefs on the walls describing with clinical realism all the stages of pregnancy. Posters show the right way and the wrong way to deliver a child. All medical care is free.

It is getting late. Only time for a lightning tour of the co-operative shops, which are in keeping with everything else: clean, well-lighted, staff in white overalls, a good stock of everyday necessities. No time, alas, for the markets, but I console myself by saying that markets should be visited in the morning.

The sun is low as we leave Sweet Fountain Village and the last thing I see of it is its grey blocks amidst the trees that in a few years will hide the bare walls altogether. Mothers sitting on the lawns with their babies wave farewell and the kindergarten, now released, streams across the paths to get a last glimpse of us, their shrill calls of farewell rising above the noise of the slow-moving car.

CHAPTER XIV

The Street Committee

I HAD heard so much indirectly about Street Committees by the time I reached Shanghai, that I thought it was time to find out how this ubiquitous and comprehensive organization worked. In China you have only to say what you want to see and if it is humanly possible you see it, so I was not surprised one morning to receive an invitation to visit the Street Committee of Alley 756.

That afternoon we wind through streets crowded with heterogeneous traffic, and stop outside a high brick wall with strong gates. We go through the gate up a narrow alley-way enclosed on one side by a brick wall, on the other by the walls of a three-storeyed brick building with many doorways opening on to narrow roadway. A gaily decorated wall blackboard contains information for the occupants.

A heavy courtyard door leads into a room that is cool and fresh after the intense heat outside.

It is furnished in old Chinese style with solid carved redwood furniture, the chairs with marble insets in the backs. Hanging on the wall are similar round figured marble plaques in redwood frames, the strange dark figuring on the marble giving an extraordinary impression of mountains and clouds.

At the end of the room is a Buddhist altar. A silver Buddha looks down on us inscrutably, rosary beads round his neck and silver incense burners before him. It has been, and probably still is, the family altar. Incongruous is a wireless on a shelf beside it, two wicker-covered thermos-flasks, two electric fans, and photos of two men in soldier's uniform on the wall.

The Street Committee is there to welcome me. Chen I-ti, vice-director, is an earnest, rather plain woman in her thirties, neat and housewifely in a white tunic and black trousers.

Liu Chin-yu, the president of the local Women's Federation has permed hair which surrounds a most expressive face and she gestures freely with a fan as she talks.

I begin my reply to their welcome, but at the sound of my voice a canary above me bursts into song so loudly that I have to wait.

I begin again; he peers down inquiringly at the strange voice and gives a trill of surprise. Never in all my travels have I heard a canary with such volume. It reminds me more of the carolling of an Australian magpie, one of the richest singers in the world.

Each time I begin he drowns me. I give up. Everybody laughs, and Mrs Chen begins to explain their work. "This Street Committee is responsible for four alley-ways with three hundred and forty families comprising one thousand seven hundred persons. Ninety per cent are workers, ten per cent business-men—that is, shopkeepers and pedlars."

Anyone connected with trade, I find, is a "business-man". The "capitalist" they define as "someone who employs labour".

"The Street Committee is composed of a director and three vice-directors," Mrs Chen explains. "The director is a tailor and carries out his committee work in his spare time. We women are housewives. There are eleven committee members who are responsible for welfare, for public safety—fire prevention and so on —for women's organizations, for sanitation and hygiene, and for mediation. The members are elected by the people of the alley-ways."

Mrs Liu, fanning herself vigorously in spite of the gale from the two fans, adds, "The Women's Federation is a parallel organization that co-operates with the Street Committee and devotes itself more specifically to women's problems."

"All the residents are organized into groups of eighteen to twenty-eight families according to their size," Mrs Chen goes on. "For each group there is a group leader and a woman's representative, and these group leaders are considered as members of this Committee. Altogether there are fifty-two group leaders, forty-one of whom are women. The Street Committee meets three times a month. The first meeting sets out our plan for the month, the second meeting in the middle of the month is to see how it is progressing, and the third meeting at the end of the month examines what has been done.

"Once a month there is a meeting of group leaders at which the Street Committee reports what is being done and the group leaders report on the wishes and demands of the people. They act as a bridge so that the Street Committee is always aware of what the people are thinking and what they want. Women's representatives also attend the group leaders' meeting. At a set time every day two Street Committee members are available to receive people who have any questions to ask or requests to make. Of course, if anything urgent arises someone is always available to deal with it."

"Housewives' time and energy are saved in that the welfare committee collects the rent and rates and makes the payments to the requisite municipal office," Mrs Liu adds. "It is also responsible for educational work, for writing up the blackboard newspaper—you must have seen it as you came through the alley-way —on which are explained the new laws and matters of policy.

"There are about four hundred children under school age in the area and these are organized into pre-school groups to save mothers time and worry, and we arrange for examination at the clinic for babies under a year old and for inoculation and such things."

I am interested to know how the Committee functions in problems that specifically concern the New Marriage Law and succeed in getting the question out before the canary wakes up. Mrs Liu explains that one group is responsible for mediation—that is, for dealing with family quarrels, quarrels between mothers-in-law and daughters-in-law, and, after the introduction of the Marriage Law with unsatisfactory marriages and new marriages. "We had a very busy time when the law was first introduced in 1950, but now these problems are getting fewer each year.

"Coming from a Western country, you can't imagine how backward our men were!" I hate to destroy her illusions! "At first, in the Street Committee there were only three women. The men refused to let them go! My husband was entirely opposed to my going to meetings and when I defied him and went I would find myself locked out when I returned. We really used to be very unhappy because he lived a most dissipated life. However, when the New Marriage Law came in we discussed it and decided that we both had responsibilities and faults and that our responsibility didn't end with our home, as it did in Old China, but extended to the whole community. As a result we are happier than we have ever been in all our married life. My husband has changed completely and he says that since I've begun to take an interest in outside things and study I am a much more interesting woman to live with, so he doesn't want to go to brothels and drink any more."

"There are a lot of homes like that," Mrs Chen adds. "At first women were afraid of taking part in things outside their home, but now about eighty per cent of them take part regularly. Most of the balance have good reasons for their inactivity, but all support the work of the Committee. We haven't discovered any woman who is opposed to the new ideas, though at the beginning there were, particularly the older women."

Mrs Liu nods. "Yes, one of our most active members began work among the women in her village after Liberation, though she was only sixteen. Her mother was so strongly opposed to it that she immediately tried to force her to marry to keep her at home. But the girl refused. She had the support of the New Marriage Law, so she left the village and came to this area and now she has a good job and is extremely active in the Women's Federation."

"One of our main problems was persuading women to give up the old unhygienic method of childbirth," Mrs Chen goes on.

"One woman refused to adopt the new method. She had the old traditional midwife who had no knowledge of hygiene. It was a difficult birth and the midwife did not know what to do. The doctor was called, but it was too late; the child was born dead and he had a struggle to save the mother's life. But it was a good lesson to the other women.

"Another woman had borne many children, all of whom had died. We persuaded her to have an examination. The blood-test showed that the cause was venereal disease. She and her husband were treated and cured. Now they are proud parents of a plump, healthy baby."

"The mediation committee plays a particularly important role," Mrs Liu says. "For instance, in one house there was a couple with four children. Very often the man came back late. He drank too much and had affairs with other women. The wife was hot-tempered, and before the New Marriage Law was promulgated they often quarrelled. Once during a quarrel a mirror was broken. The children were very unhappy. The mediation committee took the matter up.

"A member of the women's organization talked to the wife and a male member of the Street Committee talked to the husband for a long time. The husband was told that in the new society a man had serious responsibilities to his wife; neither polygamy nor concubinage were allowed and his going with other women was absolutely against the New Marriage Law. The wife was told that her husband certainly had serious defects, but she didn't help things by her bad temper, and just as she expected her husband to control himself, so she should control herself.

"The husband could read and write so he was persuaded to help his wife to study and become literate. This gave them a mutual interest and in the course of the lessons outside matters came into discussion and in the new atmosphere he found a new interest in his wife and in the changed atmosphere her temper improved! Altogether, the home became a much more attractive place, and finally the couple were completely reconciled. Now there are two more children and the family gets along very well."

"Another case concerned that of a young widow living in the same alley." Mrs Chen takes up the story. "She was only twenty and she was always very depressed because, though her husband had died several years before, in the old days it was thought wrong for a widow to remarry and her mother-in-law kept nagging at her on this point. Then came the New Marriage Law, posters and blackboard news explaining all about it. One of the committee members explained to the mother-in-law the new attitude to marriage and to the girl that it was no longer wicked or unlucky for a widow to remarry. She was encouraged by all the progressive women to think of remarrying, otherwise, as they said, 'Your youth and happiness are buried in the ground.' The mother-in-law decided, 'I mustn't be backward', and set to work to find a husband for her. One of the neighbours had an unmarried nephew. They were introduced, fell in love, and married. Unlike the old days, the daughter-in-law often visits the former mother-in-law and the old lady is as proud and happy about the two children as though they were really her own grandchildren."

Mrs Liu smiles. "In this area there was a landlord who had a wife and two concubines. After the New Marriage Law the younger of the concubines decided to leave and start a new life. But the wife and the elder concubine got on very well together; the wife didn't want her to leave and the concubine didn't want to go, as there was great affection between her and the wife and she was timid about her capacity to make a living outside. So the household is going on much in the old way.

"In another case a rich man who was a speculator had a wife and a concubine. The concubine was young and demanded to leave him, being unwilling to suffer any longer a position she felt was not honourable. Now she has married a neighbour, a schoolteacher. Though concubinage and polygamy are absolutely prohibited by the New Marriage Law, a realistic attitude is taken, and it depends entirely on the wishes of the wives and concubines as to what is done in each particular case.

"One of the difficulties in the beginning," Mrs Liu goes on, "was that not only were we women confined to the home but a great number were illiterate. Now that most have been taught to read, reading groups have been organized by the women's organization and we meet to read newspapers and magazines together so that we know what is going on in China and the rest of the world. Before, for most of us, the world stopped at our front door. Our main job, you might say, has been to teach women to live as members of a community, emphasizing a number of points we called 'The Five Good Things'. These are: One, to co-operate with our neighbours. (In the old days families lived their own lives with no feeling of responsibility to their neighbours.) Two, to do our housework well, observing the new laws of hygiene and sanitation. Three, to bring up our children well. (Corporal punishment has been forbidden and we are taught to reason with our children instead of beating them.) Four, to encourage our children and our husbands to study well and put their heart into their work. Five, to study hard ourselves.

"It is the responsibility of committee members to set a good example. There's a saying, 'A catty of example is better than a picul of talk.'"

"You might say each Street Committee is a little revolution in itself," Mrs Chen says in her gentle way. "Since through it we have learnt to play our part in society. In the past we lived in a small family circle concerned only with our personal affairs and our children. We took it for granted, for we had always been taught that we were inferior and could play no part in life outside the home. But now all that is changed."

"Indeed it is!" Mrs Liu laughs. "It wasn't until I saw my name on the electoral roll, after the introduction of universal suffrage, that I realized that I, too, had a place in society, and the New China we were building was as much my responsibility as anyone else's."

It is time for me to go. I take my farewell of the committee members from the midst of a surging crowd of men, women, and children, all of whom seem anxious to impress the stranger with their friendliness and enthusiasm at her visit.

CHAPTER XV

The Girl in the Butterfly Opera

MEETING actresses off-stage is always something of a wrench to the imagination. The magic of the footlights persists to confuse reality. Glamour hangs like a mist between you and the person.

When I was on my way to meet Yuan Sui-feng my mind was full of flickering images of her as I had seen her in the delightful colour film *Liang Shan-po and Chu Ying-tai*, more commonly known in the West as *The Butterfly Lovers*.

I'll admit I had a moment of shock when a tall, grave woman rose to meet me. Mature and dignified in her severe white *chi-pao*, she bore little resemblance to that glamorous figure my mind refused to relinquish. She wore no make-up. Her hair was parted on the side and two small plaits tied across the back with narrow purple ribbon, nails cut square like a schoolgirl's, a man's gold watch on her wrist. Only her soft, beautifully modulated voice and the movement of the hands as she fanned herself with an ivory fan recalled the heroine of the film.

She greeted me with an air of modesty and reserve, almost of aloofness. Was this the glorious creature whom the film had made known to the Western world as her work with the Shaohsing opera had made her known in China?

She tells me her story simply.

"I was born thirty-three years ago in a very small village in Chekiang Province whose main activities were tea-growing, silkworm culture, and farming. It was typically feudal in attitude, with the peasants little more than slaves to the landlords. Women were despised, so that if a mother bore three girls the third would probably be killed. It was not that the mother had less love for the girl-child, but the girl-child was an economic problem in an area where it was a struggle for the peasant to live. And with all of them so poor, many felt that it was the only thing to do.

"I was the third daughter, and it was only because my father was a teacher in the primary school and a man who did not accept the feudal ideas that I survived. My father said, 'Let her live.' And my mother, an industrious peasant, was only too glad to be spared the horror of putting her own child to death.

"My father and mother were regarded as a deplorably improvident couple, for, though mother gave birth to seven daughters, all were allowed to live. There was only one son, who died from illness because my parents in their poverty were unable to pay for medical help.

"For many generations they had been landless, but, since my father was a teacher, from the age of four I began to study. He was a very kind and just man and very advanced in his ideas. 'In future, you are going to have to depend on yourself, so learn!' he would say. While my mother, typical of her generation, would repeat, 'The only future for you girls when you grow up is to marry and depend on your husbands.'

"There was always a conflict in me between a sense of inferiority which my mother's words left in me and the sense of self-respect my father tried to inspire.

"When I was seven I saw my first performance of a Shaohsing opera, in which all the roles are played by women, as today. It originated in Chekiang Province and compared with Peking opera is quite young—not more than sixty years old.

"I was fascinated. Here a new world was revealed to me. And from then on my ambition was to become an actress. My father was horrified. He wanted me to become a scholar, but I ran away and joined the opera troupe. But of course I came back next day."

She plays nervously with the end of her fan, but, as she becomes absorbed in her story, the wall of reserve breaks down a little.

"During these years my father was the only income-earner for the large family. I wanted to learn something so that in a few years' time I should be able to earn and help the rest of the family. But all I wanted to do was to act.

"At ten I finally joined a travelling troupe, in spite of my father's objections. Even at ten I was a strong-minded child and did what I wanted to, though it hurt me to hurt him because I loved him deeply.

"Once with the training troupe, I became rather worried myself. I found that it wasn't the training class it was supposed to be. Some of the girls were being treated as nothing but prostitutes for the landlords.

"My father was extremely disturbed when he heard about this and gave money which he could ill afford to the master of the troupe to allow my youngest uncle to join the troupe to look after me. I was the youngest in the troupe, and the eldest was sixteen.

"At first I was very naïve and inclined to be rather undisciplined. I thought all masters were like my father, good and upright. But as I saw the older girls allowing themselves to be used as prostitutes without protest 'just like the willow-tree that blows with the wind', I began to realize that there were wicked people in the world. In the circumstances girls easily lost their self-respect, but as a child I had been told by my mother and grandmother, 'Keep pure and unspotted as a white gown', and by my father, 'Keep your bones straight and be upright.'

"When I was twelve the biggest landlord in the province offered a big price to adopt me as his 'daughter'. Actually, he wanted me as a concubine. He forced many presents on me, but even at twelve I was too strong-minded, and whenever the landlord tried to seduce me I would shout loudly and thus let everybody know what was happening.

"I saw many girls become concubines of rich landlords and, after a while, be thrown out when the landlords were tired of them, then, since the troupe would not take them back, drift into prostitution.

"For the first six months with the training troupe I played the part of a boy, mainly acrobatic roles. It was a hard and ugly life, redeemed only by the pleasure of acting. I began to know the darkness of society that I had never known before. I often wondered why I had chosen such a career, the lowest in society, where, no matter how hard you worked, you still were regarded as no better than a prostitute. I made up my mind to change my occupation and began to study once more. This was in 1938, but by then my father was very ill with T.B. and all the family was depending on me, so I continued to act. I had to earn money, and this was the only way I knew to earn it.

"Later I came to Shanghai, but it was no better than the villages. Worse, indeed, for now there were a greater number and wider variety of predatory men who regarded young actresses as their lawful game.

"But I had seen the unhappy fate of others in the troupe and, although I was only fifteen, there was no trace of childishness in me. I began to dress like an old woman so that I wouldn't be recognized once I was off the stage. All the year round I wore dark clothes, cotton shoes, and a large pigtail. To avoid invitations to eat in cafés with men who invited us after the theatre I became a vegetarian and said I was a Buddhist in religion.

"My only comfort in these days were my letters from my father, whose care for me was one of the spiritual bases of my life. I loved him very dearly and by now he was very proud of me, since I was trying to make the profession I had chosen an honourable one and critics began to appreciate my work."

She smiles behind her fan as she goes on and her whole face changes. It is the smile of Chu Ying-tai. She has lost her reserve now and with it her aloofness. Her voice is infinitely melodious, with astonishing varieties of tone.

"During those days I tried to escape from reality, living only for my work, and refusing to have anything to do with the world, which I regarded as utterly evil. While I still loved my art, I was sick of the stage-life which was so corrupt—the more so as the Japanese had now occupied Shanghai. But I kept on for my father's sake. I sent most of my money to him, but instead of spending it on medical attention for himself he spent it on the family and in 1942 he died.

"The year 1942 was the worst year of my life. My father died and I was found to be suffering from T.B."

She pauses a moment, lost in her memories, then takes up her story.

"I decided that I would act no more. My family must manage the best it could. I would take my own life and be done with it all. Then I thought of my father—of his courage and the faith he always had in me, the way he had always taught me to be brave and strong, so I put away the idea and decided to keep living for my work.

"By now I was one of the best-known actresses, and Shaohsing opera had begun to be very popular in Shanghai. Because of its comparative youth it had no set traditions like Peking opera. It had not even a written script. It was then very simple, just a reflection of the life of the village, like folk-opera. There was no director and no backgrounds. At this time I happened to see some modern plays and decided that we must try to do something to modify Shaohsing opera and give it a higher artistic standing. I said to the master of troupe, 'If you'll get a playwright to help me, you can cut down my wages to pay him.'

"I began to consult with playwrights and we decided that we should put on plays which, though traditional, reflected the feeling of the China of those days, which was then fighting the Japanese. We decided also that in addition to the suitable script, new backgrounds and lighting must be evolved, and the make-up should be more realistic than that of the Peking opera, and that the dress should faithfully represent the people of the period. At that time it was not very clear just what should be the final form of Shaohsing opera, but the changes that I made revolutionized the whole troupe.

"The master previously had been the dictator and the actresses merely his employees, and sometimes he would order them to play at the houses of rich men in the hope they would offer to buy them for concubines, from which he would receive a big commission. But now I said actresses should have the highest place in the troupe, and the master did not raise objections, since the opera was becoming increasingly popular and he was making good money.

"In between 1942 and 1945 we made great headway in dramatic reforms, even though we met many difficulties. New themes were introduced, the form of the acting changed. New scripts were written, costumes, setting and décor evolved their own styles, different from Peking opera or modern stage productions.

"The worse things got in Shanghai, the more I resented my inequality, not only as a woman but as a Chinese in my own country." Her eyes are blazing. Her extraordinarily flexible hands mime the story of her struggle.

"As the war against the Japanese intensified we chose historical plays with special significance—for example, *The Taiping Revolution*, and others with themes from the Tang Dynasty regarding the fight against the invaders. These plays were very popular.

"The troupe began to attract the attention of the Japanese, and the order went out that every play had to be submitted for censorship. But they were so popular with the people that they had to allow them to be produced.

"Then in 1945 the Japs were defeated." All the drama of victory is in her voice, her flashing eyes and her gestures, but the folded fan is pressed against her breast as though to subdue her emotions.

"But their place was taken by the Kuomintang, and things for the theatre were as bad as ever. The Kuomintang detested our opera group because of its strongly nationalist themes. One play about the Three Kingdoms was a direct hit at corruption and brutality. We also put on a play by Lu Hsun called *The Benediction* about a woman in a village reduced to nothing by oppression.

"Because we had a repertoire of plays that had a content of progress and protest we attracted the attention of the liberal and progressive forces in Shanghai. The Kuomintang, realizing the popularity of my troupe, tried to win me to their side by organizing a General Opera Association and trying to make me an associate member. I refused to join.

"From 1945 to 1948 were very hard years. We continued to

produce the plays and the Kuomintang tried all kinds of revolting means to discourage us. They sent hoodlums to molest me in the street in all manner of ways, even going so far as to throw excreta over me.

"I never knew what would happen next. My mother would wait anxiously for me to come home from the theatre, terrified that something had happened to me, and I rarely got a night's sound sleep.

"Armed men threatened me, but I knew they dared not injure me openly because I was too popular. On another occasion they plotted to throw acid on me, but in some mysterious way the plot became known and they dared not because of popular outcry. I had a series of escapes I thought providential at the time. Always something happened at the last moment to protect me. The pedicab driver took a different route from the usual one; warnings reached me from people I did not know.

"It was only many years later when I met Premier Chou En-lai in Peking that I learnt that somewhere about this time he had seen two of our plays and thought our work valuable as national art and that he told the underground Resistance workers to support us, and, incidentally, to protect me. It was then that many things that had puzzled me became clear and I realized I owed my life to something different from Providence.

"In 1947, during the summer vacation, I decided to get in touch with the actresses of other troupes, with whom I was very popular. My aim was to get rid of the troupe masters. I got as many as I could together and we gave a combined show. It was a great success and that encouraged us.

"The K.M.T. had articles published about me in the papers, saying I must be a Red and I was getting money from the Communist Party. They demanded a letter from me confessing that I was acting for the Communist Party. I refused. I knew nothing of the Communist Party. So far as I knew I had never met a Communist in my life. I was concerned only with my art and the production of significant Chinese plays.

"So I survived until Shanghai was liberated, becoming more and more aware each day of the truth of what my father used to say, 'True immortality is in courage and struggle!'

"When the New Government took over control of Shanghai they asked me, 'Is there anything you want?' I replied, 'Nothing except to act.' They asked me to attend the People's Political Consultative Congress in Peking which represented all political opinions. I refused, saying, 'No politics for me, thank you! I am interested only in art.' " She frowned reflectively, moving her fan almost imperceptibly.

"Many of my friends tried to persuade me, pointing out that it was the first time in history that a despised actress had been invited to an important congress with the highest in the land, and that I owed it to my art to go, since the invitation clearly showed that New China was going to give their rightful place to artists of the theatre. So eventually I went, reluctantly, in my mind still the thought, 'Politics are a dirty thing, I want only my art.'

"The work of the Congress lasted for forty days. I watched, saying nothing and feeling very doubtful about it all. But gradually as I saw how they went about tackling the problems of the country I began to change my ideas. As the discussions went on and I listened to the plans for the building of New China, I realized that these people wanted what I wanted, a free China where Chinese could lift up our heads with pride and need bow to no one. But I still did not want to be involved.

"I met Chairman Mao, who congratulated me on my work, and Chou En-lai. For the first time in my life I found myself treated as an equal. In the past no reputable Government leader would have deigned to meet an actress.

"In 1950 and 1951 things were very difficult professionally, though for the first time in many years I could sleep sound at night and go about my work with an easy heart during the day. But with all the problems involved in the cleaning up of Shanghai theatres faced a difficult time. Realizing this in 1950, the Government accepted our application to become a State-owned theatre, and from then on we received a subsidy from the Ministry of Culture.

"For the first time in my life I was free to do what I wanted," she says with her gravely beautiful smile.

"I am a woman who has experienced two different Chinas. When in 1952 my troupe took part in the All-China Theatrical Festival in Peking I realized that this was a new world and I had my place in it.

"It was then that the Government honoured me. All the other recipients were veteran players, like Mei Lan-fan, who had made a great contribution to the Chinese Theatre. I felt very humble and inexperienced and asked myself, 'Why should I be awarded such an honour?' But it inspired me to do more. I felt that although I had done something for my country and my art it was not enough. It was then I made the film *Liang Shan-po and Chu Ying-tai.* It was particularly important because it was China's first colour film. Despite the praise it has received I still feel that my role in it is not good artistically. I am constantly concerned with the necessity to improve my art. Besides, there is so much work to be done, not only with the development of Shaohsing opera, but with rediscovery and improvement of the many local operas which had previously been lost. Since the Government had given help for this over five hundred local operas have been rediscovered. Some of these are more suitable for treatment in the traditional manner and others on modern lines.

"In 1954 the highest honour of all came to me. I was elected a deputy to the National People's Congress. Now I no longer try to escape from reality. I try to make reality better, for I have realized that today in my country there is no conflict between politics and art." She glances at me uncertainly and hesitates a moment.

"Now a new life has opened for me personally as well as artistically. My health has greatly improved because I am no longer under continual strain." She breaks off and a flush creeps up her pale cheeks.

"In the old days I had determined never to marry, but to devote myself to my work. My experience of men—except my father—was such that I could never entertain the thought of getting married. But I met a man whom I felt I could really trust. He is a journalist. We are married and I am happier than I ever believed possible."

For the first time she laughs—the full-throated laugh of Chu Ying-tai.

"Next February there is going to be a baby."

I have a flashing memory of Chu Ying-tai running to her lover's tomb that opens to welcome her. And I'm glad that, for once, life is much better than fiction.

A POEM TO HER BEAUTY

Your loveliness has never been surpassed
by any woman;
enough to make men forsake all
are mere stories of your beauty.

I grieve that time passes so swiftly
life is so full of care, and all is over
in a hundred years; so
I would that you smile more often
and all sorrow pass you by.

You lift your head and gaze
up to the heavens; your lovely neck
bends lower as you stroke the strings
each movement has its charm,
would that I could be
the border of the gown
about your neck, so I
might catch the fragrance
of your lovely hair; but then
you would throw me off at bedtime, and
I should suffer through the night
waiting for you to use me again.

Would that I could become a pair of silken shoes
so I could be with you as you walked—
yet I would always dread the empty hours
when you must rest and I lie
beside your bed, unused.
If only I could make the clouds
bear you the story of my love!
But they are quiet and still
for only a moment, then they drift
away, and leave me to my reverie
and longing for you
whose existence is so far from mine.
I wait for a clear wind
to blow away my woes; let
my love ride back to you
on crests of waves! Out
in the open country I will come
to you, my love, singing
the songs of Shaonan, giving up
all for you, true to you
for ever.

—TAO YUAN MING (Fifth Century).
Translated by REWI ALLEY.

CHAPTER XVI

Shanghai-Hangchow

SHANGHAI platform early on a Sunday morning, bustling with life. Crowds going out of the city for the day. Crowds coming in. Girls in gay florals, boys in coloured shirts.

Out through the crowded suburbs. Mixture of modern city and ancient slum. Matting houses, airy workers' flats.

Rice country. An irregular checker-board of watery fields where the growing rice makes a symphony of green.

Sunday, but, as in Italy, the fields are full of peasants. Wide sun-hats, bright-blue, faded-blue tunics. Here, as in France, blue is the working colour.

Grey-white houses, with curved roofs and ridge-poles, set among clumps of trees. Grey cylindrical tiles like rows of bamboo in clay.

Water-wheels and -buffaloes. Fantastic windmills with curved white canvas sails dotting the green every fifty yards. A pagoda piercing the pale sky.

The train radio plays an aria from the Shaohsing opera, *Liang Shan-po and Chu Ying-tai*. Yuan Sui-feng as Chu Ying-tai sings despairingly before the tomb of her lover.

An argument in the train. A man has taken a reserved seat. The rightful claimant grows heated. The conductor comes and reasons mildly. Eventually the usurper leaves, flinging over his shoulder an angry protest.

Tea and more tea. The service boy sweeps up an empty cigarette packet and the wrapping of a sweet and looks round at us all reproachfully.

Houses with low thatched roofs. Camel-backed bridges. Memorial arches white against the green. (If a widow lived chastely and did not remarry the Emperor would give permission to erect a *pailou*!)

Across the carriage two young lovers hold hands and gaze out of the window seeing, I should say, nothing.

Fish dams made of matting and bamboo. Reversed umbrella nets like those I have seen in Chinese stone-rubbings two thousand years old.

Here, life is catching up. The graves are still dotted throughout the fields, but now pumpkin and melon vines riot over them in a fashion I fear is not accidental. They tell me Southern China was always less conservative than the North.

A storm is driving out of the south under livid clouds that intensify the colour. Suddenly the fields blossom with oiled-paper umbrellas, yellow and blue and red. The jute crops bend under the rain that slashes down in a slanting silver screen. Hangchow!

On the shores of the lovely West Lake at Hangchow, sheltered by acacias beneath which children are playing, is the tomb of a famous heroine, Chiu Chin, executed in her thirty-first year by the order of the Manchu Government in 1907. Her influence—in death as well as in life—was such that she has been called a pattern for the New Age.

Daughter of an official family from Shaohsing County, she was educated in the classics and the writing of poetry, and married at eighteen by family arrangement to a man from a wealthy Hunan family. China's humiliation at the end of the century stirred her passionately patriotic soul. Beautiful, cultured, she gave up the leisured, sheltered life of a woman of the upper classes and obtained a divorce. In 1904, having sold her jewels, she left for Japan, then the place of pilgrimage for Chinese revolutionaries. When in 1905 Sun Yat-sen organized the China Revolutionary League, she was one of the first to join—their aim, the overthrow of the Manchus.

She founded the first women's newspaper. "Moved by affection I rise, I run forward calling loudly to elder sisters, younger sisters, companions of the womb. . . . I desire that they be leaders, awakened lions, advanced messengers of learning and intelligence; that they may serve as lamps in dark chambers. . . . We Chinese women should become the vanguard in rousing the people to welcome enlightenment."

She and a cousin, Hsu Hsi-lin, a wealthy man of official rank, planned a rebellion to overthrow the Manchu rulers. The Government discovered the plot. Hsu Hsi-lin was killed. Chiu Chin was arrested.

At her trial she refused to answer questions. She was tortured to force her to reveal details of their organization. She refused to speak.

She was executed on 15th July 1907. Her biographer writes, "We can say that her hot heart was given, a whetstone, that the country could sharpen its dull sword." She died, but she did not fail, for the women who died in the abortive rising against the feudal régime in 1910 and those who a year later joined Sun Yat-sen's army against the dynasty were her disciples.

CHAPTER XVII

Lily-foot

A s I sit on the balcony of my room in the modern hotel over-looking the lake, waiting for a visitor who is coming to tell me about foot-binding, I think of Chiu Chin, who wrote a paper attacking the custom.

No custom of Old China fascinates outsiders so much as this. Of all the sexual fetishes men have invented to adorn or deform women, to us this is the least comprehensible. But when Western women first came to China in the seventeenth century and criticized foot-binding Chinese women retorted that it was not so bad to bind the feet as to tight-lace the waist and thus injure the internal organs!

No custom was so hard to eradicate. The Manchus imposed the wearing of the pigtail on Chinese men, but they did not dare interfere with the habit of foot-binding among Chinese women.

The pigtail was abolished with the Revolution of 1911. In the main, it disappeared. Foot-binding was also abolished, but it continued. After 1949 cases of foot-binding were found in remote provinces in spite of the Government's prohibition.

There is no subject about which it is so difficult to find information. Perhaps male scholars considered it too unimportant or too shameful to write about! I've searched for hours in the National Library. I've asked the Women's Federation. I've asked all my Chinese friends. All I can find is that it probably commenced in the period of the Five Dynasties following the Tang Dynasty. The encyclopaedia tells us, most inadequately, that about 907 the last Emperor Lei had made an enormous golden lotus and asked his court ladies to dance upon its petals. Their feet were bound for the purpose—it is not stated why—and from this the custom is said to have originated.

Tiny feet became the craze. Women suffered to conform to the ideal of beauty, as women have suffered all over the world. (There flashes across my mind the story of the lady-in-waiting at the court of Catharine de Medici who died because a broken rib penetrated her lung when she was squeezed into the steel corset that would reduce her waist to the size demanded by fashion!)

It is the way of the world everywhere to glorify the particular sexual fetish the race has adopted, and poets called such feet "golden lilies" and "golden lotus-buds".

Over a thousand years ago an Emperor employed groups of lily-footed girls to pull his barge along a canal because he liked to watch the way they swayed so beautifully on their bound feet.

From the Court the fashion spread downwards, as fashions did elsewhere, till even poor families sought an aura of gentility by having a bound-foot daughter and thus having hopes of a better marriage.

The Laws of the Empire are silent about it. It had no religious significance. It was simply a custom, but a custom of tremendous power and popularity.

An old lady told me that "golden lilies" were desired in a bride. Matchmakers were not asked, "Is she beautiful?" but "How small are her feet?" If a man found that his wife's feet were larger than he was led to expect at the betrothal ceremony, it was considered grounds for cancelling the marriage.

Women were its most rabid supporters, as in the West they once clung to the wasp-waist and today they cling to the four-inch heel. But more than sixty years ago progressive Chinese women began to fight the custom.

I asked a Chinese friend—something of a poet himself—why a man should like it. He laughed, holding out his cupped hand. "He liked to feel a woman could dance in the palm of his hand. So small, so dainty, so helpless! It made him feel so big and strong."

My visitor is announced.

Tung Hsiao-niu comes along the balcony, walking with a stiff, Chaplinesque walk, knees rigid, ankles stiff, wedge-shaped feet turned out at an angle of forty-five degrees. She is a tiny woman, not more than four feet ten in height, grey hair drawn tightly back to a chignon, the hair-line squared above the forehead.

Her wrinkled face is full of life as she smiles, and she sits down beside me, a doll-like creature in black silk trousers and grey silk tunic, fanning herself with a white goose-feather fan.

"She says she has had eleven children," the interpreter, Lao Chang, tells me, "eight of them living. A remarkable family. She knows you will be interested to hear about them."

My interest is in foot-binding, but I try to look suitably impressed while gazing significantly at her four-inch feet in their black satin slippers.

She plunges straight into the story of her remarkable family—
"no woman ever had a better family".

As soon as I can interrupt politely, I remind Lao Chang that
I've been promised a story about bound feet. Both interpreters—
—Mrs Tung speaks a difficult dialect and one interpreter trans-
lates into Shanghai dialect and Lao Chang then interprets in
English—speak to her gently, but, I hope, firmly.

She sweeps them aside. Bound feet? Who on earth wants to
hear about that? She brings up one tiny foot and places it on her
knee and puts her wrinkled little hand lovingly on the satin
slipper.

"Would I ever have dreamt in the past of wearing satin slippers
with embroidery on them?" she says challengingly, and pursues
her own line.

Again the interpreter interposes and has a long conversation.

Tung Hsiao-niu holds out her arm for me to see. It is to inform
me that never in her whole life, never, never, *never*, would she
have dreamt of wearing silk. She pulls her trouser-leg out wide
and admires it, laughing merrily. Her pleasure is infectious.

"And feel my arm! See how plump I am." To me it feels light
and fragile. "That's because I'm so well fed now. My sons had
a conference when they all met in 1950, for the first time in many
years, and they arranged they each should give so much money
to me. That was on my sixtieth birthday. What a day that was!
I hadn't seen some of them for years and years, because they all,
at one time or another, had left home to join the Resistance in
the fight against the Japanese. The first ran away when he was
twelve, the second when he was fourteen. Even my elder daughter
—she was nineteen then—joined them when the Anti-Japanese
War broke out, despite the fact that she had bound feet. She
took off the binding and ran away into the hills and, though
she often fell because of her feet, she stayed with the Resistance
armies until the Japs were out of the country."

"But surely Sun Yat-sen banned foot-binding in 1912?"

"True enough! But, alas, my mother-in-law forced me to give
my daughter away to another family when she was a baby. She
was supposed to be affianced to their son, but actually she was
little better than a slave in the house. This family it was that had
her feet bound when she was eight. When she was eighteen her
elder brother bought her back with the twenty silver dollars he
saved. And it was when he ran away to join the partisans that
she went with him.

"What a day that was! The Kuomintang soldiers came into the

house, threw things about, took what they fancied, and slapped my daughter's face and knocked her down when she protested."

She jumps about from date to date in her story and the two interpreters hold her up, to her very obvious impatience, while they untangle things.

At this stage she folds her legs under her like an acrobat to illustrate some point. Her eyes flash. Her voice rises. She chuckles. The interpreters look at me despairingly.

"My eldest son is now forty-three and has a very responsible job in Shanghai. They are wonderful boys, all of them. When they had run away I never knew what had happened to them. Never had a word from them, except one that came back once to hide. That was my seventh son. It was the first time I had any idea that they had joined the partisans. I was terribly upset when he told me, but he explained that they were fighting for China. I never saw any of my sons or daughter again until after the Liberation.

"When the People's Army was approaching the village all kinds of rumours were about. They said all girls of eighteen would be forced to marry old men, that only one knife would be left to each eighteen families to prevent them being used as weapons, that if your dresses were long they would be cut and if you protested you would be shot. I was terribly worried, thinking of all my children with a bandit rabble like that running all over the country.

"Then when the army did come, they were quite different—never went into houses, never took food from anyone, unless they paid for it, and they were so polite and helpful! I felt happier then, but it was not till my sons and daughter came home that I understood why the People's Army was so different from any other I had seen. They had strict rules of discipline and were severely punished if they broke them. They mustn't take a single needle or a piece of thread from the people. They must speak to the people courteously, be absolutely fair in all business dealings, return everything they borrowed, pay for everything they damaged, not swear at people or beat them, and must respect women. We couldn't believe our own eyes.

"After they had been there a few days it rained heavily and there were those poor boys sitting out in the rain. Then people started *asking* them to come into their houses. I invited two, because I really wanted to know had any of them ever come across my sons or my daughter. No one had heard of them. I was very depressed.

"Then one day I got a letter from my eldest son which a neighbour read for me. So I knew he was alive. A little while later he and my third son came home. They told me that my second son, whom I had not seen for twelve years, would be coming back. It was then that I found that they hadn't known whether I was alive or dead, because when they made inquiries about me in Hangchow I had disappeared. Really what had happened was that I had gone back to my native village.

"I was full of excitement about my second son. I kept thinking of him as I had last seen him, a boy of fourteen. I sent my fourth son to meet him, but they actually sat down next to each other at a tea-house and didn't recognize each other!

"So I was alone in the house when I heard a call at the door and went to it. There was a big strong man in army uniform and a young woman with him. I looked at them, wondering who they could be, I didn't know who he was until he held out his arms and said, 'Mama!' And then I was so happy I just burst out crying. And he said, 'Mama, this is your daughter-in-law!' Such a nice girl. And clever! They had been in the army together and she had nursed him. That was a romance for you, wasn't it? Very different from the way I had been married off without even seeing my husband."

"Bound feet," I murmur to the interpreter.

He passes on the query. But Tung Hsiao-niu takes her own course.

"You know, I can't understand now how I could have been so silly as I was in the old days. Before they joined the Resistance my sons were working in the Underground, and I hadn't a single idea what they were up to. It worried me frightfully. They used to work right into the middle of the night and go out when respectable people were in bed. My elder daughter was up to the neck in it, too.

"I became suspicious and scolded them. I said to them, 'I hope you're not up to anything bad. Remember we've always been respectable. And your father would turn in his grave if he thought the good name of Tung was being harmed.'

"My son assured me it was all right and asked me not to tell anyone about them. Oh dear! Was ever a woman in such a position? But I always reminded myself that they were perfect children and never said a word to anyone.

"Then posters began to appear in the town. And then when I was washing my daughter's dress I found a bottle of paste in one of her pockets, and I knew she had been pasting up forbidden posters. It was a terrible shock. Then when my son opened a book-shop in Hangchow where we were living at the time and began selling prohibited books I should have had to be very silly indeed not to have known what they were doing. Often books would be hidden under the floor. It was very worrying, because several times the K.M.T. sent search parties.

"When they left to join the Partisans they hadn't any money and I was worried again that they wouldn't have any food, so I sold up practically everything and sent two hundred and fifty silver dollars after them with a trusted friend who told me he was going to join them.

"I have been given a medal for the work I have done for service-men's families when their men are away, for who should under-stand better than me the grief of seeing all your children leave you?"

She sits back with a triumphant air and composes herself as though to say, "There, that's my story!"

"And now about your early life?" I say, glancing significantly at her bound feet, dangling like two silken wedges.

"My early life?" she repeats and sits looking at me under frown-ing brows, fanning herself reflectively with the goose-feather fan. Then she shrugs her shoulders as though yielding out of politeness to an importunate questioner and rushes headlong into the story.

"My father came from a well-to-do family in Fukien Province. He was very feudal-minded, even though he was a schoolteacher. My mother was the daughter of a well-to-do peasant. She had bound feet and in consequence was used only to very light work. She was married at twenty-two and had eleven children of whom only one brother and myself, the youngest, survived. By the time of my birth my father was a very sick man. He grew more and more feudal-minded and he wouldn't have me taught anything, because it wasn't fitting that a girl should know anything. It used to worry him very much that our house was too small and we were too poor to observe the old rules about girls and boys not eating together or using the same pegs for their clothes or the same place to bathe in, as used to be done in his old home when he was a boy. But he treated my brother and me quite differently."

She shakes her head wonderingly. "Seeing how free and im-portant women are today it's hard to believe that it's so short a time ago that these things could happen. Would you believe it that if someone came to the door and asked if anyone was at home, I would answer, 'No', since I didn't count as anyone? And to think that now I, who once counted for nothing, have been elected to the Hangchow People's Congress! And I know it's not only because of my wonderful children." She catches my eye and pulls herself up.

"Yes, indeed a girl had a hard life in those days! When I was fourteen my father died—he had been an invalid for ten years—and my mother went to live with her married brother and, of course, I went with her. My uncle wasn't rich and as I had been trained only to do needlework and kept always at home life was very difficult. I had to work or starve. So I got orders from a shop to make cakes of nut-meat and I did this till I was seventeen.

"When I was seventeen my uncle told me I must get married so that he could get some money to repay him for all I had cost him in keep. My mother protested, saying her daughter was not for sale. But what could she do? In spite of her protests my uncle found a family that was prepared to give the amount he wanted as a marriage gift and arranged a marriage for me, and at seventeen I married Tung, who was twenty. Neither of us had seen the other until the marriage day. I gave up my family and became daughter-in-law to Mrs Tung. A girl was lost to her own family. 'A daughter married is like water poured out the door', they used to say, and 'A wife married is like a pony bought; I'll ride her and whip her as I like.' And they did very often. Not that my husband was ever cruel to me.

"My father-in-law had a grocery store, and they were quite comfortably off. After his death the property was divided among the sons and we had to get a little business on our own. When my husband died, more than twenty years ago, I had to earn a living for myself and my family." She brightens. "But, of course, my sons and daughter were wonderful. Did I tell you—"

"But your married life, Mrs Tung," I say firmly.

She sighs and shakes her head slowly. "What a life it was! The Tungs were a big family—father, mother, grandmother, and three brothers. And I was expected to do the work for the whole household, alone—the cooking, making the cotton slippers and the socks made of cotton cloth. Be the personal maid of ma and grandma. Help them get up and wash. Prepare the breakfast, clean the house, do the needlework, prepare the lunch. In the afternoon I had to make the shoes, then get the supper ready and in the evening clean up everything and prepare the old ladies for bed, and if I couldn't finish my mother-in-law would say, 'Are you coming in a sedan chair?' Indeed, the daughter-in-law in a family was nothing but a slave." Her little hands make a pantomime of subjection.

"I hadn't the right to say a single word, no matter how wrongly

I might be scolded. For it was believed that if the daughter-in-law answered back the family would never be prosperous. When the relatives came I had to hide.

"Looking back on it, I realize that practically all the women I knew suffered as I did. Many, indeed, far worse. It was taken for granted. My husband's mother had had a terrible life when she was married, and so had the grandmother. It looked as though women lived just for the day when they would have a daughter-in-law and take out on them all they had suffered. Sometimes I wonder if I would have been the same if things hadn't changed. Today—" She pulls herself up.

"There was no end to a mother-in-law's power. You couldn't be legally made first wife of your husband without her consent and her presence at the ceremony. If she didn't like you and you didn't get on well together, she could insist that your husband sent you back to your own home. There was nothing left for you to do but kill yourself. Yes, indeed, I had an unhappy life, but really, compared with a lot of other women, it was a bed of roses. Many women were so badly treated by their husbands and mothers-in-law—beaten, insulted, day in, day out—that they were driven to suicide. Then a woman had her revenge. She counted for nothing alive, but once she was dead her own family had the right to demand heavy compensation, an expensive funeral, everything. Not that it did the girl much good, poor thing." She sighs.

"I had eleven children in all. In those days you weren't allowed to lie on the bed for a birth, but had to kneel on the floor, for it was said if you lay down the blood would come out of your mouth. After the birth you sat on the bed for twenty-four hours. For one hundred and twenty days you could eat only plain things with no salt." She shakes her head impatiently. "But it's all different now. The Marriage Law has changed all that."

She makes large, free gestures and the white goose-feather fan is waved vigorously. "I've been invited to work on the mediation committee of my district, which settles marriage problems, and my own experience is a great help to me, particularly in dealing with some of the feudal-minded people who are still about. I have a wonderful life today. Everyone calls me Ta-ma—Honourable Mother. I'm president of the Street Committee. And, you see, with the sixty yuan a month my sons give me, I don't need to work." Her voice drops as if giving me a confidence. "Actually, I don't need sixty yuan, so I have plenty of money to give away to help other people, because I don't even have to buy food. At the family conference on my sixtieth birthday it was arranged that my fourth son, as his contribution, should be responsible for feeding me. Such a ridiculous menu they made out! Once a week at least I must have a chicken and a piece of the fat part of pork. I must have fish another day and all the fruit and vegetables and tea that I want. I often have the neighbours in to help me eat it all. When I protested that I couldn't possibly eat all that my sons said, 'You've never eaten good food in your life. Now you must eat what you want.' Mind you, it was true enough what they said about the food, because even though the Tung family ate well, the daughter-in-law would never dare take anything but the poorest things on the table."

She opens her mouth and points to her toothless gums. "My children are getting a set of false teeth made for me so that I can really enjoy the lovely food."

We all laugh together.

"My own experience, too, with my children makes me very sympathetic with children and I am often asked to advise in their sicknesses. You see, both my daughters were given away to other families because the Tung family didn't want the trouble of rearing girls who would be only an expense to them. I was broken-hearted, but my mother-in-law and the grandmother forced me to part with them. I tried to console myself with the thought that, if I didn't give them away, the poor things would have terrible lives, scolded all day, beaten, and it was better to let them go to a family that would care for them. You couldn't imagine just how different things are today, when girls are wanted and loved and have opportunities to become anything instead of being called 'unprofitable goods'.

"But that was the way it had always been and no one thought it would ever change. My eldest daughter's feet were bound when she was five, and she still remembers what she suffered, but people did it for her own good."

She smiles her mischievous toothless smile at me and unexpectedly says, "Now I shall tell you the story of my bound feet."

She picks up one tiny deformed foot with extraordinary agility and puts it on her knee. Her face shows repugnance as she puts both hands protectively round the pointed slipper and stares at it silently for a space.

"During the old days you must have feet as small as possible. The perfect bound foot should not be more than three inches. Of course, my feet are more than three inches, I haven't bound them for twenty years. Not since I became a widow at the age of forty-three. In those days a widow was not allowed to remarry.

She didn't even dare to speak to a man for fear of being thought a bad woman. What awful misery it caused! I knew a woman who was bought as a wife for the young son who was only eight at the time and very delicate. Really, she was bought to be a nursemaid to him till he was old enough to live with her. But he died when he was twelve and there she was! Neither wife nor mother, and with all her life before her just a despised slave. In another case, a widow who dared break the feudal rule that a woman should die faithful to one husband was killed by her own brothers because she had disgraced the family. But now no girl will ever suffer from that again, the New Marriage Law has done away with all that.

"Lily-foot was such a nice name, I sometimes wonder if the poets knew what it meant to the girls." She looks at me with her small bright eyes, doubtfully. "Have you ever seen a bound foot?"

I shake my head.

With a sudden gesture she takes off her slipper and waits for my reaction to the sight of the lump in the mauve sock. I feel a little sick.

The interpreter explains rapidly, "She has never shown her feet to a stranger before."

She looks at me searchingly, and then takes off her sock. The distorted lump of flesh and bone is the worst form of foot deformity it is possible to see. The heel is drawn down in a solid block with a deep cleft of puckered reddened flesh under the arch, which is pushed up in an abnormal ugly curve. Only the big toe is normal. The other four are drawn under and pressed into the sole. I put out a hand and touch it. We smile at each other a little uncertainly. She goes on rapidly, putting on her sock again.

"Foot-binding started generally when you were about five. The younger the better. But not too young, or the foot would not have the proper shape. The work of binding was done with strong cotton strips about five feet long and seven inches wide. These were drawn over and over the four toes, leaving only the big toe free, till gradually the toe bones were broken and they lay as flat as possible under the sole. They were drawn so tightly round the heel that the pressure curved the arch bone."

She puts on the slipper. Her voice trembles a little. "I have never in all the years that have passed forgotten the pain. It was agony to rest on the bed, and for a long time both feet were like lumps of burning coal. I couldn't bear to put a blanket over them in even the coldest weather. One night they pained so badly that

I took off the cloths, but next morning my mother beat me and I never dared do it again.

" 'You'll never get married, if you have big feet. No decent family will look at you,' she scolded. But, oh, the agony of it!

"My parents made me walk in spite of the pain and at first I would totter along the hall holding on to each side. It was a long time before I could walk without holding on to the wall, and then I could walk only on my heels. For years I cried all night and my daughter told me she did the same. During the hot weather the feet had a very bad smell because they couldn't be washed every night and some sort of powder was put between the bandages to take the smell away.

"If once the bandages were removed the feet began to grow, so it was necessary to keep them always bound and always more and more tightly. So as you grew older the shoes were made smaller and smaller, and if when you put them on there was a little space it was stuffed with cotton to make it tighter. It depended on the person how long the feet hurt, but generally for four to five years. If your feet were fat it was better, but if they were thin the heel-bone hit the ground and it was very painful for a long time. There was an old saying, 'For every pair of bound feet in the house a bucket of tears.' "

She sighs. "But now all that is over. Little girls and little boys are equal. They have the same love and care. They have the same education. One of my grandsons is teaching me to read and write, and I can write my name and simple letters."

She proudly takes a pen from the pocket of her tunic and, leaning over, carefully prints the three characters of her name in my note-book in rather shaky characters.

"There," she says triumphantly, "they bound my feet but they couldn't bind my mind!"

Will I excuse her? She has a meeting of the Street Committee.

She gets up, puts out her two bony little hands and takes one of mine between them. We stand looking at each other and suddenly she puts her frail little arms round my neck and presses her cheek against mine. I watch her go with her stiff-kneed walk on her wedge-shaped feet, feeling that three thousand years of women's suffering go with her.

CHAPTER XVIII

Hangchow-Canton

HANGCHOW STATION and a crowd of our friends to see us off. Two nights and a day of travelling ahead of us! A hot clear evening. All villagers out of doors. The sun setting, red as a bush-fire sun, turning the rice-fields to lakes of fire.

A bronze frieze of naked boys sitting on a railless bridge over a rivulet, each with a fan that moves in concerted rhythm. Below them glistening bodies in the brown water.

Water-buffaloes wallowing luxuriously in the river after the day's labour, only their heads and backbones visible, while buffalo boys splash in the shallows.

Night. The rumble of the wheels. Hot wind rushing in to displace the hotter air.

After tossing stickily in the sleeper, finding even the towelling coverlet too hot to lie on, I unwind the length of smooth matting I have till now disdained and cover my pillow with the smaller mat. It is cool and pleasant and the blue cotton sheet with bright flowers is covering enough.

Morning. Solid grey villages set among red ochre fields. Low huts of the same red mud.

Green and red fields running away to fantastic hills tilted like a Punch's cap. This is three-crop-a-year country. Hour after hour, endless fields, innumerable peasant men and women stringing along the elevated paths that divide them, bamboo pole on the shoulder, with its laden baskets dangling from each end.

A train kept incredibly clean in spite of the crowds and the heat and the dust. Glass after glass of steaming green tea.

Midday. The thermometer shows 102°F. The dining car finds iced watermelon for me and delicious peaches chopped up raw and soaked in a syrup that has a faint flavour of ginger.

On the platform fruit-stalls with luscious pink watermelons and small yellow melons and green star-fruit and peaches.

Buffets on the bigger stations. Two-thirds of the train descends. Attendants in white overalls and caps at the glass-covered food-stalls. Bowls of rice eaten steaming on the station. Cold rice in paper boxes to carry away. Hot noodles in bowls. Steaming soup.

Flat wheaten cakes as big as a bread-and-butter plate. Long coiled ropes of crisp brown batter. Fish dishes and prawn dishes and brown bean-cakes and meat dumplings.

Night comes down over the fields that reflect the rose and apricot of the afterglow, against which are silhouetted streams of wide-hatted figures going home.

"Too hot to eat!" I say, though I go with the others to the restaurant car. An iced shandy. Then the waiter comes, bearing dish after dish of wonderful Cantonese food. My appetite revives. Steamed chicken that melts in your mouth. Diced liver with chillies. Bamboo shoots. Sweet-and-sour pork. Fish with a ginger sauce and a crisp crackling skin. Rice, each grain separate, light and fluffy. Iced watermelon.

We insist on writing a eulogy of the food and the restaurant staff that could turn out such a meal in such overpowering heat. We name them Model Restaurant Crew!

When we leave the car everyone, from head-waiter to cook, shakes hands with us.

Eleven o'clock. The train stops for ten minutes at a station. The passengers flow out. We do the same to stretch our legs and get a breath of fresh air. The night is still hot. Everywhere waving fans. The perfume of the "night-breathing flower" comes to us.

Another stifling night. Even the matting is hot. I awake to green crops, grey soil, fields dotted with wells, each with a primitive long pole structure that somehow recalls pictures I have seen of irrigation in ancient Babylon.

A long human chain is building a dam. There should be a monument to the man—and the woman—with the shoulder pole.

Varicoloured fields stretch to smooth rounded hills. The chrome yellow of ripening rice, the dark green of jute fields, lotus ponds, green-blue of onions, yellowing stubble. Here necessity has overcome ancestor worship and very often the graves are smoothed and cultivated without pretence.

By a river, rust-brown fishing nets draped like the tents of Genghis Khan.

And, suddenly, grove after grove of eucalyptus-trees. The familiar unforgettable smell of gum-leaves burning and I am homesick for my country that is washed by the same ocean eight thousand miles away.

Canton.

CHAPTER XIX

Village on the River

EARLY morning. From my window on the ninth floor of the hotel in Canton, I look down on the Pearl River where already, against water the colour of milky tea, the incessant shuttling of river-craft weaves the tapestry that, leaving aside the steam-boats, it has woven for uncounted centuries.

As far as I can see the sampans lie side by side, nose to tail. Each is a home as well as a boat, and here, in a space about twelve feet by five feet, Canton's waterfolk for uncounted centuries lived a life where the river was all their world.

The junks along the edge of the river are like an encampment with cooking fires, families sitting out on the prow or on the middle deck with their bowls of rice and their chopsticks, the washing already drying on bamboo poles.

Large passenger boats, the after-part like an apartment house, draw into the wharf after their voyage from distant villages of Kwangtung that lie along the rivers that lead into the Pearl. Up-to-date steam-ferries shuttle skittishly across the river. The steam-boats are parvenus of a century. But for two thousand years— probably more!—the sampans with their plaited bamboo hoods that shelter cargo and family, the high-prowed junks with their bamboo-slatted sails have plied the river.

A breeze ruffles the water. Sails leaf-brown and veined like a butterfly's wing, swell. An endless procession of boats, big and small, junks and sampans laden with vegetables, bags of rice, jars of oil, jars of wine. Loads of long strong bamboos for scaffolding, sawn timber, tiles, mysterious products in matting bags of all shapes and sizes.

I can see the smoke blowing from the round stove in the stern of a sampan moored below me. At nine o'clock last night I watched them manoeuvre for position, riding lights flickering, cabin faintly illuminated, children looking like cocoons in their quilts, mother and father still working. They tied up to another craft, the sixth in the row. A splash. Someone dived into the river. A dog barked and a second splash sounded.

This morning they are astir early, the dog barking at passing craft. A woman leans overboard to wash a pastry board. She straightens, raises the cover of a pan and sniffs, turns and calls to a woman on a neighbouring boat. Evidently she is "out of something". Her neighbour, a young woman with a baby in a carrying cloth on her back, comes to the stern of her boat, ties a packet on the end of a sixteen-foot bamboo poling-stick and passes it across to her friend. Housewives everywhere have the same problems!

Just at that moment a seller of vegetables comes by, his boat piled with long green cucumbers. Both women add cucumber to the breakfast menu. From the shouted comments I am sure they are complaining about the price!

Lam Yoo comes to take me to see the waterfolk. She is one of them herself.

"My ancestors were all waterfolk. Generation after generation of Lams lived on a sampan and ferried people across the river."

She is a little brown woman with a strong, stocky body and large muscular hands. The black mole between her dancing eyes makes them still brighter. They do not cease their dancing when she tells me with her wide smile, "In the old days we were the Untouchables." In her new life she has no time to brood over past wrongs. Now she is a deputy to the Canton People's Congress and the world is hers.

"We never came ashore," she goes on, "but spent our whole lives, sleeping, eating, living, dying, on the sampans. We were despised by the land-people, mocked and jeered at and even assaulted if we dared to put a foot ashore. They called us *Tan-ka*."

Young Chen explains in a shocked voice that this is a word one couldn't translate. It has been abolished by law.

"If we came ashore the city folk would spit contemptuously. We had no civil rights, but they used to levy taxes on us, the main one being a poll tax. Everything reminded us every day that we were Untouchables."

She strides powerfully in her modern leather shoes as we step out of the hotel, a trim, competent figure in her bright-blue tunic and navy trousers, her short, strong black hair swinging with each stride.

"I never put on shoes till Liberation," she says, smiling broadly at me. "And the first time I wore them to a meeting on shore they nearly killed me."

To reach our launch we walk under the broiling sun along the river-quays, looking down on the moored junks and sampans and rowing boats and big river boats. All the varied life of Canton

passes us by on the sizzling asphalt road. Little girls carry baby
brothers on their backs, bunched up in gaily flowered or embroidered carrying-cloths suspended from their shoulders. Baby is used
to it and his head lolls backwards as he takes his afternoon nap.

Canton has always been a city of working mothers and welfare
facilities have not yet caught up with the legacy of poverty and
misery the city inherited from the old days.

"But we will soon," Lam Yoo says confidently. "Who would
ever have thought we waterfolk would have a clinic for mothers,
and schools—we who were practically illiterate?"

Heavily laden hand-carts, men and women straining at the
ropes, the sweat dripping from sun-bitten faces.

"Cantonese people are still poor," Lam Yoo says frowning, so
that the dark mole links her brows. "But the beggars are gone!"

Men with exquisitely woven baskets dangling from shoulder
poles, one full of green melons, others of pineapples, bananas,
star-fruit, yellow-fruit, papaws, mangoes, guavas, lichees, water-
melons, white melons, yellow melons, peaches, pears, apples, tomatoes. . . .

We cross the wharves where two old men look at us curiously.
One is smoking a bamboo pipe about eighteen inches long, drawing in the smoke from a smaller pipe about two inches long, set in
the middle of the long stem.

To go aboard we have to walk through three boats moored
side by side. The captain of our launch and his offsider shake
hands and welcome me in rapid Cantonese. Out in midstream the
two worlds of Canton open up: the city with its tall European
buildings lining the shore and behind them the narrow crowded
streets where most of the "land" Chinese live, the river where sixty
thousand waterfolk still cluster together in their floating homes.
Sixty thousand—a fair-sized city by any count—the majority living
by ferrying passengers from one shore to the other. It costs two to
five cents to cross the river, according to the distance. The others
are sailors on the river junks, fishermen and dockers.

Sea-going junks move with a stately motion down the river, like
Spanish galleons with their high prow and stern, the stateliness of
their progress not marred by sails that look as if they had been
made of patches of discarded old clothes.

A raft of big logs goes by, with a shack built in the centre, the
living quarters of the crew. Two women and a man are working
on the big oar that is part propulsion, part guidance.

Lam Yoo takes up her story. "Our lives in the old days were not
only poverty-stricken but full of fears. All the police did was to

come down and collect the taxes, and if you had no money, your oars, your means of livelihood, would be taken away until you had finally borrowed or in some way earned it! Is it strange then that many women were driven into prostitution? Those houses over there were brothels—" she points to dilapidated shacks built over the water on piles—"and in addition there were hundreds of so-called 'flower-boats' where private prostitutes received their customers. They're all gone today. It was a bitter life for everyone. They used to say, 'If you go upstream you're afraid of being arrested by the police, and if you go down stream you're afraid of the gangsters.' Because of the frantic struggle to live there was always quarrelling and people would fight each other for the customers who were offering.

"The little ferry wharves were controlled by racketeers and we had to pay sixty per cent of our day's earnings for the right to pick up passengers, for if we didn't we would be beaten and denied access to the landings. In addition, the police menaced us with revolvers whenever we put a foot on land.

"We were oppressed, yet we could do nothing. We had to lick the feet of the despots to get passengers and the police gave us neither help nor protection. Now all the landing wharves are managed by the waterfolk themselves and the little ferries take passengers in rotation.

"Our family was like many others. My mother had more than ten children and only four of us survived. Most died at birth and the others when they were infants. My mother had to deliver the child herself on the sampan, and, an hour after birth, resume her ferrying, otherwise they would starve. My father did odd jobs, but he was always scratching for a living, though he was a good honest worker. He originally had to borrow money to marry my mother, and then settle that dept by paying—at heavy interest—from what he earned.

"Six of us were crowded on the little boat and we had only one blanket to cover us, and the winter nights on the Pearl River are very cold.

"Our boat was hired from a small boatyard owner and we were always in debt—like everybody else. I started to row at eight with a big piece of light wood tied to me so that if I fell overboard I would float. Many children were drowned. As I got older sometimes I sneaked ashore and ventured to walk a couple of hundred yards along the bank, but even if no one recognized me as one of the waterfolk and hunted me back, after a short distance the entirely new life so bewildered and frightened me that, like a little jungle animal, I would rush back into the world I knew." For the first time Lam Yoo's sunniness is clouded and for a few moments she is silent.

"But now things are different. My father has a permanent job with the Canton Sundries Company and though my mother is still working on the boat, she has a much easier life. I am now completely literate. In the old days we married only among ourselves, but I married a land-man. My husband works in the same company as my father, and we have a boy one year old. He is very naughty." She smiles indulgently. "Not that I mind, since the doctor explained that it is because for the first time in history Chinese babies are properly fed. And that is how it should be."

We passed what used to be a K.M.T. Officers' Club and swimming-pool. It is now open to everyone, and crowds of swimmers are in the water and a long queue waits at the diving boards. A floating café goes by, selling soft drinks which must be close to boiling in the sun that beats on them.

An endless stream of ferries plies back and forth, women standing up at the long oar. At one a child of about eight is helping. It is now holiday time, Lam Yoo explains, and children work on the boats as they did in her day.

We are now closing in to the River Village. Most of the boats are of plain unpainted wood, weatherworn to a soft grey, but some are elaborately decorated with yellow and blue and orange and green, and have neat curtains on their cabins. From some of them triangular nets are drying, henna brown against the blue sky. Some even have pot-plants on the ledges. Children peer curiously at us, the young ones all with a harness attached to the side of the boat.

"Now tap water is available all along the banks," Lam Yoo says. "But, alas, some of the older people are hard to educate and still drink the river water, with the result that we have not yet succeeded in eradicating the diseases that come from it.

"Since we knew no hygiene in the old days, we washed in the river and drank the water. And as the river was filthy, being a drain for the city apart from a disposal place for corpses of human beings as well as animals, there was much illness, and typhoid and dysentery added their victims to those who died of beri-beri from bad food.

"Our only clothes were made of black cotton cloth. No one would have dreamt of wearing bright colours, and right up to Liberation all the men wore long pigtails which they didn't dare cut because they were so superstitious, even though Sun Yat-sen had abolished the pigtail in 1911."

The launch slows down; some words are shouted and we are invited by several voices at once. It is siesta time and most of the women are resting in the intense heat, but one is already moving and the oarswoman turns and sculls towards us. She poles the boat skilfully alongside, and holds out a hand to me to help me aboard. It is as hard and muscular as a timber-cutter's, and she all but lifts me over the narrow gap.

She is strongly built with a smooth tanned face and broad, shapely brown feet. She wears a twisted gold ring on her right hand and pearl ear-rings and also has a wristlet watch, signs of prosperity here! She is a widow and her son is a sailor, she tells me as she introduces us to her passenger, a maternity nurse, a slight grey-haired woman with two badges on her pale-blue tunic. She smiles at me warmly, half of her teeth gold and half aluminium, and explains that she is on her rounds by sampan; her job is to visit expectant and nursing mothers on their own boats to see that all goes well with them and the baby.

The boat is about twelve feet long by four feet wide, enough for three people to lie down side by side, with woven bamboo mats on the deck and paper flowers stuck in the lathes of the roof, where the family portraits are also displayed. The cabin is open, with bamboo blinds that can be left down at night. Bent bamboo coat-hangers hang from the arched bamboo ribs that form the roof. My hostess pushes forward wooden stools with legs about three inches high. A flowered thermos is produced and hot water is served in little flowered bowls. The reflection of water-ripples plays on the roof and the lap of the tide is peaceful.

Another boat sculls over. Introductions. Invitation. I step from one boat to the other, aided by the strong arm of the owner of the second boat, a dark woman with a pock-marked, sardonic face under permed hair.

To my queries she replies, "I have been a waterwoman like all the others and our mothers before us since we came from our mothers' wombs."

It is a delightful boat, the cabin wood inlaid with mother of pearl, attractive woven mats on the floor. The kitchen is in the stern, a space roughly three feet by two, where the rice-bowls and the tea-bowls, plates, and chopsticks are neatly stacked in narrow shelves on one side, the cooking utensils on the other. A shining brass kettle. A water jar. The stove is a large brown earthenware

pot in which charcoal is burned. A deep covered pan is sunk in
the mouth and simmers gently.

The bedclothes are padded cotton quilts and are stored away
under the floor of the central cabin, where my hostess's extra
clothes are also kept. All the women wear the thick, lustrous black
silk tunic and trousers with the backing of brown that is said to
be a protection against the heat and the rain.

Her friend, who is visiting her during the siesta hour, tells me
that she has two children at school. "Before the Liberation," she
says, "we should no more have thought of going ashore than of
eating rice!"

Their takings now average twenty-five yuan a month. And since
they now all own their boats and have no debt burden or hire to
pay they are well off compared with the past, for one can live very
well in Canton on fifteen yuan a month.

Lam Yoo glances at her watch. Time to be going. We have a
lot of visits to make yet. We are sculled back to the launch where,
in spite of my protests that I'm quite capable of getting aboard
alone, Lam Yoo and the widow hoist me up like a bag of rice.

Late next day our big launch noses its way slowly and very
carefully through what is really a city of watercraft in a shallow
river-bay where thousands of small craft are moored, one against
the other, a hundred yards out from the shore.

These are the craft that transport goods across the river, unpainted, utilitarian. Families come out to wave us greetings. Children shout. Amidst much laughter we are poled off with long
bamboo poles whenever the slow-moving launch finds the going
too difficult in the narrow passageway.

All the life of the waterfolk goes on uninhibited around us. A
half-blind grandmother is mopping herself with a wet cloth.
Naked little children in their harness are tied to beam or mast,
bigger ones swimming in the dirty river, women dipping into
large stone water jars, pans steaming on the stove, small girls
watering flower-pots.

We pass a workers' club, a rickety building on piles, where men
are sitting drinking hot water from large enamel mugs.

At last we are manoeuvred into the landing stage of the Waterfolk's Cultural Club, a low weatherboard structure on a bamboo
raft.

The director, a girl with a heart-shaped face, looking much too
young, meets me and takes me through the reading-room. The
readers look up curiously. A small girl with two long plaits smiles
at me, and puts out a welcoming hand. A grandfather with a

straggly beard nods his welcome. Some youths look up from the long table covered with magazines and clap as I pass through.

The Club is a bright, airy building looking out on the river. A bright cloth covers the reading-room table. There are pictures on the walls, pot-plants on the window-sills.

It is clear the waterfolk are proud of their Club—the first they've ever had, the director tells me, as we sit down in the lending section before another mug of steaming tea. (This tea is becoming a problem.)

"Our main task is to distribute books," she says enthusiastically. "Quite a problem, since our borrowers are likely to be here to-day and gone tomorrow, so we have organized the libraries to suit our mobile clientele and boxes of books are packed and sent to groups to distribute. The Club is also used for opera practice. We have a flourishing opera group, and a drama group, and there is also an organized section for recreational activities."

At the other end of the room two girls in big plaited-straw hats are borrowing records, a loud-speaker and a gramophone, for a dance they are holding that night. I compare Lam Yoo's girlhood with theirs.

On their way out they stop and with some giggling ask me if I can come to the dance—"only a small one in the hall of our union. When we hold a big dance we borrow the Y.M.C.A. hall, which, although it is very busy, is very obliging. Can you come?"

Alas, I can't. Tonight I am going to the opera.

They go off, shaking my hand and looking back to wave fare-well. Young and buoyant, they hurry along the footpath, afraid of nothing and no one.

"We have many activities here at night and mothers with children bring them along," the director continues. "If you could come along I'm sure you would be interested."

I hear a familiar tune. A young man has come along to borrow a record and hums the first few bars to the girl in charge.

Back to our launch. By now the homecoming sampans have gathered so close that the launch can barely squeeze through to open water. What looks like imminent danger of collision is a cause for great amusement, and much expert pushing and shoving with long poles. There is laughter and waving of chopsticks as many interrupt the evening meal to shout greetings. In the excitement a small boy falls into the water and is fished out with a bamboo pole. Undaunted he stands on the prow, his wet naked body glistening in the evening sun and I hear his shrill voice follow us, "Good-bye, Aunty, good-bye!"

Next afternoon, after a visit to the Waterfolk's Maternity Clinic, a model clinic where two newly born babies are squalling lustily, Wung Mei-tse and I glide over the glassy water towards a sampan moored on the outer rim of a "water-street". It has the look of a settled home about it, with its flowering pot-plant on the forward deck, the indigo cotton curtains that keep out the western sun, and gay cotton squares flapping from a bamboo pole in the stern.

A woman watches our approach, standing poised on tanned feet, the thick lustrous silk of her tunic and trousers whipping against her slender body.

With the long oval of her face, even brows, dark hair parted in the middle, and a tiny baby on her arm, she looks like a thirteenth century Byzantine Madonna, except for the two short plaits that barely touch her shoulders. When she smiles the wrinkles show in her cheeks and you realize with something of a shock that she is not a young woman.

She helps me aboard with a small hand, bony, muscular, hard and strong as a man's.

This is Liang Ta-ma, Mei-tse tells me proudly, chairwoman of her "Street" Committee, a director of the Women's Federation, and a deputy to the Pearl River People's Congress.

She beams at the older woman with affectionate pride. Liang Ta-ma bows in acknowledgment as she motions me to the usual small stool, with a courtesy that would not be out of place in a palace.

"And this is Ah Sung, two months old and the only survivor of five."

Ah Sung means "Life". His mother's face softens as she tells me and I sense all the joy and hope that lies behind the choice of his name. Like a Chinese doll with his pineapple hair-cut and bright patterned jacket and split pants, a wad of printed cotton, strategically placed, showing through the split, he stares unwinkingly at me out of jet eyes. Then he thrusts a plump fist into his mouth and the silver bracelet on his wrist sinks into its dimpled folds.

Wung Mei-tse feels his rounded legs, raises him, and estimates his weight. His mother proudly tells her how much he has gained, and she exclaims in wonder.

Ah Sung suffers it with dignity then, after staring at us expressionlessly in turn, suddenly wails.

With beautiful unselfconsciousness, Liang Ta-ma unfastens her high-necked black tunic and the blue cotton jacket underneath, looking more than ever like the Madonnas I have seen in Italian churches who look down on the Infant Jesus at their breast with faint smiles of pride and contentment touching their faces.

She looks up to tell me she is sorry her husband is not here. He would have liked to meet a foreign friend on their boat, for what could more surely tell them that the old days are past?

"But this week he is away. He is a sailor and the junk on which he works trades up the river. A very different life today from what it used to be. In the old days we lived between the devil and the deep sea. His was a very dangerous life, because when carrying cargoes into the back areas ships were often attacked by bandits and pirates and the crew assaulted and killed. But now there are no more bandits and pirates and he has a regular job, whereas before we were often almost starving. Before, the crew were exploited by the captain or the company. Now the owners have changed over to joint State-private and the wages are determined by the work done, and as my husband has always been a steady worker we are doing well."

"So you can stay at home and look after Ah Sung and attend to your various activities?"

"Oh, no." She stops in the act of massaging Ah Sung's back. "I was on morning shift today. A nursemaid looks after baby when I'm at work. You see, I'm a docker."

"A what?" I stare at her slight body incredulously.

"A wharf-labourer," she repeats. "Many women work on the wharves in Canton."

She is looking at me with her serene eyes as though wondering at my reaction. "I was born on a boat like my mother and grandmother before me. From when I was a child of eight I used to ferry people across the river but I couldn't earn enough that way so I had to take up wharf-labouring. We had a very bad time. We received less wages than the men, but now we have equal pay in our work as in all others.

"We used to work very long hours while now we have definite shifts. Before, if we wished to rest during breaks between jobs we just stretched out on the wharves. Now we have special places where we can lie down and rest between jobs. Of necessity we had to work up to the day of childbirth. Now the law provides that we are not allowed to do heavy work after the sixth month and we get the usual leave of fifty-six days before and after birth.

"Our trade union gives subsidies for special food for the mother and child during this period. Before we had only rice gruel to eat. When I look back on it it's hard to realize what a terrible life we lived.

"Forced marriage was the general rule among the daughters of the waterfolk. Strange as it may seem, in the crowded life of the river many of the boys and girls had never seen each other before. My husband was chosen by my parents when I was eight, but I never saw him until the day I married him when I was twenty. Our life wasn't a happy one. In spite of being a hard worker he was often out of work and poorly paid when he was in work. He was also overbearing, as was customary with men of those days, when the wife wasn't supposed to answer back or she would be scolded. I was one of those people who could not keep my tongue still when he was unjust, so we often quarrelled and even, at times, came to blows. Things weren't helped by the fact that all the four children I had died. The eldest would have been eighteen," she says wistfully and she puts a hard forefinger gently on Ah Sung's cheek.

"What could we do? We were so poor that we could not get treatment for them. And as we were very superstitious we went to the temple to burn paper money, but it did no good." Two tears run down her cheek and she wipes them away with the back of her scarred hand.

Ah Sung twists uncomfortably and is held up while she pats his back. He burps. She makes clucking noises to him, an adoring expression on her face. He now gets that tense expression that every mother recognizes. She lays him on her lap and removes the red-and-blue wad of cotton cloth from the split in his pants, folds it up neatly and replaces it with one of equally gay printed cotton from the line. This she attaches round his waist with a tape. He closes his eyes and goes to sleep, looking like a little ivory image. Her thin hand with the broken nails strokes his bristling head.

"When he is old enough he will go to the kindergarten our trade union has established and then to one of the schools they run. Later," she says, smiling, "I would like him to be a doctor, but his father prefers engineering. He always wanted to be an engineer himself.

"After the proclamation of the New Marriage Law my husband and I looked at each other and wondered what was wrong with us. We sat down and began to criticize ourselves. Then we decided to forget all about the past and start over again, even though we were middle-aged—I am forty. We found it so interesting and got on so well that we were named as a Model Married Couple."

She casts a swift, amused glance at me. "That's not one of the least of the miracles of New China! We have both learnt to read and write because we realized that to do our best we must be educated. That was the hardest thing I've ever done in my life and, oh, the mistakes I made when I first started to learn! I thought I would never learn to distinguish one character from the other."

She stretches out a hand for my note-book and writes the intricate characters of her name swiftly and firmly.

"At first when we heard rumours of the Liberation Army, we waterfolk couldn't see that it affected us. As long as anyone could remember our lives had been the same—Untouchables we had always been, Untouchables we would always be. That was our fate, and who could fight against Fate?

"Our first surprise was when the Liberation Army sent a special message to the waterfolk saying that we could go ashore without any fear of being molested by anyone, which not even the oldest among us had ever heard of happening in the past.

"So we went ashore and lined up to watch the troops come. They treated us like everyone else. No one was hit, no one was arrested. We weren't hunted back to our boats. All the gangsters had disappeared and we thought this time at least some of the other kinds of rumours about Canton being cleaned up *were* right!

"Then they told us we had the same rights as everybody else and that we were equal to everybody else. We hardly dared believe it. But when the Republic was proclaimed the law gave us equality. For the first time in the long history of the waterfolk we celebrated wildly with fireworks, drums, cymbals. Every boat was decorated with flags and lanterns. So we got together and decided to work hard and do anything the Government asked us.

"At the local Congress election more than ninety per cent of the waterfolk over eighteen voted. And the missing ten per cent was represented by those who were absent on river work.

"Today the feudal attitude to women has gone, because men must abide by the New Marriage Law. Also, you can't beat children or sell them. And people are no longer forced to expose children in the hope that someone will take them. But even in the old days it was very rarely that a baby was deliberately drowned, unless the mother was a prostitute. Now there are no more prostitutes and every baby is cherished.

"Sometimes it all seems like a dream after the lives we had. Everything so quiet, so good. During the Anti-Japanese War the Japanese had bombarded the wharves and the bridge and destroyed many of the boats and killed many of the waterfolk. And when the K.M.T. blew up the river bridge without warning many small boats were destroyed and so many waterfolk killed it was impossible to count them."

I ask, "What has happened to your own people?"

Her face grows sombre. Her throat works. Suddenly she puts her two hands across her eyes and sitting bolt upright, weeps bitterly, her body racked with sobs, the tears running between her rough fingers. I sit shaken, ashamed of myself, and stretch out a hand to touch her arm in sympathy.

When at last she controls herself, she sits with eyes lowered looking down at the sleeping baby and speaks shakenly. "My father died at the beginning of the Japanese invasion and my mother and my four brothers and an uncle died of starvation during the Occupation."

A silence descends on us. She breaks it at last, saying gently, "I am sorry I distressed you just now." She raises her eyes still wet with tears. "But that is why the thought of what we suffered gives us strength, for now all we waterfolk realize that everything we do will make a better life for us and above all, for our children." Her arms close round the child and she rests her cheek against his. "All I ask is a good life and peace for Ah Sung."

As we go homeward the sunset gilds the shabby woodwork of countless sampans moored twenty deep along the shore, and in the low light the smoke of cooking-fires drifts over them in a golden haze.

Out on the river the mercantile flags of New China—five gold stars and yellow wavy stripes on scarlet silk—flicker in the wind like flames.

CHAPTER XX

Canton-Wuhan

SUNDAY, 8 a.m. The train glides out. This time we are in the oldest sleeper in China—all wood with only a central window, which makes sight-seeing difficult.

The line follows one of the tributaries of the Pearl River. Naked children are swimming from its white sandy beaches, rusty-tan fishing nets drying on bamboo poles, sampans tacking in the reaches.

We slow down close enough to look into a little floating home with the wooden-covered pan steaming over the cooking jar, a toddler tied to an upright, a dog barking beside him, a young man stripped to the waist poling against the strong current, and a woman, a sleeping baby strapped to her back, working the fixed stern oar.

The railway winds into deep river gorges with sheer cliffs. Out into a valley surrounded by fantastic broken mountains flecked with cloud-shadow, tortured peaks piercing the low clouds, ridges writhing under straight-trunked pagoda-like pines.

I had always thought the landscapes of Chinese paintings were figments of imagination, but now I know they are photographic, like the dreamlike Umbrian backgrounds of Renaissance painting. Vista after vista unfolds, each one a potential Chinese scroll. A painter of the Sung Dynasty once did ten thousand sketches of pine-trees! An artist-friend, Lei Tsun-tsai, last vacation made two thousand.

Towering pinnacles of ebony rock wreathed with scarves of mist. An amphitheatre of pine-covered hills enclosing a valley with moon-arched bridges white against the brilliant green, and a small cluster of grey stone houses under corrugated tiles black and shiny as obsidian.

A steaming day. Two little girls, aged three and five, from the adjoining sleeper, sit in the corridor clad only in panties and eat their bowls of rice with china spoons. The radio plays an air from the Cantonese opera we saw two nights ago and a young soldier sits in the corridor playing the same air on a mouth-organ.

Rain, and the green fields are dotted with golden oiled-silk hats like monstrous mushrooms, cocoa-brown palm-leaf capes.

Lunch, and in the restaurant car we are adopted by a group of laughing teen-age girls. It is a basketball team from Taishan going to Peking for the All-China Competition. They surround our table, long black plaits falling round us in thick ropes, asking numerous questions, till the waiter patiently pleads that he has no room to pass.

In spite of the heat and the crowd the meal is as good as usual.

We return to find the soldier has been adopted by the three-year-old and is sitting in the guard's seat in the corridor with the small girl on his knee listening absorbedly to a story.

At the other end of the corridor the guard has four small children round him, listening with the same absorbed look on their round brown faces.

A night of stifling heat. We have left the rain behind and the air is dry and full of an impalpable red dust. I sleep; the bunk is wide and comfortable but even the cool matting is soon hot. I dream that I am on my way to Broken Hill in New South Wales, the fine dust filling my nostrils, the night scarcely cooler than the day, and wake to Wuhan on the Yangtze, the triple city composed of Hankow, Wuchang, and Hanyang, six hundred miles from the sea.

My window looked out over the East Lake at Wuchang and the garden that ran down to it was ablaze with flowers.

Sculling at evening on the placid water mirroring the hills and an island pagoda, a faint breeze stirring the rushes by the shore, I thought how much I would give to know the story of the nine women of the Taiping Revolution whose hundred-year-old grave on the Loja hill at last bears a monument but no names.

Soong Ching-ling wrote of the nameless nine:

> *Here in the heart of our land*
> *in times gone by were*
> *nine women of China whose names*
> *are lost with the years, who would*
> *not kneel nor bow their heads*
> *but who fought for the people*
> *giving their all.*

"Wuhan cherishes the names of heroines nearer to our time," my companion tells me. "In an anti-monarchist rising at Hankow in 1900 several women patriots were killed, notably Chou Fu-tien, Mo Che-yung, and Lui Wei-fang. In 1922 Shiang Ching-yui, another woman heroine, organized meetings and discussions. She was arrested at the time of the split in the Kuomintang in the French Concession at Hankow. The French police, backed by the K.M.T. tortured her to make her divulge the names of her fellow workers. She knew French because she had studied in France, but she answered only, 'All I do is for the freedom, equality, independence, and liberation of China. What I work for is the same as you worked for during your Revolution.' On 1st May 1928 the French police handed her over to the K.M.T. and on the same day she was executed. Her death, like that of Chiu Chin, rallied many women who were moved by her courage and endurance."

CHAPTER XXI

Fight Against the River

Our ferry chugs crabwise against the racing river that at the moment is running with a five-mile current. Swollen, red-brown waters glitter under the sun that blazes down from a sky ominous with storm-clouds.

"The ferry from Wuchang to Hankow crosses the Yangtze Kiang at its narrowest part," says Lan Chuin, a smart young woman with permed hair who has come from the Water Conservation Board to show me the dykes that protect the city. "Here it is so deep that big ocean-going steamers can come right from the sea."

Clouds roll over the sun. At this season every cloud is a menace. May to August are the danger months for floods, with the snow melting in the foothills of Tibet where the river rises, and the summer rains sweeping up from the sea.

I have never feared a river before. But then I have never seen such a river before; so wide, so fast, so deep, so—so savage. The word comes unsought to my mind as I watch the innumerable junks and sampans fighting the same battle their predecessors have fought for thousands of years.

Beside us a sampan, piled with rice-bags, edges its way inch by inch across the river. They use the wind to help them and the sail swells in a sudden gust. The sampan surges forward and one wonders at its progress under a sail that is as much hole as cotton.

They lose the wind. The boat is tossed like a chip on the water. The man bends to the oar, chin dug in, lips pulled back in a snarl, his body glistening with sweat, the muscles of his arms like cords. The woman clings to the stern oar that serves as rudder, pressing all her frail weight against it, her head thrown back and her eyes closed in an agony of useless effort. The racing current takes them and while we watch they are carried a half a mile down stream.

All round the same drama is being played out on a larger or smaller scale.

We pass a big trading boat, high of prow and stern, rowed by eight men on a long swinging oar who walk backwards and forwards across the deck without cease, propelling the vessel across to the shore we have left. What a few hundred tugs could do here in the saving of human energy in the daily struggle against the big river that must wear out the body and the heart!

Chen Mei-yin of the Women's Federation tells me with what I feel is quite misplaced pride that the temperature is well over a hundred in the shade and, with a burst of chauvinism, I tell them that I know many places in Australia that are hotter. The fluttering of fans stops for a moment. I feel that I am not believed. *No* place can be as hot as Wuhan!

Lan Chuin points out the landmarks: along both banks European-type cities; everywhere scaffolding of huge new constructions. It is planned to make Wuhan, already an important business and trading centre with a population of a million and a half, one of the great industrial centres of Central East China. Upstream the gigantic pylons of the Bridge-that-couldn't-be-built are advancing, span by span, over the River-that-could-never-be-spanned.* They tell me a girl is driving the travelling crane that is perched high up.

Along the shores a forest of masts of river-craft of all kinds, and all around us the ceaseless fight between man and the river that is as old as man himself.

I find it easy to understand when they tell me that not so many years ago the folk who made a scanty living from the river endowed it with a malignant personality, so much so that if a man fell overboard they would make no effort to save him. The river must have its sacrifice lest worse befall!

The clouds spill over and the squall whips the water in a fury of driving rain. It beats on the ferry roof like hail, hisses through the sodden air, soaks the clothes of the oarsmen, blots out the bridge and the shores.

"Seven times in history has the Yangtze flooded the triple city," Miss Lan goes on, "drowning uncounted thousands of people, destroying tens of thousands of acres of land, and property and crops, so that floods were always followed by famine. Throughout the centuries when the waters began to rise, from mighty Emperor to poverty-stricken fisherman, men bowed their heads to the will of the gods. In 1850 the Manchu Emperor had cast a large iron ox, which was placed in position by Manchu officials to check the floods. It did not succeed!

"In 1931 Wuhan suffered in the greatest flood of all time—till then. Kuomintang officials brought Buddhist monks to the dykes to burn incense and pray. The level rose to eighty-three feet. It

* A year later it was ready for traffic.

was officially estimated that thirty-two thousand were drowned, and no one counted those who died of starvation.

"In 1954 the successful struggle of Wuhan against a bigger flood marked a turning-point in history. In all, 289,800 men and women rallied, 174,000 of whom never left the dykes. All China swung into action. Three million cubic yards of soil were transported by trucks, junks and tugs, bullock-carts, hand-carts and pedi-cabs, hundreds of thousands of baskets on shoulder poles. Six thousand anchors were sent from Shanghai to anchor the huge rafts which were placed along the dykes to break the force of the waves which the wind raised.

"Night and day the struggle went on. There were deeds of incredible valour by women as well as men. I think it's safe to say that never before in all China's history had so many women of such different types—some of the older ones had never before ventured out of their own homes—worked together for so long."

Our car speeds out through the Europeanized streets of Hankow into the open countryside, where a silver heat-haze shimmers over the low-lying flat.

Miss Lan points out a weather-beaten stage that during the flood served for theatrical performances to entertain the workers.

"One very old play was particularly popular. The story dates from the Chou Dynasty in the tenth century B.C., but though it is three thousand years old, everyone who saw it felt it might have been in their own lifetime. It is called *The Betrothed of the River God*, and tells about a very poor and miserable town that is flooded nearly every year. Thousands of people are drowned, crops and houses destroyed—just like here. A temple has been built to the River God where the priests receive gifts to appease him. But the God isn't satisfied with ordinary gifts. He demands each year the sacrifice of the most beautiful maiden in the village. Crowned with flowers, she is put on a raft of straw and sent down the river where the rapids swallow her.

"A new Governor is sent to the town and he soon discovers that the annual sacrifice is a source of profit to the priests. They always begin by choosing the daughter of a rich family. If the family discreetly offers them enough money they announce that the River God is not pleased with their choice and select another maiden. This goes on till they arrive at a family too poor to be able to influence their judgment, and the little Betrothed of the Gods is sent to her doom.

"Since all the sacrifices have not succeeded in preventing the flood, the new Governor decides that he will himself assist in the choice. Just as the raft is about to be launched, he announces that the maiden isn't beautiful enough to satisfy the God. Consternation!

"Still more consternation when he orders the High Priest to go himself to consult the God's wishes! As he does not return with an answer, his attendants are sent to follow him. The applause of the audience as one after another they were unceremoniously forced into the river was enthusiastic.

"Then the Governor goes into the temple to ask the God's wishes himself. When he comes out and announces that the God commands that twelve canals should be dug to prevent the waters of the river from overflowing the cries of *'Hao, hao!'* ('Good!') could be heard a mile away."

Lan Chuin smiles and unfolds her map once more.

"Today we don't consult the priests any more. The Water Conservation authorities have planned that more than . . ."

On the outskirts of a little village whose mud huts cluster in the shelter of the enormous earth dyke, three women await us. Lin Hsiao-tse, a tiny woman with a heavily freckled face, shuffles on her bound feet to take my hand. Beside her is Hsiah Wang-ying, a middle-aged woman whose brown face is stamped with an unmistakable air of long privation and suffering, and Han Ji-ying, a dark-faced, sturdy girl of twenty in a blue-and-white tunic and bright-blue shorts, exuberantly young.

"She was awarded the honour of 'second-class veteran of the floods'," Miss Chen whispers to me as we walk towards the village whose roads not even a jeep could negotiate.

Hsiah Wang-ying insists that before going to the dyke we should go to her village, rest in her house, and take some refreshments. She is a thin woman and I am surprised to find that her arm under mine is like steel.

We skirt a large pool covered with the broad leaves of the lotus, where water-buffaloes wallow. Each has his own youthful guardian, some dozing on the broad backs of the gentle beasts, others stretched on the grass. They line up to greet us as we pass, clapping enthusiastically, not the slightest bit inhibited by the scantiness of their garb, for the smaller ones are running naked in the blistering afternoon.

"Lotus roots are one of the products of our village," Mrs Hsiah tells me. I had had them in the salad at lunch, crisp white slices with a sweetly acid taste reminiscent of the flavour of a not-quite-ripe Granny Smith apple.

We go across a clay track where chickens scratch in the hard fawn clay and a fat sow grunts protestingly as she is shooed out of our way.

Past a small pool where a crop of yams shows vigorous growth. Through the rough village street, and up an incline to my hostess's house. She tells me proudly that it is only in the last few years that they have been able to build such a beautiful house. Before they lived in a crumbling mud hut.

She beams with pride as she leads me under the shade of the big acacia-tree that droops above the thatched wattle-and-daub house and into the main room. A chicken scurries with shrill squeaks across the earth floor to escape by the back door.

Rough wooden partitions divide the house into three. The light streams through a window opening where lengths of bamboo form a pattern against the sky. Inside it hangs a gauzed wooden safe. On the wall are scarlet silk banners with gold lettering, many pictures, and a portrait of Chairman Mao in the place of honour, with other national leaders round him.

I have a choice between a six-inch stool or the bamboo-slat bed with a woven mat cover. I sit on the bed. From there I can see the crowd of beaming faces blocking each door and smaller brown faces appearing suddenly between the legs at threshold level.

My hostess lifts the lid of an earthenware kettle that steams on the clay stove. She pours the hot water into bowls that have been standing, carefully covered, on the side table—presumably against flies, yet although this is a village with all that that means, not one fly is visible—and hands a bowl to me with the dignity befitting such a ceremony. Then her ten-year-old son comes in carrying a bunch of lotus flowers.

Mrs Hsiah presents the bouquet to me with a little speech whose meaning I guess without translation.

Miss Lan breaks the stem and draws the broken pieces apart. The viscous fibres stretch out like a spider-web without breaking. "She says it is a symbol of friendship, that though you be parted you remain linked for ever."

The villagers are introduced to me. A trestle bench is brought out for the more honoured ones to sit on.

Mrs Hsiah tells me: "There are almost eight hundred persons in our village, which is prosperous, now. Since we can farm our land without fear of annual flooding everything has improved and we are able to concentrate on cultural things such as learning to read and write. Lin Hsiao-tse is our best scholar."

Mrs Lin's freckled face beams as she sits on the trestle, tiny feet not reaching the floor. She tries to look modest as they proudly announce that she has learnt a thousand characters! Asked to tell me about it, she says, "I can write as well as read. Sometimes I wish I wasn't fifty-two, for there is nothing a woman can't do in this new world." Then she twinkles at me. "But whenever I think of the past and compare it with the present I feel I am growing younger and younger."

My hostess is director of the village's Agricultural Co-operative and has received many awards. She is also a member of Wuhan City Council and director of the Women's Federation for her district, and a deputy of the Provincial Congress.

"We have a wonderful life now," she says. "Before Liberation my husband could hardly feed the seven of us—we have three sons and two daughters—even though he is a very honest, hard-working man. We were bowed down with debt we could never reduce. After one of the bad floods we borrowed a picul of rice from the landlord and had to pay back practically the same weight each year in *interest*, good harvest or bad. As a result, at Liberation we owed thirty-nine piculs of rice to different people because we were always borrowing to pay the interest. We could see nothing ahead of us but hunger and ever-increasing debt."

"How does your husband like all your activities?" I ask.

Mrs Hsiah smiles affectionately. "Oh, there's nothing feudal-minded about my husband. I wish you could meet him but he's away today buying seed. He's a farmer above everything and is only too happy for me to be busy with social and political activities. Indeed, he helps me in the house all he can. Sometimes when I have to be away two or three days at conferences he takes over all the household tasks. When he needs my help I help him and so we advance together, study together, and have happier lives than we ever believed possible."

Under the fierce sun that beats down on us out of a sky temporarily clear of clouds, Lan Chuin, Chen Mei-yin, Hsiah Wang-yin, Han Ji-ying and I walk along the high dyke that is wide enough for a car and an ox-cart to pass. Like a rampart of earth and stone it stands on the edge of a vast lake. Here it was that two years ago my companions helped in the fight against the raging waters that threatened to overwhelm their homes.

When the Government first announced its plans for mastering

the river not many people believed it was possible, Mrs Hsiah tells me.

"Do you remember the first meetings we held about it, Lin Hsiao-tse?"

Lin Hsiao-tse nods. Han Ji-ying recalls that it was one of the first meetings she went to. She laughs buoyantly as one who never had any doubts.

"The official who talked to us explained that the Government had plans to control the river that would in the future save us from floods. But they could only be carried out with our help."

Mrs Lin joins in: "Only the young ones like Ji-ying here really believed him. My father-in-law said *nobody* could control the river—the Emperors and the Kuomintang had all failed and he didn't believe even Chairman Mao could do it. A lot of the old ones agreed.

"Then the official said, 'Have you any reason to love that old river since you won't fight it?' And that started us off. One after another we got up and we poured out our hate of the river. We told what it had done to us. Drowned our fathers, our mothers, our children, ruined our homes and our crops, condemned us to starvation time and time again no matter how hard we worked the land.

" 'And now it's *your* land,' the official said. 'You own it.' "

Ji-ying laughs again. "It was the first time in my life—I was only fourteen—that anybody had ever told me I owned anything."

Mrs Lin nods. "That thought made every one of us feel that we'd do anything we could to defend it against flood as well as anything else or anyone else that tried to take it from us."

"It was then that the plans for a real drive forged ahead," Lan Chuin says, unrolling her large map to illustrate her explanation.

Chen Mei-yin takes up the story. "When the rising water kept moving up beyond the old levels the Government issued the call: '*Wuhan must be saved!*' Everybody worked. I'm telling you only the story of the women because that's what you've asked for, but the men were the same, except that they did the harder work.

"In the old days, women would not have realized that the call was for them, too. But now women of all ages and spheres of life responded magnificently. Some, like these three, actually worked on the construction of the dyke."

I look at the two older women, seemingly so frail. Impossible!

Blushing, Mrs Lin stammered, "I only carried soil. So did Hsiah Wang-ying."

"They were both team-leaders and organized groups of women to carry soil as well as carrying it themselves," Miss Chen says.

I try to imagine them both struggling up the steep banks bowed under the weight of the heavy shoulder baskets, Lin Hsiao-tse's bound feet stumbling on the slippery track.

"What made you take on such hard work?" I ask. "Surely there was something else . . . ?"

Lin Hsiao-tse's smiling face hardens.

"In the old days I was a beggar with no land at all. For eighteen years we worked on the landlord's land, but everything was extorted from us by the landlord, and to live we had to go out on the road and beg. I was married to Shen Ta-shing when I was twenty. While he was still young my husband fell ill and was bedridden for twelve years. I wove and sold grass slippers to keep our family of six. But life was so difficult that I had to sell our third daughter to keep the family going. Even when she was sold life was still very difficult and I had to wander about in the streets with the three children begging for food. I kept my family by weaving and selling grass slippers and by begging. After the Liberation I was classed as a poor citizen as far as my class status was concerned because I had no land and did not till the land. And now—" she chokes, her soft rapid voice stops.

"Now," Miss Chen takes up for her, "now she is director of the Agricultural Producers' Co-operative and last summer she grew a tomato weighing two pounds!"

We laugh. It breaks the tension. Mrs Lin laughs with us.

"It was Han Ji-ying who was the heroine," she insists, drawing the sturdy young woman up beside her. "And she was only eighteen then."

They all look at Ji-ying affectionately and her smooth brown cheeks flush deeply.

"I shall never forget that terrible week," Miss Chen continues. "It was at the beginning of July, and July is the month of typhoons. Rain fell continuously for over a week and the flood-level rose alarmingly. In addition a gale was blowing and whipped that great expanse of water into huge waves that battered the dyke and threatened to destroy all of our work. Teams of men were working frantically to lay down matting rafts to break the force of the waves while others brought earth and stones to raise the level of the dyke. But it was clear that unless something more was done to protect it, it would give way under the battering.

"So, in order to protect it, six hundred youths and girls linked arms to form a human chain. For a week they stood in shifts with their backs pressed against the wall of the dyke and took the force of the waves on their own bodies. For a week they never left the dyke. When the waves receded they came out and lay on the bank. When the waves rose they went back again. On 7th July, when the wind was at its strongest and the waves highest, Ji-ying stayed in the water all through the night and into the day.

"Once she was so exhausted that she slipped down the bank, but the wave caught her and threw her back and her companions pulled her out again. That time they were sixteen hours without a break. Food was taken to them and they ate where they stood. When the waves were high they could not eat.

"When at last they came out they could not raise their arms, they could not use them. They had to be put to bed and fed like babies. It was for this that she was made a veteran flood-fighter."

"Anyone would have done it," Ji-ying stammers.

I look at the embarrassed girl. What did she feel in the hours when the wind howled across the waters and hurled the waves against them?

"Well," she says, "it was very hot above the water and cold under it and you just ceased to feel anything after a while. You just knew you had to stay or the dyke would be battered to pieces and villages and farms destroyed. So you stayed."

As simple as that!

"Before, my family was very poor," she goes on. "When my father died I was only seven and our landlord kidnapped my mother and took her to his house, leaving me and my two elder brothers to fend for ourselves. I looked after the landlord's cow and if anything went wrong I was beaten by the landlord. My brothers and I never had enough to eat. We were all illiterate. It was a long time before my mother succeeded in running away and coming back to us. The landlord was tired of her by then. We all lived in one very low, dilapidated hut and most of the time we hadn't enough to eat and only rags to wear. Now we have two brick houses, we all work. My brother could afford to marry, which he couldn't have thought of before. We can all read and write.

"With all this to defend, who would not stand as long as her strength would let her and take the waves on her body?"

She makes the declaration in a ringing voice, head thrown back, strong legs planted wide as though to assert her right to the earth she treads.

"Besides, what I did was very little when you think of Lu Yiu-shieh. She was only a girl like myself. One day she discovered that there was a leak in the dyke and she dived down with a gunnysack to plug it. She would have been drowned only that a companion went after her when she didn't reappear. But one lad was not so lucky. He was only sixteen. When he dived down to try to plug a hole in the dyke the pull of the water was so strong that he was drawn into it and drowned. More than a hundred lost their lives in the struggle."

There are tears in her eyes as she looks over the calm lake lying silver under the afternoon sun, seeing in imagination, as I see, the long chain of boys and girls, arms linked, bodies pressed against its sloping side, battered by the waves.

"It was not only the dyke we were defending," she says at last. "It was our right to live as human beings."

CHAPTER XXII

Wuhan-Peking

LATE evening, and the train glides through a world of golden lakes in which the dykes loom black and gigantic. Only the long procession of far-away sails above invisible junks distinguishes the river from the flood-waters. Diaphanous in the slanting light, they float like burnished wings against the threatening storm-clouds.

An international journey in every way. A spanking new sleeping-car bearing on the side in Chinese and Vietnamese, "Hanoi-Peking", made in Hungary, the chrome steel ladders engraved with the name of an English firm! A ruby-red carpet in the corridors and apartments, seats upholstered in a light-blue leather with blue-and-white loose covers. White curtains on the double windows—a sign that it was made for colder climates than this. Flowers in a porcelain flower-pot on the table, a reading lamp, an electric fan—superfluous, one would have thought, since the car is air-conditioned, but the heat presses down and we are glad of it even at night. Nowhere in the world have I had such a luxurious apartment—the "night-breathing flower" I was given before leaving Wuhan fills it with cool fragrance.

Morning, and the sun comes up red and swollen through the mist that covers the swirling flood-waters of the Yellow River, China's Sorrow. I look at the mile after mile of flooded countryside with an occasional village on higher land surrounded by muddy yellowish waters.

The service boy comes round early. This time, in keeping with dignity of the new carriage, he goes over everything with a vacuum cleaner.

Happily we are a long way from the restaurant car and we go to breakfast earlier than usual and see all our companions travelling "hard". The train is crowded. Every couchette is occupied. They are made up by adjusting the seats, and three tiers of bunks lie open like a vast dormitory. Old and young, men and women and children, are busy breakfasting. They have brought their own food with them or bought it at the railway stalls and now they form little encampments round each lower bunk, enamel tooth-mugs ranged neatly against the wall, rice steaming in bowls, bright-eyed toddlers nibbling steamed bread.

A small baby is being held over its bright enamel chamber-pot. In one bunk a woman lies prostrate. "A very bad headache," her husband explains as he wrings out a hand-towel and tenderly places it on her forehead. It is all clean and busy and happy. The radio gives the morning news. An unending chatter rises above the noise of the wheels.

A long hot afternoon with the sun blazing down on the beige-coloured northern plain and donkeys and horses taking the place of water-buffaloes, dry cultivation that of rice, and the glossy black clothes of the southern peasant yielding to blue and white, the wide peaked bamboo hats to dome-shaped woven reed ones that look like an inverted basin.

Evening, and the western mountains a purple line against an apricot sky, and towards ten o'clock, far off on the edge of the plain, the lights of Peking coming up.

CHAPTER XXIII

Shu-feng, Ex-concubine

THE car crawls down a narrow, winding hutung in Peking. It is half past nine in the morning and all the housewives are out with their bamboo or reed shopping baskets. We almost stop to let a mothers' meeting disperse with its low bamboo go-carts in which plump babies sit upright, their hair plaited in ridiculous little upstanding plaits, the ends bound with red or green wool. I wish I had a colour-movie of the scene, the younger women in their gay floral tunics, the toddlers in their scarlet and green and purple flowered split pants. Fifty yards farther on a street market on the footpath, carrying an extraordinary variety of goods.

We have difficulty in passing a wedding taxi, gaily decorated with many coloured streamers and paper flowers, that waits outside a gate on which is the large red character for happiness.

But today I am less interested in the street than usual. My mind is ahead of me with the woman I am going to meet. She is the former concubine of a Peking merchant and has agreed to see me only on condition that I do not ask her to talk of her past life!

The New Marriage Law put an end to the custom of legalized polygamy that had so long a history in China. During the centuries the number of concubines allowed varied. One finds references to the "thousands of beautiful women in the King's harem" and in later days of the Empire some say the Emperor was allowed seventy, but others say there was no limit.

The official sanction of concubinage was to ensure that there was a male heir to carry on the Ancestral Sacrifices. "The Sacred Commands" published by the Emperor K'anghsi say: "You must not forget the great rule of human life. If people marry it is to beget offspring. When the Ancients had reached forty years without sons they had to buy a concubine to provide for the future. Mencius says: 'There are three crimes against Filial Piety: to leave no posterity is the worst.' "

The car pulls up. A woman greets me looking unworried and competent in her striped grey-woollen slacks with a badge on the pocket of her blue tunic. It is clear that she is expecting me and she introduces herself—Lei Shu-feng. Her smile makes me forget the feeling of slight irritation with which I had set out.

We go in, past the spirit screen, across a small courtyard where faces peep at us from doorways and windows. The usual crowd of small children follows me as they would a circus. Past a second gateway into a room about ten by twelve with a stone-paved floor and two wide windows, partly glassed and partly open woodwork, already papered against the cool winds of autumn.

I am introduced to her mother, who is changing the diaper-pad of a protesting baby. Mother greets me with dignity but obviously without warmth. She is a tall, heavy woman, hair pulled back in a bun like a pickled onion. I ask the baby's age. She thinks I'm asking hers and says in a tone of rebuke that she's sixty, then picks up the baby and stalks out into the courtyard, keeping barely within the limits of courtesy demanded for a guest. Mother plainly thinks it impertinent to seek any story from her daughter.

It is a simple room, the walls newspapered almost to the attic-roof, decorated with coloured prints. A photo of mother in her prime stands on the top of a chest. Just inside the door is a large earthenware crock with a wooden cover that holds the daily supply of water, and on a dresser near it two vacuum-flasks.

Lei Shu-feng waves me to a seat on the double bed, hard and solid as a kang. A new bed, she points out, that she's been able to buy since she got a rise in wages. She shares it with her daughter, who was so excited last night when she heard a foreign friend was coming that she couldn't sleep.

"This is her photo." She passes me a snapshot and shows me a laughing girl with two long plaits. "She is very bright at school, but she loves to play and is in the school basketball team."

Mother has returned and stands on the doorstep, ostensibly to keep away the group of children who peer in and lift the smaller ones to look through the window panes, but actually to keep an eye on me.

I take the opportunity of saying that daughter and granddaughter get their looks from her. Her grim expression relaxes.

"Both my daughter and granddaughter are very smart," she says. "Shu-feng was illiterate, but when she got the chance to go to classes she learnt very quickly. And my granddaughter, she's a remarkable child. I wish you could have met her. But of course she wouldn't miss a morning at school."

She brings the tea in two fine porcelain cups with a large character in red. I admire them, saying I have never seen any like them.

"They were wedding presents," Shu-feng says. A shadow comes

over her oval olive face. I feel we're on dangerous ground and compliment Mother on the excellent tea. She smiles and takes up the crowing baby, who refuses to go to sleep, and kisses and snuggles him.

I get as far from the subject of marriage as possible and ask Shu-feng what the badge means that she is wearing. She explains that it is something to do with her job in a construction company that is responsible for much of the new building in Peking.

"A very responsible position," Mother puts in from the doorway. "She gets more than sixty yuan a month. And I make ten yuan baby-minding, which means we're very well off. We pay seven yuan a month rent, electricity and water. Indeed, fifty yuan a month covers all our expenses.

"The time workers have today!" she goes on, coming back to sit on her bed. "Why, there's been another increase even this year! And Shu-feng used to work nine hours a day. Now she works only eight hours and for more money. And every Sunday we go off to enjoy ourselves in the parks or boating on the lakes, and sometimes even go to the temples in the Western Hills. If a fortune-teller had told me that a few years ago I would have told him he was a quack!"

By now it seems to me that all the residents of the court are at the door. She rises, clucking her disapproval. She remonstrates with the women and reproves the children. A Chinese courtyard has no privacy—never had!

Shu-feng takes up the story. "Yes. I'm very lucky. I have a good job and now I can read and write. Sometimes I think that had the old life continued I wouldn't be alive today."

She hesitates. I, too, am silent. A small white half-Persian cat bounces into the room, up onto the bed, over the pile of brilliant cotton-padded quilts and onto her lap. She strokes him abstractedly and he watches me with round golden eyes, then decides that my lap looks more comfortable.

I ask what he is called. "Pai-tse", says Mother, and I'm delighted that my limited Chinese enables me to understand that this means "Whitey". I tell them I once had a white cat we called "Snow" and the ice is broken once and for all.

"When I see my daughter's life today," Shu-feng says, "I find it difficult to believe that there's only a generation between us. It's a new world for girls. As a child I had a hard life. It was almost impossible for a girl to get any kind of job unless it was sheer slavery. When I was fourteen the owner of an opera troupe came to my mother and asked her to let me join his troupe to be taught to sing and dance. It wasn't a very high class troupe but it was better than no job at all. We used to play in the open air. Sometimes our faces would crack in the cold wind. We earned barely enough to eat and live."

"I'd never have let her go if there'd been anything else for her to do," Mother breaks in. "But at that time other families I knew were being forced to sell their girls to brothel-traders to keep them alive."

At that moment the cat bites me playfully, and I give a slight yelp. Shu-feng reproves him. He looks at us both with his golden eyes, then jumps over and bites her as though to make it clear that there is no favouritism. Shu-feng's shapely brown hands move over his long fur. Her face is reflective. I tickle the cat, who decides that he will come and sit on my lap again. He snuggles up and goes to sleep. Mother goes out into the courtyard, drawing the door behind her. Shu-feng is silent for some time.

What lies behind that smooth face, I wonder? What thoughts are moving behind that broad brow that brings such a look of pain into the eyes?

Abruptly she turns to me. "I wasn't going to tell you my story," she says. "But if it will help you to understand the change in the lives of Chinese women I think I should, even if it does hurt me."

I nod my thanks.

"Because I was in an opera troupe," she began, "I wasn't in the position of the ordinary Chinese girl who was protected by her family. When a man asked me to marry him—I was sixteen—we didn't make proper inquiries. He seemed very nice and we took it for granted that everything was all right. He was an army tailor and made a lot of money. There were great festivities for our wedding. But I soon discovered that I wasn't a first wife but only a concubine. His wife and children were away in her native village and when she returned I was so horrified I tried to commit suicide by taking opium. Then I thought I would leave him, but what could I do? According to the ideas of the day a wife or a concubine who ran away was the guilty one and there was no choice but to become a prostitute. Indeed, our husband threatened that if I went on with this nonsense, as he called it, he would sell me to a brothel, which he could have done without my being able to make any protest. I was in a state of complete despair at the time. But the wife was a very nice, kind woman and she was very good to me. We sympathized with each other, because he had given her a terrible life." Her eyes are fixed on the window and she speaks rapidly.

"It was an unhappy household. I helped to take care of the two children. He made plenty of money from army contracts, but gave very little of it to his home. He soon tired of me as he had of his wife and he spent his money giving parties at tea-houses and expensive brothels. Sometimes we had barely enough to buy food. And he got meaner and meaner so far as his home was concerned. Indeed, he got worse and worse in every way. Not only did he go to brothels, but he humiliated us both by bringing prostitutes into the home and making me wait on them.

"I had a daughter, but her father despised her because she was only a girl. He was an unnatural man. He even treated his eldest son so badly that the boy hated him."

Mother has returned and seated herself on the other bed. The baby had gone to sleep, and she is smoking a two-foot pipe with a jade mouthpiece.

"Added to our personal suffering, there was the misery of the years of Japanese Occupation. Food was terribly scarce and you never knew whether you'd be able to buy anything, even if you had money. The wife and I did our best to feed the children properly, but it was next to impossible. Although she wasn't a strong woman she insisted on doing the shopping because a young woman wasn't safe in the streets. It was very brave of her, because up till then she had never gone outside her own gate. Occupation or no Occupation, our husband seemed to have plenty of money, but when we asked for some to buy food he would threaten to sell me to a brothel, saying it was the only thing I was any use for.

"Then the Japanese went, but things weren't any better for us, though he began making more money than ever. When it began to look as though the Kuomintang was going to be defeated our husband was terrified and he told us horrifying stories of what the People's Army would do when it came to Peking. We weren't very much interested. By then we didn't care at all what they did to him, and we couldn't be less happy than we were. Anyway, it had nothing to do with women, we told ourselves, and dismissed it. But when I heard that the new Government had proclaimed the equality of women I began to take an interest in things.

"Then I was asked to help with the organization of a Street Committee, to my great surprise. And I found that I was regarded as an equal, and that the organizers didn't look down on me because I was only a concubine. They explained to me that it wasn't my fault and I mustn't be ashamed, that it was the fault of the old society.

"Then I decided to go to night-school. Our husband couldn't

do anything to stop me, but he made it as difficult as possible. He used to ridicule me, saying, 'Now just what use do you think it is for an old hag like you'—I was twenty-eight—'to go to school? You haven't got the brains of a turtle.'

"However, now I knew that the law had given me rights and I wasn't afraid to do things I had never dared do before. I went to the classes and when later I was elected director of the Women's Federation for our district he got frightened and never dared say anything to me again. But he took it out on his wife, who, poor woman, was so browbeaten by all she had suffered over the years that I could not persuade her to oppose him and take advantage of what were now her rights.

"The Women's Federation told me I was free to leave him and I could obtain the custody of my little daughter, even though officially by the Old Laws she belonged to the first wife. But I felt I couldn't go and leave the wife alone, knowing that bad as it was, it would be worse for her if I left. He got worse and worse to her now that he could no longer carry on his old tea-house, brothel-visiting life, and he didn't dare say a word to me.

"My new work took me away from the house a lot and once in my absence, after a particularly bad time, she drowned herself. Then I had nothing to hold me any longer. So in 1954 I left, taking my little daughter with me. His son, who was then twenty-two, also left. He was a mean man, a really bad man. He wouldn't even let us take my little girl's padded cotton quilt with us!

"The Women's Federation appointed me to do work among the older, backward, cowed women, for they thought my own experiences would help me to calm their fears and solve their problems.

"Then they suggested that I should train myself for some job. But as I had no education I had no confidence in myself. I thought I was too old. But they kept on encouraging me and finally I joined one of the short-time training classes. I learnt a lot in the class, above all to understand that life was very valuable and that I had a part to play in it. When I'd finished the course I was given a job in the Construction Bureau. I kept on studying, for I was weak in maths, so I joined night classes to improve them."

She is silent. The pain has gone from her eyes, the frown from between her willow-leaf brows. Suddenly she says, "I think my happiest moment was when I was given my badge for being a good student. I really worked hard, because even though the Government said my husband could be compelled to pay me money I would not touch it; I wanted to keep myself, my mother, and my daughter by my own efforts."

"Was your husband punished?" I asked.

"Oh, no. After all, in his own way he was a victim of the old society, too. But since he had so many bad habits it was decided to send him back to the village where he was born to be re-educated by labour. Now, when I see the progress my daughter is making at school and how ambitious she is, I'm glad to see that she does not take after her father in any way."

I close my note-book and with it the unhappy chapter of a life.

We go out of the door arm in arm. Shu-feng's face is smiling once more and the little cat rubs itself against my legs. Her mother looks up from the stove. She takes my hand in both hers and I know she has forgiven me.

GRIEF

Who have you just come from,
whose eyebrows have you just
been helping to paint?
I know well your goings-on;
that you have been among
sing-song girls. Why, all
have heard your horses neighing
when tethered in that street!
With half the night gone, so do you
come back drunk, coming in
so carefully, so silently,
walking softly: I wonder if
you know how you have lost credit
or whom you resemble? You should know
that you have small excuse,
lying there on your bed
without even bothering
to undress.

—CHIANG SIAO-SAN (Yuan Dynasty).
Translated by REWI ALLEY.

CHAPTER XXIV

A Leader of Women

I HAD travelled from one end of China to the other, seen tens of thousands of women at their normal occupations, spoken with hundreds, interviewed scores, before it began to dawn on me that I needed a background for it all.

By now I knew from the stories told me by older women what it used to be. I could judge for myself what it is. But all the books I had read gave me only glimpses of the process in between, and no one I had met had the key to it.

I was discussing my dilemma with a Chinese friend. "Of course the person who could tell you all about it is Teng Ying-chao," she said. "She has been the leader of the Women's Movement for nearly forty years."

"And who," I asked, "is Teng Ying-chao?"

She looked at me, surprised and rather pityingly.

"Teng Ying-chao is a vice-president of the Women's Federation," she explained and added, with a glint of malice in her eye, "and the wife of Premier Chou En-lai."

"Excellent!" I exclaimed. "I shall write to her tonight."

I wrote. The answer came promptly that Madame Teng would be delighted to see me. Unfortunately, at the moment she was ill, but as I was staying some time in China perhaps later. . . .

I shrugged my shoulders and said to myself, "The polite rebuff!"

I had almost given up hope when months later the telephone rang and a voice said in excellent English, "Madame Teng wishes me to tell you that if it is convenient for you she would very much like to see you. Would you like to arrange a day next week?"

On a sunny May morning a car comes for me with two interpreters, Miss Ling and Mr Yang, both speaking excellent English, and Miss Liu, who looks young and earnest and speaks only Chinese.

"This is going to be very formal," I say to myself. And I react badly to formality.

As we drive through Peking streets where the trees are bursting into a green shower, I regret I haven't looked up my protocol on meeting a V.I.P. It wouldn't help matters to start off on the wrong foot from the beginning.

Along a narrow street that skirts the wall of the Imperial City, through the massive arched gateway topped with a giant red star, khaki-clad guards on the gate, and into the vast grounds of the State Council that extend along the shore of one of the old Imperial Lakes. Along a tree-lined drive, through many court-yards, and at last through a large garden where lilac and yellow hedge-roses and peonies are in bloom, wistaria riots over a trellis and invisible birds are chattering in the flowering acacia-trees.

The curved drive takes us up to the wide steps leading to the terrace of a large building in the traditional style.

As I mount the steps I am putting on my best Government House manner. Then a middle-aged woman with a wide smile of welcome on her face comes out of the magnificent doorway and walks across the terrace clapping her welcome in the fashion that has greeted me in village and slum.

She takes my hands in both her small ones saying, "Welcome! Welcome!" and when I reply in my best Chinese that I hope that one day I shall welcome her to Australia, after a moment of astonishment she gives a ringing laugh that sweeps formality from the boards for ever.

Indeed, with Teng Ying-chao I think the greatest stickler for protocol would have difficulty in maintaining the manner con-sidered suitable in highest diplomatic circles. She radiates friend-liness and you have the pleasant feeling that she is as much interested in you as you are in her!

Into the vast reception room where, she tells me, Chou En-lai receives official guests: a stately room with tall white pillars, high windows, and deep-pile fawn carpets. All the chairs and lounges are in white loose covers—this is the month of Gobi dust-storms—and the general impression is one of lightness and freshness. Flame-coloured cacti on priceless carved ebony stands, graceful trellised woodwork high above the windows, figured marble screens, vases of great beauty, several statuettes, exquisitely wrought porcelain flowers.

Seated on a comfortable lounge, I have a chance to study my hostess. I had expected someone much older—nearly forty years as leader of the Women's Movement is a long time. She is of moder-ate build and dressed in well-cut grey slacks and tailored jacket beneath which is a mauve silk blouse; her tiny feet are in flat black court shoes.

Her black hair, sprinkled with grey, frames a face that seems always on the verge of laughter, her oblique eyes are twinkling and humorous. She gives you the impression of exuberant vitality.

She sets herself to make us all feel at home. The two interpreters and Miss Liu, who takes down the interview in Chinese, are clearly not at all overawed and laughter is quick and frequent.

Tea is served—she speaks to the boy who brings it just as she speaks to the rest of us. He brings in peanuts the cook has roasted specially (I get the recipe) and kaoliang sweets from Shantung.

For some time I am in the position of answering questions behind which I feel the working of an acute mind, thirsting always for fresh information. Then, with her wide smile, she asks, "And what do you want to know about me?"

"Everything," I say promptly.

She looks at me with an air of summing me up. I have a feeling that she is accustomed to lightning judgments.

"In that case I suppose we start from the beginning." She turns over the note-book she has beside her.

"China was still a feudal despotism when I was born in 1904. I was an only child and I had an unsettled life from early childhood. My father died when I was young, and that meant the end of our easy home life for my mother and me, for he died bankrupt.

"In those days it was not considered proper for women to come out of their homes, so you can imagine how difficult it was for my mother to decide to leave Nanning, our home town in the South, and come north to find a job to keep us both." Her eyes are brimming with love and her voice tender as she speaks of her mother.

"She found a job on the medical staff of an orphanage in Tientsin, where she got only enough for us to live on. There was no money over to send me to school, so she taught me herself, for she was determined I should be educated.

"Later, she came to Peking to teach in the Free School for Common People, set up by the Socialists and supported by contributions from progressive people.

"That was my first school and it influenced the whole of my future life. Many of the teachers were progressives and often talked to us about the ideals of world brotherhood, and young as I was, I began to realize that life was wider that our personal lives.

"The school was in existence for only six months. Yuan Shih-kai closed it down, the principal was arrested, and the other teachers forced to go into hiding.

"My mother was not only warm-hearted and upright, but she

was just and courageous and, in spite of the danger she ran by doing so, she came forward and tried to save the principal. It was in vain—he was shot.

"Once more she had to look for a job. We returned to Tientsin and, by working on the medical staff by day and at night as a tutor, she managed to earn enough to send me to the primary school affiliated to the Normal School in Tientsin.

"I studied for two years when the 'devil's claws' of lack of money forced me to leave school. My mother, recalling her own difficulties in earning a living, spent all the money she had on a machine for weaving towels, saying to me, 'If you have a trade you'll be independent. You won't be at the mercy of others and you won't have to rely entirely on your husband.'" She gives her rich, deep laugh. "I learnt to weave good towels.

"Then a school friend said, 'Why don't you sit for the entrance for the Normal School? It's free.' So I sat and I passed.

"For two or three years life was as calm as a pool of waveless water. I studied very hard with two ideas in mind: one, to be an independent, capable woman; two, to be able to keep my mother. Perhaps I studied too hard. After the first-term examination I had a haemorrhage and it was found that I had tuberculosis."

I tell her that one of my novels has as a heroine a young girl who has tuberculosis and that the book is based on experiences in many sanatoria. She is deeply interested and says she would like to read it, adding, "I'll get it translated."

She takes up her story, telling it rapidly and vividly. Her face mirrors her thoughts and she speaks with her hands in quick expressive gestures.

"When I was just sixteen the great patriotic protest of 4th May 1919 upset my calm student life. The Japanese made their notorious Twenty-one Demands on China. Our national feelings were outraged. Patriotism was already a green shoot in my heart, so I set aside my books temporarily and came out of my class-room to organize girl-students and housewives of Tientsin into a patriotic society. Girl-students and boy-students combined their organization, and in this fight for independence and freedom I first got to know my future husband, Chou En-lai."

I would like to stop her and ask how, but she goes on.

"As the months went on, protests grew, and the pressure of war-lords and officials on schools—to say nothing of families!— became heavier. I was lucky. My mother, remarkable woman that she was, in spite of her natural fears for me, supported me in this as she later did throughout the whole of my revolutionary life.

"We decided to hold a big demonstration on 10th October, anniversary of the Revolution of 1911. We girls prepared banners and banner-holders of bamboo. We didn't know at the time that they would also serve for self-defence. The meeting was surrounded by soldiers who threatened us with bayonets, then the police rushed out and we used the bamboo poles to knock off their caps.

"Just as we were trying to break through, Chou En-lai and the boy-students returned to the meeting after touring the city in a truck distributing handbills. Seeing our predicament, they turned the truck about, thus making a path for us and we all rushed out after it. We demonstrated throughout the city and surrounded the Police Administration Building for twenty hours as a protest."

I venture a query. She smiles.

"It was in the autumn of 1919 I actually met Chou En-lai. In order to concentrate our efforts the organizations of boy-students and girl-students amalgamated. Chou En-lai was then editor-in-chief of the newspaper of the Students' Federation and I was director of the Public Speaking Department. The first time I saw him he was covering a meeting for his paper. At the time he was very popular with the girl-students, who thought him very handsome as well as courageous. A schoolmate nudged me and said, 'The one in the blue gown and wearing a cap is Chou En-lai.'

"The second time we met was when about a score of us young people formed the Awakening Society to study new ideas of democracy, science, and so on. The authorities banned the Student Federation in Tientsin, so representatives of the boy- and girl-students went to the Provincial Government to protest. Chou En-lai was arrested. I had stayed at our headquarters so I escaped. I have a photo here of the Society you might like to see."

We peer together at the faded photograph from which a score of faces look out. So young. So stern.

I would not have recognized the urbane Premier of today in the burning-eyed young man who gazes at me challengingly. Only the famous eyebrows are the same. In the serious young girl with the oval face and the grave wide-open eyes I can see no resemblance.

"When he was released half a year later he left for France. It was not till 1925 that we started our married life."

My dramatist's soul is affronted by this skipping of climaxes. I look at her reproachfully. She is already launched on an account of her first teaching appointment.

I ask boldly, "Did you get engaged before he left?"

Madame Teng looks at me in genuine surprise. "Do you really want to know all that about my private life?"

I nod firmly.

She pauses, looking at me quizzically, then says, "No, we weren't engaged before Chou En-lai left. We fell in love only after he went to Europe. You might almost say we fell in love by post. We wrote to each other frequently. I told him all that was happening in China and he told me what was happening in the world. He proposed to me only after three years of correspondence." Her eyes are soft, her smile at me faintly mocking.

"My mother gave me all her loving help and sympathy at this time. She had suffered much from an arranged marriage. She used to say, 'Your marriage must be one of free choice, but I will be your adviser.' I think she was a very good adviser.

"In the meantime I had graduated from Normal School, and went to teach in the primary school affiliated with the Normal University in Peking. When we students were appointed we were asked if we had any remarks to make about the work and the pay and we said, 'As we shall be doing exactly the same work as the men teachers we should receive the same pay.' It was the first demand of its kind in China.

"As well as teaching in Peking and Tientsin I organized the Feminist Movement in Tientsin and published a weekly called *Women's Stars* and a women's daily. I joined the Young Communist League of China in 1924 and became a Communist in 1925. Once more my mother was my adviser. I never concealed anything from her and she supported my joining. After becoming a Communist I worked as secretary of the Women's Department of the Party in Tientsin.

"The period 1924-5 marked a new stage in Chinese history—Kuomintang and Communists combined in the Northern Expedition to overthrow the Northern war-lords. An association of women of all circles was organized in Tientsin to urge the convocation of the National Assembly. The Kuomintang set up a Provincial Headquarters, in the province in which Peking is situated and I was elected to its committee.

"In May 1925 there was another outburst of popular indignation over a tragic incident in Shanghai, and as about this time the authorities began to take notice of me because of my activities I was forced to make a move. I left Tientsin for Canton. I went there mainly to attend the Second National Conference of the Kuomintang."

She hesitates. "Besides, my comrade and companion Chou En-lai was there waiting for me. We had been separated for six years, but we felt very sure we knew each other well enough to enter a partnership we wanted to last for life.

"We started our married life in 1925. We had no marriage ceremony at all, only inviting our friends. We promised to love, to respect, to help, to encourage, and to console each other, to have consideration for each other, to have confidence and mutual understanding."

(Later, a friend of Teng Ying-chao in those days told me, these "Eight Mutuals" were to become the basis of marriage among young revolutionaries.)

"For women Communists marriage was not incompatible with work. I still took part in the revolutionary movement at Canton, working as secretary of the Women's Department of the Party of Kwangtung Province. During the work I came to know two remarkable women, Ho Shiang-ning, now over eighty and still a leader of the Revolutionary Kuomintang Party, and Soong Ching-ling, the widow of Dr Sun Yat-sen, herself a courageous revolutionary who never ceased to fight for China's freedom."

The pattern begins to take shape as I hear of these women of different political beliefs working together for the one end.

Her face grows stern. "In 1927 Chiang Kai-shek betrayed the revolution and unleashed a terror. The friend of yesterday became today's enemy. Our home was searched and sealed. We became the prey of the vultures. I had just given birth to my first baby after a difficult labour. It died and I had hardly time to dry the tears I shed before I had to drag my weakened body out of bed and flee. Fortunately I had already brought my mother from Tientsin and I was lucky enough to meet a kind doctor who risked all difficulties and dangers to help me out of hospital and to get me on board a boat for Shanghai. Thanks to my mother's care, I weathered the trip to Shanghai.

"After the escape from Canton came a long period of sunless days. For almost five years we had to conceal ourselves in Shanghai, leading an underground life. We had secret lodgings, we were cut off from all contact with acquaintances, friends and relatives—all except working contacts. We dared not even keep a maid and had to learn to do our own cooking and housekeeping.

"Even so we couldn't escape notice. The 'running-dogs' of the K.M.T. were always on our trail, and we dared not stay in one place too long. Sometimes they were so close to us that we had to leave with nothing. I remember very clearly how once, in 1931, we had to leave in a hurry. My mother was not quick enough and was arrested by the police of the Foreign Concession, who tried to force her to tell where her son-in-law and daughter were. Another time she had left the house for ten minutes and the police entered and took everything.

"Our home or resting-place, whatever and wherever it happened to be at the moment, was home and office. Once some important documents had to be delivered, so, late at night, I decided to take them out myself. While I was riding in a rickshaw with them a squad of police on bicycles came along. I looked very calm and unconcerned and the police passed by with only a glance.

"Although my mother worried a lot about our safety, we worried also about hers. Shanghai was under an ever-increasing K.M.T. terror. Chiang Kai-shek was more intent on wiping us out than in driving out the Japanese. It became almost as difficult to find a safe place as for the proverbial camel to get through the eye of a needle. My mother decided to go to Hangchow to stay in a Buddhist nunnery.

"In the spring of 1932, with the invasion of the Japanese Army and with the increasingly frenzied terrorist activities of the Chiang Kai-shek régime, the pressure became too heavy and it was impossible for us to carry on any activities. Consequently we had to leave Shanghai for our revolutionary bases in Kiangsi. Eventually we reached Juichin, at this time the headquarters of the Revolutionary Government.

"We had always before lived in cities and this was the first time we had ever led a village life. Though at the beginning we felt out of place we quickly adapted ourselves. I felt so free in spirit in this area after stifling Shanghai that I felt always that I wanted to sing.

"During my two years in Juichin I worked in the central body of the Party and the Revolutionary Government. There was much work to be done organizing women, as we introduced free marriage in all the areas we liberated.

"Chou En-lai was fighting the K.M.T. as all manpower was sent to the front. The K.M.T. blockaded the bases, so life for people in the rear was very hard. Oil was scarce and we had great difficulty in getting salt. Due to heavy work and malnutrition, with my already weak constitution, in 1934 I had a serious relapse of my T.B.

"At the end of October that year the main troops of the Central Red Army were forced by the pressure of Chiang Kai-shek to leave our revolutionary bases in the South. We began the Long March.

Ill as I was—I had just had a bad haemorrhage—I went with them. In a year of unbelievable hardship and fighting we travelled from the South to the North, eventually to reach Shensi Province. The shift northward was for the double purpose of preserving the revolutionary army and establishing a safe base from which to carry on the war against the Japanese. There were thirty women in the ranks who acted as nurses and collected provisions from the peasants, explaining to them what we were, what we stood for.

"Being so ill—in the early period I was unable to walk—I lay on a stretcher for four months. Everybody was greatly worried, afraid I wouldn't stand such a strenuous journey. But, in the light of the situation at the time, they did not have the heart to leave me to the inevitable fate I should suffer if I fell into the hands of the K.M.T." She is silent for a moment.

"Only my belief in what we were trying to do and my will-power enabled me to triumph over the suffering of those first months. We were constantly bombarded by K.M.T. planes. When this happened the stretcher-bearers would be ordered to take cover in the woods and those of us too ill to move would just lie on our stretchers.

"One day I couldn't bear it, so I crawled into the woods and when I came back the man on the stretcher beside me was dead and there was a bullet hole right through my stretcher where my body would have been. If I hadn't taken that quick decision I wouldn't be here to tell you the story.

"Strangely enough, I began to improve. Maybe the fresh air and the sunshine played their part. Anyway, I got much better and by the time we reached Kweichow, four months later, I decided I would learn to ride a horse so that no one would have to carry my stretcher. The rest of the distance I walked or rode."

I think of another revolutionary heroine, Anita Garibaldi, riding beside her husband in his campaign for Italy's freedom.

"I shall never forget the hardships and difficulties of those months. We were constantly pursued and attacked by the K.M.T. troops. At the beginning we had to march at night and we made detours to trick them. When we had to go across the Great Snow Mountains of north-western Szechuan the sufferings of the troops were terrible. When we left the valleys it was hot weather and we went through passes full of glorious flowers we had never seen before. Then as we mounted higher and higher we ran into showers of snow. We were all lightly clad. There was insufficient food. In the snow-covered trackless mountain regions we had four seasons in a day, snow, then sunshine, then storm and blizzard. Our clothes would be soaked one hour and then the sun would come out and dry them. All round and above us stretched towering snow-covered peaks, glistening in the sunlight. Indeed, sometimes the scenery was so magnificent we forgot our suffering.

"The rarefied air made it difficult for us to breathe, and for me, with my sick lungs, it was particularly hard. During this time I rode on a mule or a donkey and when I would get off to give the poor beast a rest my legs would be so stiff and numb from the cold that I couldn't bend them.

"As we progressed things got worse. It was difficult to get food, difficult to cook it when obtained. Men fell and we thought they were exhausted, but they were dead." She pauses a moment, her eyes have a far-away look as she relives this epic of human endurance.

"Only our ideal upheld us. We hoped for a free China, an independent China from which poverty and exploitation would be abolished. If we failed, the hope died with us. And never in the worst times we went through did we believe we would fail. Optimism was like wine to us and we forgot our misery.

"Eventually we came down into the plains. A minority race, the Lolos, who had suffered much at the hands of the Han people in the past, hated and opposed us till we explained our policy of equality between the nationalities and that we were fighting for them as well as the rest of China. Then they could not do enough for us, since they, too, saw in our triumph their hope for deliverance from oppression.

"We crossed swampy plains where we were forced to kill our baggage animals to live. Many of those who succeeded in surviving the terrible mountains got ill in the marshlands. I myself got influenza and ran a high temperature and for seven days couldn't eat. I often wonder how we came through it all. When we left Kiangsi there were a hundred thousand of us. Less than thirty thousand arrived at Shensi.

"When we arrived at our base I had no chance to recuperate, for urgent work awaited us all. Immediately I was at my fighting post. Not until the Sian Incident in 1936, when Chiang Kai-shek's own patriotic officers kidnapped him and held him until he agreed to stop the Civil War and turn the Kuomintang forces against the Japanese invaders, did I get a chance to seek treatment. Chou En-lai flew to Sian to negotiate with Chiang Kai-shek to combine the Communist forces with the Kuomintang and form a united front to fight the Japanese, and then I had the opportunity to go to Peking to consult a T.B. specialist."

She laughs suddenly, and so infectious is the sound that we all laugh, too.

"I was afraid of being recognized and wore dark glasses, and the first person I ran into when I went through the gates of the P.U.M.C. Hospital was an old schoolmate! I averted my face and hurried away. The doctor sent me to the Sanatorium in the Western Hills in Peking, where I went under the pseudonym of Mrs Li. I was there only about three months when the Anti-Japanese War broke out and I had to leave."

"How had your condition been affected?" I ask.

"The specialist said I was practically cured and asked what my treatment had been. I told him, 'I'm optimistic. I'm not afraid of T.B.' What I couldn't tell him was that I had spent practically a year in the open air, through all weathers day and night, and maybe that was the most important factor in my cure."

"And have you never had a set-back since?" I ask, incredulous at this most unorthodox of cures.

"Never. Of course, the calcified spots remain on my lungs. Of course, I have had to discipline myself never to catch cold. I never go near anyone with a cold—not even my husband. Though it's almost twenty years since I was cured, obviously my health was undermined. So now you understand why I couldn't see you before."

Her words remind me that I have been remorselessly interviewing her for hours. If she is as tired as I suddenly realize I am ... I close my book and apologize.

"I am tired," she admits. "I haven't had such a long conversation for months. Would you like to continue another day?"

That evening a friend brought me recollections of those months in the Sanatorium written by Teng Ying-chao's room-mate, a young graduate of Chinghua University in Peking. They were published in 1941, after her death. It is a moving narrative of a politically uninformed girl whose illness had cut her off from life, and it reveals a side of the remarkable woman's character that otherwise might have been hidden from me.

I quote Hsing-feng:

One day during our rest period I heard the nurse's voice saying: "This is your room-mate." I looked round and saw a woman in a deep-blue silk *chi-pao* lined with peacock-green, and I said to myself, "I don't like that combination of colours." My heart sank when the new-comer said, "My name is Li Tai-tai." I had hoped to have a young, unmarried girl like myself, not a "Mrs". But in ten minutes my disappointment had changed to joy. Madame Li had such a delightful laugh; she was so kind, so sincere, looking at you with big, round, intelligent eyes. She wasn't beautiful, but immediately I had a warm feeling towards her.

She said to me, "This is a double room, but I want you to forget I'm here. If you want to talk to me, talk; if you don't, don't. Feel it's your room at home. Otherwise it's bad for your health."

I thought, "What an understanding person!" So did all the other inmates. Everyone felt very close to her. She was so warm, so sympathetic, so helpful. She attracted everyone. She was particularly kind to the service boys, and if she had something specially nice to eat she shared it with them. She wanted to know how they lived, and how much they earned. She was just as nice to a peasant who came as she was to the doctor.

She was well on the way to recovery so the doctor allowed her to go down the slopes for a walk—a privilege rarely given to us.

What Hsing-feng didn't know, it emerges later, was that "Mrs Li" was in contact with the local Resistance section.

She liked to sing "The Fisherman's Song", a song telling about fishermen's lives, and I used to sing "Pussy, Pussy". Later, we grew so friendly that she called me "Pussy".

I had no idea who she was. Even when she asked someone to buy her a book about the Sian Incident, I still had no notion that she had any link with it. And, of course, I hadn't any idea that the person who negotiated with Chiang Kai-shek at Sian to combine the Communist Forces with the Kuomintang was Mrs Li's husband, Chou En-lai.

When she spoke of her husband she always gave me the impression that they must be a very happy couple. And she was always trying to persuade me to get married. She would say, "You don't know the real joy of life, Pussy, till you are married."

She was always telling us how good-looking her husband was, with his thick eyebrows and his broad shoulders. She said he was very intelligent and able to deal with any situation in the world and that his patriotism was so strong that there was nothing he would not do for his country. Whenever she spoke of him she seemed very happy. But when it rained she used to say, "I wish I could be with my husband, Pussy, what can you do to comfort me?"

One day it was raining and the other patients came and said, "You're thinking of your husband again. Why don't you show us his photo?" Mrs Li replied, "I didn't bring one with me." So they teased her, saying, "We don't believe it. He's so handsome, you're afraid we'll fall in love with him."

She gently probed into the reasons why I was uninterested in life but never probed into my private affairs. She loved friendship, but I was sceptical because through illness I had lost my friends. What she said to me helped me very much.

Mrs Li got a lot of letters but few people came to call. One lady who used to call she always spoke of as Shing Tai-tai, and when she came, she called Mrs Li Fifth Elder Sister, and grasped her hands and wouldn't let them go. They would look at each other for a long time without speaking. I could see the happiness and affection on their faces. I came to the conclusion that Mrs Li's inner life was a much richer one than mine.

On 7th July 1937 the Anti-Japanese War started. Mrs Li seized the newspapers as soon as they came. After reading them she could almost repeat what was in the papers. Besides, she could tell many things the papers did not say. She could even predict political changes and military movements.

When news came that in the village near by there were a lot of wounded Chinese soldiers, she became very active and proposed that we start a fund to buy comforts for them. One man—a patient—gave her much help.

One day she said her husband had written her to go back to Sian. As the news became worse, she decided to leave. We were all very sad. She shook hands with every patient. I kissed her hands twice as I saw her off and wept. I waved until she was out of sight. When I came back, I felt the room was so empty.

When she left she said we should write to each other, but the addresses she left seemed vague, so I didn't like to write first. T.B. patients denied friendship are very sensitive. Then one day my elder brother came with a letter in strong handwriting that didn't look like a woman's, and in the lower left-hand corner was written "From Teng". I knew no Teng!

I opened the letter. It started: "Dear Pussy", then I knew. It was signed "Teng Ying-chao". So I knew that Mrs Li was an assumed name. I wrote to her to find out whether she was Miss or Mrs. I wonder what Teng Ying-chao said when she got it. Not to know the leader of the Women's Movement for twenty years—Chou En-lai's wife! Later, by sheer accident, I found her name in a book, and realized who she was.

Touchingly the dying young girl concludes: "I hope all my friends will fight on for the liberation of China."

The next day she is waiting in the drive to greet me as the car draws up. It is warmer and she wears a wine silk tunic over her grey slacks.

"My husband is receiving foreign guests this morning so I'm

going to take you to our private apartments," she says. "I hope
you don't mind."

She puts her arm through mine and we walk through the garden, stopping to admire the peonies that are a mass of blooms. A
high archway leads into a large walled garden.

She points to the buildings that run round three sides of it,
saying, "Those are all offices", and as we mount the shallow steps,
"This is our apartment. We have two rooms for ourselves."

The large room we enter is wide and deep, two L-shaped partitions on each side, a third of the way back, dividing it into dining-
room and sitting-room. Its ivory walls and woodwork give it
brightness and the large windows look out on the garden.

"This is where my husband and I have our meals," she says,
pointing to a small dining table, "and on Sundays our nieces and
nephews come to visit us. We have no children."

Lovely old-rose carpets embossed in wine cover the floor, the
same burgundy-coloured lounge suite I have seen in many other
places looks out to the garden, behind it a large bronze bust of
Chairman Mao. To the side is a piano, and on a stand a modern
wireless. The only touches of Old China are two cloisonné vases in
which stand peacock feathers and a large cheval-glass with a
heavy carved frame. There's a homely touch about the coats and
scarves hanging in a corner of the alcove.

Tea on a low utilitarian table, the peanuts I liked and the
kaoliang sweets.

"Where do we start from?" she asks.

"From your leaving the San," I reply promptly.

"Good. I went first to Sian—"

"But how did you manage to leave Peking with the Japanese
there?"

She gives her laugh, so full of gaiety, and says, "You are meticulous, aren't you?"

"I'm a dramatist," I retort, "and I'm not going to miss a scene
like that."

"Well, at first I didn't think of leaving Peking, but the situation
got very tense and as the gates of the city would be closed once
the Japanese entered and I had to catch a train in the city, on the
day of the official entry of the Japanese I got a rickshaw and entered with them and the rest of the crowd. It was the anniversary
of our wedding."

She stands and with her face alight and rapid gestures describes
the scene. "Just as my rickshaw got to a cross-road a Japanese tank
came along the other road. My heart was beating very rapidly,

then they turned off and went another way. I just managed to squeeze through the gates with the rest. I went to my friend's place and burnt all my books and papers. After two days I left for Tientsin. It took us ten hours instead of two and we were packed like sardines and had to stand all the way. We had no food, no water, and the stations were crowded with Japanese soldiers. . . .

"From Tientsin I went first to Sian, then to Wuhan, seat of the Kuomintang Government. Chou En-lai was there and other Communist leaders, and we were warmly welcomed by the people. I was one of the six Communist members on the Political Consultative Council of the War of Resistance to Japanese Aggression on the eve of the Government's withdrawal to Chungking. There I worked in the office of the Communist Party, where we carried on our work, though the city was constantly under Japanese bombardment."

She does not tell me that, in the midst of all this, she found time to write to "dear Pussy".

"In the summer of 1939 we went to Yenan, which had been flattened by Japanese bombs, and shortly after, I went with my husband to the Soviet Union for treatment. He had had a fall from his horse and broken his arm. We stayed there half a year before returning to Chungking. Here in 1940 my mother died." She is silent a moment.

"From 1941 onwards things got more difficult for the Communists in Chungking. We were pressed from all sides. Between 1941 and 1943 we were forbidden to leave the city and prohibited from speaking in public. It was not until 1943 that I got a chance to go back to Yenan."

Rising from her chair, as she often does during the interview, she walks across the room, talking as she goes.

"In 1945 I attended the Seventh National Congress of the Communist Party and was elected Alternate Member of the Central Committee. A few months after the capitulation of Japan and on the eve of the holding of the Political Consultative Conference I came to Chungking as delegate for the Communist side. During this period, though I was very busy, I still paid much attention to women's work. On International Women's Day in 1946 I spoke in public again for the first time in many years.

"We stayed at Chungking trying to save the last hope of peace. But negotiating for peace with a dictator like Chiang Kai-shek was like trying to turn a tiger into a vegetarian. When his real face was unmasked the Communist delegation withdrew to Yenan. I was elected to the executive committee of the Women's International Democratic Federation and intended to go to Paris, but the K.M.T. refused to grant me a passport."

She adds fresh hot water to the teapot, refills our cups, and takes up her story.

"Almost eleven years have passed since we withdrew to Yenan from Nanking. Those years fall into two periods. First, the War of Liberation, and second, the socialist reconstruction of our country.

"During those years I have been mainly engaged in the Women's Movement. In the three months after leaving Nanking I spent most of my time reading, since there was no suitable work for me to do. In the meantime the evacuation of the city was going on as the K.M.T. Army was beginning to invade it. We had been in Yenan close on ten years so it was not only an army we had to withdraw but families with women and children.

"I left with the last group before the K.M.T. Army arrived. The provinces of Shensi, Kansu, and Ninghsia became guerrilla areas and all women had to be withdrawn to Shansi Province east of the Yellow River. For six months after the withdrawal we were continuously on the move. To help the women with children we used the large Northern mules and fixed on them special saddles with side panniers in which the children travelled."

She grows extremely animated as she tells this part of her story, moving to and fro, gesticulating, reliving it all.

"We organized ourselves into teams of fifty to sixty to make the problems of travel simpler. Madame Chu Teh was leader of our team and I was the political commissar.

"We couldn't march during the day because the K.M.T. planes were constantly strafing us. All night we plodded on over the rough tracks and before sunrise we had to find lodgings and go into hiding till night. These areas had long been liberated and the peasants were on our side, but we still had terrific problems. No one dared go out of the house during the day in case of air-raids.

"On arrival we had to count and check, and exchange meal-tickets for food. One of our strictest regulations was that we took nothing from the peasants without payment.

"At last we settled in a village and engaged in rear-service. In the summer of forty-seven a national conference on the land question was held at which we summed up our experiences and planned for the future.

"I was four months in the village taking part in the work of land reform, and then I learnt how full of wisdom and understanding our peasant women are. When they came to understand the real sources of their oppression and suffering, then they were full of courage and spirit to struggle against them. But when they didn't understand, but only blamed their miserable lives on their ill-fate, not only would they not stand up themselves but they dragged the legs of their loved ones who wanted to stand up.

"Our job wasn't easy: giving them a sense of *their* importance, and awareness of what we wanted *our* country to be. At first their role was underestimated by the peasants. 'The women know nothing but household affairs,' the men would say, explaining their absence from meetings to discuss land-distribution. Then next day they would come back with a long face and say, 'I've changed my mind. My mother says—' or, 'My wife says . . . '. So the women were brought into the meetings and surprised everybody by their knowledge of the land. They had practical ideas, too. They insisted on using wooden measuring-rods so that they couldn't stretch and that the measuring-rod should always be measured first.

"During all this we were putting into practice what Chairman Mao had taught us—he had been reared in a village and understood the peasants better than anyone else—that the most important thing was to encourage the peasants to act for themselves in a democratic way. Not easy when for thousands of years they had not dared do a thing for fear of the landlord.

"But when the landlords were overthrown they gained confidence and when they got their land they realized that a new era had begun. They learnt—some very fast, some slowly. For women, the greatest teacher was the fact that every woman was given her own piece of land so that she had her economic independence.

"It was amusing to watch the excitement when a baby was expected, for children were also given their share, and everyone would be hoping the baby would be born in time. The father and grandfather would stand outside asking anxiously, 'Is it born, is it born?' where once they would have been saying, 'Is it a boy?'

"It was interesting, too, to notice how the conception of women's inferiority began to disappear. Peasants began to say, 'Now daughters are just as good as sons.'

"There was no medical care in the village at all when we came. None of our group was fully trained, but we brought ordinary medicines with us and before we knew where we were we were elevated to a medical team! Some worked as surgeons, others as physicians and I was pharmacist. To peasants who had had no care our simple treatment and the results we obtained by teaching them ordinary rules of hygiene seemed like a miracle. Our prestige was enormous and it was infinitely touching to see the way they greeted us and tried to press on us gifts it was against our rules to take.

"Their improved standard of living led to new demands: they wanted to learn to read and write. They wanted a school for their children.

"I spent the Chinese New Year in the village and it was exhilarating to see the efforts they put into organizing plays and dances and other festival celebrations—most of them for the first time in their lives. Even old peasants would come hobbling on sticks from other villages to see the shows and I've never seen such an enthusiastic audience.

"Most of them for the first time had the traditional New Year meat dumplings and ate bean-curd. As they recalled their bitter lives of the old days, some wept. I remember one old woman saying, 'Before, we believed in Fate, we worshipped gods, and burnt incense. I've burnt incense all my life to the Kitchen God, but he never put anything into the cooking-pot. But Chairman Mao has given us food, so out the old god goes!' And out he went!

"In 1948, after the completion of Land Reform in the liberated areas, I began to take part in the organization of the Women's Federation. As I told you, I am mainly concerned with the problems of women, though I take my part also in the social and political movements of my country. I am a deputy to the National People's Congress and a member of the Standing Committee as well as being a member of the Central Committee of the Communist Party. I think perhaps we'd better leave details of the Women's Movement for another day."

Next day, as I stepped onto the terrace, a photographer snapped us.

"I thought I'd like a memento of your visit," Teng Ying-chao said, slipping her arm through mine. "I've never met a foreigner who is so interested in our women."

When we were seated she opened her note-book and began: "Though the All-China Democratic Women's Federation was founded only in 1949 it had many smaller predecessors all concerned with the welfare of women and children. During the War of Resistance there was a Women's Federation in every township, no matter how small, in the liberated areas.

"In K.M.T. areas the official organization was established by Soong Mei-ling (Madame Chiang Kai-shek). Then there were the two Christian organizations, the Y.W.C.A. which had—and still has—branches in about fifteen cities, and the Women's Christian Temperance Union, both of which did useful work for women and children.

"The problem raised by the enormous number of child-orphans and refugees after the Japanese advance in the South brought women of all parties and creeds together to form the Wartime Child Care Association. This came to an end with the Japanese capitulation.

"In addition to these, there were the organizations in Japanese-occupied areas which continued their activities in more or less clandestine ways. The representative figure among these was Shu Kuang-ping, widow of the famous writer Lu Hsun, and now one of our vice-presidents.

"As the K.M.T. grew more reactionary their women's organizations refused to co-operate with ours. So we formed the Chinese Women's Social Association whose representative figures were Madame Li Te-chuan, today Minister of Public Health, and Madame Shih Liang, our Minister of Justice.

"As the liberated areas grew larger and larger with the retreat of the K.M.T. we set to work on the drafting of the New Marriage Law, which took us seventeen months, because we collected views and opinions and suggestions for it from all over China, so that it would really be based on popular opinion.

"In 1949 the first All-China Women's Congress was convened in Peking and to it came five hundred representatives from all over the country, including progressive women from K.M.T. areas, Y.W.C.A. and W.C.T.U. delegates as well as delegates from the Women's Federations in the liberated areas.

"From the Congress emerged the Women's Federation of the People's Republic of China which now guides women's work all over the country. The Federation has representatives throughout China from the smallest village up and all delegates are elected from basic units so that it is truly democratic.

"Our task is to explain to women not only the rights that emancipation has brought them but the responsibilities that go with them. I think you must have seen for yourself how that is done."

She closes her note-book and pours fresh tea for us, saying, "I think that's about all."

"Not quite," I say, glancing at the piano. "What do you do when you're just being Chou Tai-tai?" (That is, "Mrs Chou".)

She looks up surprised, the teapot poised, and then laughs as though to say, "Is there no satisfying the woman?"

"I've never found my household life and my political life incompatible," she says as she sits down again. "Though I have for a long time engaged myself in political activities, I always take good care of the running of our house. Especially between 1927 and 1932, when under extremely difficult conditions we worked underground in Shanghai, I had to do my own housework, go to the market, do the shopping and do our own cooking.

"In fact, I don't see why any woman should find it difficult to organize her time between housekeeping and outside activities." She pauses, leaning forward to emphasize her point. "However, it is necessary that her husband should have the right attitude. Both husband and wife should be responsible for the proper running of their house and the upbringing of their children.

"Of course, wives and mothers have the chief responsibility for the home and we respect them and their work. And we advocate their managing the household with thrift and industry so that they may contribute to the building of the country.

"But to return to my story. When we were in Chungking and our movements were limited by the K.M.T. authorities, we always gave our household help a rest at New Year and invited our friends to visit us, each one contributing a dish to the dinner."

"And now?" I ask, wondering whether being wife of the Premier has altered her simple ideas.

"Now? I don't do so much work, but I run my home myself. I plan the menu for the week for my husband and me. I keep an eye on the kitchen to see everything is clean. I check the laundry. I keep a household budget to see how our expenditure goes. Sometimes I consult with the maid on how to make clothes. Last week I helped her to make a pair of trousers.

"Sometimes I play the piano and I read a great deal. Sometimes I take a walk with my husband in the garden. Sometimes we go to a movie. We have no children, but sometimes our nieces and nephews come to dine. Sometimes I give the cook a rest: the dish I particularly like to make is fish or meat with soya sauce.

"Because for so many years we Communist women led such a hard, adventurous life, it doesn't mean that we don't like home or housekeeping. But during the revolutionary wars home life was out of the question, though wherever we were for any length of time I tried to make the spot feel like home.

"Now that we can have a home we prize it all the more. After such experiences as ours we know the suffering that war has brought to women and children. We really value peace and are prepared to do all in our power to defend it and all that it means to China and the world."

CHAPTER XXV

Peking-Shenyang

A SUNDAY evening at the end of August. Half past nine, and I am in the train for Shenyang, the Mukden of old days.

"The Blue Train", made in China, is modern in every respect: smooth polished woodwork, maroon carpets, on the bunks heavy silver-grey camel-hair rugs patterned in purple that have a silken texture and sheen.

The whole train is staffed by women, with the exception of the engine crew. A man is also in charge of the security of the train. A pleasant voice over the loud-speaker system welcomes us to the train and the whole smooth routine of travelling in China gets under way.

Our car conductor—a fresh young girl in blue slacks and a white linen coat—introduces us proudly to the mysteries of our wash-basin, tells us how to close doors, put on lights, ring bells—in short, how to travel.

The Red Cross attendant, in crisp white uniform, looks in.

The tea-pourer, a fringe showing under her white cap and a tip-tilted nose giving her a comically youthful air, arrives to give us refreshment.

A peaceful night.

Next morning I look out through double windows on a flat sunlit landscape stretching away to pale hills. Here in the North-east autumn is on the way, though in Peking it was still high summer. Tall yellowing crops sway in the breeze. This is grain country—wheat and millet and kaoliang (sorghum). Here the fields are large—gone are the small holdings of Southern China.

Along the road solid Mongolian ponies trot, usually tandem, pulling low-wheeled carts with a sweet jangling of bells.

Everywhere old Japanese pillboxes, relics of the Anti-Japanese War.

Big herds of cattle, business-like villages, plain undecorated houses.

All the train crew stirring and smiling.

Breakfast with the countryside unwinding like a film. Neat helpful waitresses.

I am presented to the train director, an attractive woman who has been a year on this train, eleven years on trains altogether. She is on duty for two trips from Shenyang to Peking and back, then she has four and a half days' rest. I am shown the comfortable cabins in which members of the service crew take their rest during the night.

Roadside ponds, a carpet of cobalt water-hyacinths. A motor lorry standing incongruously beside ancestral graves. Spindly electricity pylons receding in the distance. A tall pagoda.

Precursors of a big industrial city—factory chimneys coming up, dozens, hundreds of them, their wavering smoke scrawling arabesques on the pale sky.

Shenyang! The industrialized North-east begins—the Chinese do not recognize Manchuria, a word coined by the West, any more than they recognize "Manchukuo" coined by the Japanese. For them it is, as it has always been, the North-east Provinces.

CHAPTER XXVI

The North-east: Girls and Machines

THROUGHOUT the North-east I travelled, visiting the great
enterprises that in another ten years will completely trans-
form the face of China, for here they are not only turning
out machine-tools and steel but training the technicians who will
in their turn establish similar enterprises throughout the country.

Let me confess it here at the beginning of my North-east tour:
to me, to whom the simplest mechanical device is a mystery, one
factory is very like another. It is the human being who interests
me and the change that mechanization makes in human lives.

I am too familiar with the ugly industrial towns of Europe—and,
alas, even Australia, where we have no excuse to perpetuate the
horrors of Victorian England—not to recoil from the word
"industrialization", which is so dear to my Chinese friends. "But
here it is different," they protest. "Here the machine exists for the
human being, not the human being for the machine. And we *must*
industrialize our country to raise the standard of living for everyone."

I am still dubious, particularly when they tell me that women
have taken their place even in the heavy industries once regarded
as suitable only for men, and still regarded as the preserves of
men in the West.

"Come and see for yourself," my guide urged me. "Then you
can judge." Then began for me weeks of walking through vast
up-to-date factories in Shenyang and Anshan and Changchun
and Harbin, steel-works and motor-works and machine-tool factories, and through technical colleges and universities equipped
with the intricate tools I had seen in the factories. "All modern,"
a French engineer commented, with what seemed to me to be
bitterness, "not like so much of ours."

I saw the newly built blocks of flats where the workers live, for
as each factory is built, housing for its workers goes up. I visited
comfortable modern flats where families lived as they had never
in their lives lived before, and hostels for unmarried workers.
Every housing unit has its cultural amenities, its playing fields, its

medical service. I saw that industrial towns need not be grey and ugly, nor the machine reduce men and women to robots.

And the women? Let them speak for themselves.

I had been walking for what seemed hours through the huge, well-lighted bays of the Shenyang Number One Tool Factory, set among well-laid-out gardens, before I realized that among the blue-clad figures that handle the complicated machines so calmly are many women. We stop to watch one at work. She is Tung Wui-chin, and even the obliterating blue cap does not hide the charm of her laughing face with its pink cheeks, dancing eyes, and warming smile.

She looks rather a mischievous imp, but she is a highly skilled operative. She is just twenty.

"At the beginning," she says in answer to my question, "I learnt from the Soviet experts who were sent to install the complicated machines. Today all but eleven have gone home; they remain to handle the latest machines that have arrived. So now I must stand on my own feet."

This is too tricky a job to allow for gossip, so I arrange to see her after the shift.

Wu Hung-mei looks up from a machine she is inspecting in another workshop.

She is forewoman of a group in the milling machine workshop, twenty-seven of them men and five of them girls. I arrange to see her, too.

Transformed, Tung Wui-chin comes skipping along the corridor with her short glossy hair released from her cap, and light-blue trousers and a red-checked tunic replacing her workshop overalls. She takes both my hands in hers and looks back to throw a laughing remark at Wu Hung-mei, who follows her more sedately. They both apologize for keeping me, but after shift they like to bathe and wash their hair.

"If we told you all the exciting things about our new lives we would be here for a week," Wui-chin says, laughing. "Look at me, for instance. I come from the country. I could only work in the fields. But after Liberation I went to school, and when I went through middle school my teacher said I could now work in a factory and make a contribution to my country.

"My mother was progressive and encouraged me, saying, 'It is the chance of your life. You're the first woman in our family who has ever had the chance to stand up. Go along!' I came, and I have been here more than three years. I have done very well and now earn eighty yuan a month, so I am able to send money home to help with my young sister's education. I live in the factory dormitory.

"Altogether my living doesn't cost me much. I eat in the factory canteen, which costs me twenty yuan a month. I have been able to buy a bicycle and I have a savings-bank account. My grandmother in all her life had never heard of a bank account. My life is very busy. There's always something to do. I play volley-ball and I like gymnastics."

Somewhere outside, as though to accompany her joyous recital, a one-string fiddle begins a tune. "The factory orchestra," she explains, and suddenly the fiddle is swamped as a score of unnameable instruments take up distractedly and individually, each going its own way, to perfect its own piece.

"I sing in the factory ensemble," she adds, humming a fragment of the air the fiddle continues to play.

Although she is only two years older, Wu Hung-mei has the gravity of another generation.

"I came to the factory in 1953," she begins. "I should have come earlier, only at first my parents were opposed to my leaving the village to work alone. They had known too many terrible stories of girls who went to the town looking for work. And, besides, they didn't really believe what the Government said. 'Equality for women!' my mother sniffed. 'Don't you believe it!'

" 'Wait till we see whether this Government will last,' said my father. 'We've heard a lot of these promises before.'

"But when the Government kept its promise and my father got land and they saw women being treated really as equals they changed their minds.

"When at last I came here my parents were happy because it was proof that life had changed."

Her rather diffident manner changes to animation when I ask her why she came to the factory.

"I came," she answers, "because in the old society I had seen too many women treated like animals. But now women can do whatever work they like." She gives a faint smile. "Now our lives are our own for us to make what we want to make of them. I am married now and my husband is an office worker. We live in one of the thousands of workers' flats that the factory has built. We have breakfast, lunch, and dinner in the factory canteen and wash in the factory, which leaves me very little to do at home."

"And recreation?"

"I used to be very active in the physical culture groups and liked gymnastic work and the parallel bars, but now I am expecting a baby. I shall have the usual time off, and when I come back to work, I will leave the baby in the factory crèche during the day —we get regular times off for feeding our babies—and take it home in the evening and at week-ends. Then, when it is old enough, I will take it each day to the factory kindergarten.

"I can assure you babies are much better off in China today than any but the richest were in the old days. And then even the richest girl didn't have what we have today as our right!"

The younger generation has no doubts.

In Anshan the sinews of New China are being forged. It is a town in a delirium of construction. The old city has a bewildered look as though it hardly knows itself, so fast is a new one going up.

New streets lined with new trees. New workshops, new factories. New workers' flats four storeys high. New schools, a new university, new hospitals—a new life!

As the gates of the Anshan United Steel-works loom up through driving rain, the air is full of an all-pervading, unceasing dull pulsation, a muffled roar, a reverberating clangour.

The grounds are still in process of being drained, kerbed, street-ed and beautified—all at once. Already young trees are giving the touch of green in the plots round the huge buildings.

"Up till now we have been too busy repairing the damage done by Japs and Kuomintang to do any beautifying," my guide shouts. "When we took over in 'forty-eight the place was completely ruined, the grass was six feet high. We thought it would take twenty years." He laughs. "It didn't.

"There are eighty-six thousand workers in the United Steel-works," he shouts again—working in a steel-mill has apparently given him the habit. "Five thousand three hundred of them are women."

"What do they do?" I shout.

"You'll see!"

We go up a slippery track to the blast-furnace that looms black and enormous above us, a steady stream of molten iron flowing in an apparently casual fashion into moulds. As we mount we meet the first rush of hot air that comes from an intake where the naked fire is showing. Young workers are busy with shovels and sand near the aperture, all giving a picture of casualness as if in contempt of the giant that looms above them with such a potentiality for creation and destruction.

We mount the steps, dodging a spray of water, one straying drop of which tells us its boiling temperature, into the control-room, where an attempt is made to explain a bewildering array of instruments—alas with little success!

A girl comes towards us, buttoning her faded blue denim tunic that shows a striped shirt underneath. She is not more than four foot ten and less than seven stone and her heavy boots look disproportionately large. I imagine she is the secretary of the director I have come to see.

She puts out a tiny, perfectly shaped hand. I stare in astonishment as I hear her name. It isn't possible! This fragile creature with her delicate pink cheeks, the glasses that make her look the typical intellectual, director of a blast-furnace! I am used to surprises in China, but this is the biggest of all.

We sit down to talk. She is obviously nervous and twists a handkerchief incessantly through her fingers.

She speaks quickly in a very soft voice. It's the first time she has met a foreigner and she clearly is as intimidated by my stylo as I am by her furnace.

"I was the daughter of a landlord's family in Soochow, near Shanghai," she tells me. "When I graduated from the university I was jobless. Not that that was anything strange. We had a saying in the old days that graduation meant unemployment. No one wanted graduates from the Industrial Chemical Department, it seemed, more particularly if they were women.

"Two of my schoolmates, in the same pickle as myself, came to Anshan. It was liberated before the South. They wrote and told me there was more chance of a job here, so in 1951 I came to Anshan, too. When I came my idea was to try to get a job in the chemical department. But there was nothing there and the manager said, 'Well, there are a number of other vacancies. Choose what you like.'

"I chose the blast-furnace. Why, I am not very clear.

"Everything about the steel-works terrified me at the beginning: the noise, the heat, the danger. I was assigned to the planning section and as I got accustomed to it I began to think how nice it would be to be somewhere where I could see the melted iron flowing out from the plug. I became fascinated with the processes and had a great desire to work on the furnace itself. So I did a special course in smelting and when I was successful at it was assigned to the blast-furnace and took over the job.

"That was a really difficult part." She smiles, showing irregular white teeth. Some of her reserve slips away. "Not the work, but the men workers. They were mostly old hands, and they laughed at me. I think they disliked very much the idea of a woman working on what had always been looked on as heavy and dangerous and man's work. They used to say, 'This is a man's job. Women can never do it!' They ridiculed me and advised me to go back to the planning section, but I did my best to get along with them and began to make headway when I offered to teach the illiterates in my spare time.

"Then one day a big repair job had to be done on the furnace and I climbed round the top with the men. I cut my leg rather badly and when the men saw that I made no fuss and asked for no first aid until the job was finished they said admiringly, 'You're a tough lass, you are, even if you don't look it.'

"In 1952 I was made director of Number One Blast-furnace. Some of the men didn't like it. So I set to work to organize the furnace-workers and discuss the problems with them, got everyone to co-operate, and by 1953 our furnace was one of the best in the mill.

"At the end of 1953 I was transferred to Number Eight, which had by then been made completely automatic.

"I didn't work there very long, because a few months later I became pregnant and had to go to lighter work, and now I am studying the technique of furnace construction."

Blushing deeply, she adds, "My husband is director of the work-shop of the blast-furnaces."

I'm dying to know more about this romance. How did they fall in love with each other? Was the courtship conducted in the shadow of the blast-furnace? But she hurries on.

"We live in one of the workers' flats. Mother lives with us, but we have a maid to look after the house and the baby during the day; the older child has been admitted to the kindergarten and loves it."

She glances surreptitiously at her small gold wristlet watch, the only sign about her that, in the old days, she came from a rich family. I think of the two babies, the technician husband and her ex-landlord's-wife mother waiting impatiently for her return, and let her go.

I first saw Tsang Wun-tsen in the thunder of the rolling mill in the same steel-works. She was in the control-room in charge of the machine which cuts the hundred-foot railway lines into three.

I watched the huge, almost human machine take the incande-scent steel ingot whose heat, even sixty feet away, shrivelled my hair. It passed with a deafening clang from one gaping aperture to another, back and forth, each time shaping and lengthening until it reached its final form. Now below me the same red-hot rail glides along its track and three saws move forward and rip through it with a shattering noise and a shower of sparks spraying out like the explosion of a huge rocket.

Tsang Wun-tsen, neat and business-like in her dark-blue tunic and trousers, a blue cap covering her hair, spared me a glance from laughing almond eyes and a smile that revealed teeth absurdly like the Victorian novelist's favourite pearls.

When she came off shift some hours later I recognized her only by the smile and the mole under the eyebrow. The glare of the rolling mill had hidden from me the fact that she had skin literally like a peach with a warm rich colour high on the cheekbones, just as the blue cap had hidden two long shining plaits tied with green ribbon that matched the green buttons on her rose-and-white tunic. Full of astonishing vitality as though some of the sparks had entered into her, she radiated happiness.

"I am nineteen," she told me, "daughter of a poor peasant family that in the old days starved on the outskirts of Anshan. When I left school in 1953 my parents approved of my idea of coming to work in a steel-mill, though it was the first time any member of our family had ever left the village.

"I was very young and ambitious," she says, with amused tolerance looking back on herself at sixteen years, "and I must have looked rather silly, walking up to the steel-works with the few things I owned wrapped in a bundle. But they were very kind to me and, after a few tests, they decided that I should have a year's training. After that I was taken charge of by a Soviet expert."

"Hard work?"

"No, I don't find my work hard, and I love it. I realize that it's very important." She tries to assume an air of suitable solemnity, but the laughter breaks through. "My life is very interesting and very busy." She glances at her wrist-watch. "We have a workers' spare-time troupe for drama and opera and I'm terribly keen about acting. I have a rehearsal at five thirty. Do you mind if I hurry away?"

Till I went there, in my mind Changchun was only the site of China's new Number One Motor-car Factory, made famous by every visiting journalist as the most up to date in the world.

I was astonished when I arrived and found it is also a beautiful old city, the capital of Kirin Province. Its population has grown from 450,000 in 1945 to just on a million today. The new city is also growing fast, spreading out from the old into what a few years ago were peasants' fields. Bulldozers shouldering away the earth for new construction sites. Men with hand-carts straining at loads of stones. Men with shoulder baskets. Street after street of new red-brick worker's flats. New schools, new universities and hospitals. A teachers' college with 20,000 students. Three research institutes of applied engineering. Rubber works, printing works, large film studios. (*The White-haired Girl* was made here.)

And, dominating all, the vast bulk of the Changchun Number One Motor-car Works, China's first automobile factory, whose building, with the aid of Soviet experts, took from 1950 to 1953. Now all is completed except for a few auxiliary workshops. China is launched on the production of her own motor vehicles. We see the four-ton truck on the assembly line in the vast well-lighted bays that seem to stretch for ever.

"A pity you arrived on a Saturday afternoon," my guide says. "It takes eight hours to walk round the whole works so we shall only be able to see a small section!"

We see it, and my feet record that we've covered miles. Miles of the most modern plant I have ever seen. Seventeen thousand workers—15 per cent of them women, many in highly responsible jobs.

Here, as at Shenyang and Fushun and Anshan, the wall newspapers display a high degree of artistry. Striking designs in coloured chalks. Elegant characters. Witty cartoons. One, an acid comment on the thoughtless husband. Mother and father going home from work. Mother carrying the baby and the shopping bag while father strides ahead burying his nose in the newspaper!

It is near the end of the shift and we stop to talk to a girl in one of the interminably long bays of machines, some small, some like two-storeyed houses, all impressively intricate. The workshop is well ventilated, well lighted, clean.

Nineteen-year-old Su Yu-lan, solidly built in her blue dungarees, turns a smiling face to me and whips off the blue cap that covers her short hair. She tells me that the milling machine she is in charge of is the latest Soviet model.

"I came to the factory in 1953," she continues. "After I left school I had gone to work in the out-of-date Dairen locomotive factory. My father's native village was near Dairen. He had no land of his own and used to work as a labourer for the rich peasants and we practically starved to death. When I came here everything was very strange to me. The enormous new motor works seemed like another world. I had never had such a nice place to live as I have in the hostel for single girls. I had never seen anything like the machinery before.

"I was bewildered by the machine I was to take charge of. So I went to an old worker and asked him to help me. He took me under his wing and told me all about it, and, after twenty days, I could operate the machine which made very complicated parts. To perfect myself I came back in my spare time and learnt to master every part and every movement. In a year I had made very good progress and could turn out my products with no waste. Some of the girls couldn't manage this, so I organized them into groups and went round to see what their difficulties were and made a plan how we could all learn from each other." Her face lights up as she looks back over the vast humming hive.

"I've fallen in love with that milling machine and the happiest day of my life was when the first Liberation four-ton truck produced in China rode out of the factory. We had banners and flowers and everybody shouted with joy and I nearly burst with pride because in the engine were parts made by my machine. My only regret was that neither my father nor my mother could be there to see it. And I said to myself, 'This is a symbol—Liberation trucks made by liberated Chinese women.'"

CHAPTER XXVII

Miners' Village

LEAVING behind us the high poppet-heads of the completely mechanized Dragon and Phoenix Mine at Fushun, we skim along the untarred road a cloud of powdery dust rising behind us and passing at intervals through the smaller clouds raised by carts loaded with building material. Fushun, like everywhere else in China, is building as fast as it can.

In the open fields are excavations for buildings, beside them the crumbling mud huts that were the homes of miners in the old days.

We turn off the main road to the miners' village.

Lei Tsu-kei welcomes me to her flat on the third storey of one of the new blocks built for the mine-workers since Liberation. In her dark-blue suit with the trousers bound tight to the ankle, she looks well into the sixties. She is, I find, ten years younger!

She sits down, cross-legged, with surprising agility on a bed at least seven feet by nine, covered with a floral quilt. It is a charming room opening on a balcony gay with flowers. Attractive Chinese prints on the wall, a central heating unit along the wall. A dressing-table with a mirror above it, two other mirrors on the wall, an old-fashioned English clock.

"Just look at this," she says, the wonder of it all shining in her slant eyes. "Who would ever have thought that we, who in the old days lived in a very small mud hut, would one day have such a palace as this. Two big rooms—only my fourteen-year-old son and my daughter are still at home. A kitchen, heating in winter —we, who used to lie huddled together under one ragged quilt to keep warm with the snow heaped feet deep outside and the temperature down to thirty degrees below!"

Her pointed face, wide at the cheekbones, looks round the room wonderingly as though she is mentally pinching herself.

"If you only knew all the changes I've seen in Fushun during my lifetime! I come of a Fushun family, I married a Fushun man. After marriage I lived in Fushun. And my husband has worked in Fushun since he was fifteen! He will retire in two years and of course he will get a pension. In the old days, no matter how hard he worked, he didn't get enough to feed us properly. In fact, we nearly starved to death at times.

"Before Liberation we had no rice but only bean-cakes, and it was worse when the Japs came, our daily ration was two kilos of noodles made of coarse rye, occasionally supplemented by a coarse black bread that was practically inedible. Bean-cake was not only poor nourishment, but you never felt well after eating it. My daughter wouldn't play after eating it. It used to make her feel sick. As a result we had all sorts of illnesses. Now my husband makes ninety to one hundred yuan a month and we can have meat in the week-ends when our sons come back from Shenyang.

"My youngest son and daughter are still at school, whereas their eldest brother had to go to work in the coal-mine when he was twelve. But he's been given the chance to study, too, and now he's a mechanic in the mine. Our second son is a doctor in a hospital." She shakes her head gleefully so that the ear-rings dance.

"Our third son is an apprentice in a factory. A few years ago who would ever have thought this possible? None of them even went to school before."

She unfolds herself from the bed and goes to take the cover off an old Singer sewing-machine.

"Did you notice my machine? Now I can make new clothes. Look at my daughter's dress."

Her daughter is peeping shyly round the doorway, gangling and fresh in a gay summer cotton frock.

"Look at this!" She runs her knotted hands down her own blue tunic. "And not so long ago I used to search in the streets for discarded pieces of clothing or gunny-sacks I could sew together for the winter!"

She is so exuberantly happy that I laugh with her as she shows me one thing after another: on top of a cupboard, the stock of newly-made cotton-padded quilts, that she has just made for the winter.

"Winter comes suddenly in the North-east and it's well to be prepared. Soon I will start on padded clothing for the family, though now I buy the coats and big things like that from the co-op. Fancy me thinking of buying clothes!"

She whirls round and points. "Have you noticed our wireless? It's a modern wireless. We can listen to a great number of places I never even heard of before! Would you like to see my kitchen?"

It is the most modern kitchen I have seen in China with gas-stove, a terrazzo sink and draining board, and well-made kitchen cupboards. On the landing is a flush toilet.

"Would you like to see my grandson? He's in the other room."

The grandson is asleep in a hanging wooden cradle painted with a traditional design, his round flushed cheek pressed into the pillow. We whisper.

"I mind him for my daughter-in-law during the day. She works in the administrative section at the mine. Isn't he a lovely child?

"Have you noticed the organ?"

And there it is: a large-sized modern church-harmonium with music on the stand!

"Both my youngest son and daughter play and one of the older ones and my daughter-in-law, too. You wouldn't believe the pleasure that organ gives us!" She adjusts a reading lamp on a table. "The house is full of books. I hardly know where to put them. Not that I mind." She picks up a book and fingers it lovingly.

"Before, I was illiterate. But I've been studying hard, with the help of my son, and now I can read. Not everything, mind you, but I'm improving. But I'm so busy that I can't give as much time to it as I'd like. I do all the housework, I'm on the Street Committee, and there's always so many interesting things to do!"

Her narrow eyes sparkle. She raises her hands and laughs with sheer joy.

We go down the stairs treading a perilous way through the massed cohorts of children who are determined at any cost not to miss the stranger, and I look back to see her waving to me from the flower-covered balcony.

CHAPTER XXVIII

Guardian Angel

THE legend of my fragility kept pace with me. I find myself at Anshan in the hands of Dr Hou, who is to be my companion and guide during my stay. Sweet-faced, gentle, smiling, she is also adamant. I go to bed to order, get up to order, eat to order.

A delightful concert in the hotel ballroom, given by a troupe from Sinkiang. A flashing-eyed girl who might have stepped out of the Arabian Nights, in velvet and sequins and platter-like fur hat whirls and sings. Hawk-nosed, dashing young men stamp to the sound of leathern drums while eighty ancient farmers from Sinkiang keep turning bearded faces under Muslim caps to make sure I am enjoying it.

The Anshan spare-time chorus sings—and sings excellently. The spare-time orchestra plays strange melodies on one-string fiddles and pi-bas and Chinese guitars.

And at the interval, as I am enjoying it all thoroughly while I nibble sugared lotus-nuts and kaoliang sweets and sip perfumed tea, Dr Hou smiles and says gently, "I think perhaps you are tired and would like to go to bed." *And I go!*

Next morning I meet my flashing-eyed girl on the landing of my floor. She is all solicitude. Am I better? Apparently even Sinkiang knows!

Three grandpas with drooping moustaches and embroidered caps make room for me on a settee. Then, all grace and exquisite hand-movements in spite of a workmanlike grey frock and heavy shoes, she dances for me while a swarthy young man who has stepped straight from an Assyrian frieze thrums out a haunting melody on a pi-ba.

Some day, I promise, I shall go to Sinkiang.

It is only over our farewell dinner that I find that my companion and guardian during my stay in Anshan, Dr Hou Kwei-lin, who looks so young with her round pleasant face, is director of the General Hospital! I comment on her youthful air.

"I am thirty-two," she tells me. "My husband is also a doctor. He is head of the Public Health."

Casually, and expecting nothing unusual, I ask, "And what did you do before Liberation?"

"Oh, there's nothing very interesting about my life," she says. Still I persist. I've got into the habit of asking questions.

"My husband and I are both graduates from Shenyang University. We were married while we were students. When we graduated the Anti-Japanese War was at its height and doctors were badly needed in the Liberation Army, so, leaving our baby with relatives, we went to the areas already liberated from the Japanese."

"You must have had some terrible experiences," I suggest.

"Well, it was rather hard," she admits. "Looking after the wounded in difficult circumstances, lack of adequate and proper equipment, lack of food."

I press her for more details.

She wrinkles her smooth brow above clear, candid eyes.

"The soldiers suffered terribly. Even though officially the Kuomintang and the Liberation Army were allies fighting a common foe, the K.M.T. did everything in their power to prevent medical equipment from reaching our forces. Not that their own were much better treated! The K.M.T. Army Medical Service was corrupt and inefficient. Lump sums were paid over to divisional commanders to organize medical units, but most of the money found its way into the pockets of the officers and the sick and the wounded were left to die.

"But our doctors and nurses were all volunteers like the whole of the Liberation Army. In the first of our medical units organized in the South, workers took an oath to endure what the soldiers and the people endured.

"Our service had tremendous problems, first of all a shortage of trained doctors and nurses, so we used to recruit volunteers among the civilians and train them as we went along. These later formed a battlefield service, so that for the first time in Chinese history soldiers had first aid and many lives were saved.

"But it wasn't only soldiers we looked after, we treated civilians as well. You see, ours was a people's army. We depended on the people for all our needs just as they depended on us for protection. We taught them hygiene, how to control epidemics. Indeed, you might say the Army brought knowledge to the peasants they had never had in all their history. You really had to be many things besides a doctor. We were short of practically everything.

"Lack of drugs was a serious problem. So our chemists used medicinal herbs that Chinese medicine had used for four thousand years and worked out substitutes for others and organized a drug factory to make them."

Her calm face has never altered its expression as she tells this amazing story of medical pioneering. I express my horror at the difficulties.

She smiles. " 'Difficulties were made to be overcome,' they used to say in Yenan where the chief medical factory was established. It had a staff of nearly a hundred directed by chemists who had been trained abroad. It turned out medicines in thirty standard formulas as well as dressings and bandages, and equipment for operations.

"Probably the worst of all was operating in an improvised theatre, sometimes set up in an old temple, very often with little or no anaesthetics, and with surgical instruments made in army workshops. They turned out quite efficient, if not very beautiful, scissors and forceps and scalpels, using as models the few instruments doctors had managed to bring with them. Because of the lack of surgical gloves some of our doctors died of infections contracted when treating infected wounds.

"Although by our modern hospital standards it was terrible, it was better than Chinese soldiers had ever had in history. They knew it and showed their gratitude in appalling conditions by an amazing fortitude. And we saved countless lives that otherwise would have been lost.

"Sometimes today, when I see our hospital equipped with everything modern science can supply, it seems impossible that we did as much as we did. But when all around you is superhuman courage in face of appalling suffering, somehow you, too, rise above your ordinary limitations. You would be ashamed to fail the soldiers and the people."

I try to find out something about her personal experiences but she shakes her head.

"What I did was nothing. The worst part was when we came back we found that our baby had died." Her face saddens. "We have had three other children since, but we still mourn the beautiful child we lost. But we remind ourselves how lucky we are— other mothers and fathers lost all.

"There's nothing very interesting about my life," she concludes.

That, I should say, depends on the point of view.

CHAPTER XXIX

From Beggar-woman to Deputy

WANG SUI-WAN, fresh and clean in white cotton tunic and trousers, grips my hand between her hard palms at the door of one of the workers' flats at Anshan.

She is a tall, raw-boned woman; her broad weathered face is heavily wrinkled round the eyes, with freckles and moles scattered on the leathery skin, and framed by a mop of coarse black hair—a face on which poverty and hardship have set their mark. I am surprised to find that she is only forty-two.

She pours tea for me with big, clumsy hands that tremble as she does so. I am the first foreign friend she has ever met and she is obviously nervous. When I take out my note-book she draws in her breath sharply like someone facing a painful operation.

Without waiting for questions she begins to pour out her story, locking her hands nervously together. Her voice is rough and jerky.

"I was the daughter of a very poor peasant who died when I was only nine, and from then on I followed my grandfather. He was so old that he couldn't work, so I had to beg on the streets for my grandfather, my mother, and my younger brother. We lived in a village some distance from Tientsin.

"It was a feudal-minded world we lived in. The women in our village wanted me to bind my feet, because they thought a girl beautiful only if she had bound feet. But my mother refused, saying, 'How can she go out on the streets and beg if her feet are bound? Will any of you keep us all?'

"But when I was seventeen I, too, began to be ashamed of my normal feet. People used to laugh at me, saying, 'You're half-man, half-girl, with those hideous big feet.' But by then I was pulling a cart to support the family and I thought in despair, 'How can I pull a cart with bound feet?' But eventually the pressure of people's contempt was so strong that I bought ten metres of strong cotton strips and began to bind my feet myself. But it was so painful that I couldn't walk on them, so I had to give up the attempt to be beautiful."

Her nervousness is gone. Her powerful hands gesticulate

rapidly. Her words pour out in a torrent as though she is ridding herself of all the rancours heaped up in the days gone for ever.

"Because I didn't bind my feet no one would marry me. Mothers despised me and refused to consider me as a possible wife for their sons. Finally my mother sold me to a blacksmith seven years older than me. He had seven mou of land. I was nineteen then. The money must have been a great temptation to my mother. I didn't know that I was being sold. I thought I was being married. And my mother didn't tell me what he was like.

"When I found out that I was only a slave I was furiously angry with my mother. But now I realize that, according to her lights, she was doing the best for me. What future was there for me, dragging a cart, despised by everyone? Whatever my life would be in my new home at least I would have some security.

"But it was a terrible life. I was slave to the mother-in-law, and concubine to the blacksmith. He had no interest in me beside that. He beat me when he felt like it.

"My mother-in-law was very cruel to me. She forced me to do all the field-work in summer, and in the winter the housework and the sewing and the mending all fell on me, and she let me have only two bowls of rice a day. To fill the cravings of hunger I used to eat the wild grasses of the fields." Her face flushes darkly, her voice grows hoarse and passionate.

"In the next six years I had three sons, but even that did not make my position in the home any happier. They valued my sons, but not me. And when the Japanese came, life became worse. The father of my sons had no work and went to Tientsin to seek work. But he never sent back any money. Two of my sons died from sickness." She chokes. "I and the only son left to me were literally starving. I set out with him, looking for a job. But the country was in such a state with the war that I could find nothing. I begged on the roads for my son and myself and, finally, I came to Tientsin. I found the father of my son, but he was ill with T.B. and soon died.

"Then I met a man from my native province and we lived together." She grows more tense. "He was a good kind man, not like the father of my son.

"I sold pancakes in the street as a hawker to help us to live, but the Japs even took away my means of making pancakes.

"They press-ganged every able-bodied man, so my man started for the North-west in the hope of getting a job in the liberated areas, and told me to follow with the boy. I and two other women and my son left Tientsin. But on the road we were caught by the troops of the Kuomintang Puppet Government, who said we were Communists and demanded information about them. We had never heard of Communists and pleaded to be released.

"Our hands were beaten until they were so swollen that we couldn't use them.

"We gave them no information. How could we? We didn't know what Communism was, or what it was all about. They flogged us, even the boy. He was only a little boy.

"They said they would shoot us unless they could find someone to guarantee that we were innocent people. An old man came forward and had a talk with them. He was very courageous. He said, 'You can see they are only skin and bone and clothed in rags. Isn't that enough to show you that they are harmless, poor people?'

"We were finally released, nearly dead. It was weeks before my son could walk properly." Her mouth settles into a hard line.

"At last, in our wanderings, we came to Anshan, hundreds of miles to the north. It's all like a terrible nightmare, and I'm not really clear now how we got here. We were skeletons when we arrived. Then I found that the man I had followed all this way had died of the cruelties he had suffered at the hands of the Japs.

"But at Anshan people were kind to the boy and me and helped us. Later on they introduced me to another man. We liked each other and he was good to my boy. He treated him as if he were his own son. This time I was really married.

"My husband worked in the steel-mills, which then were owned by the Japanese. Things were better because at least we had a house to live in, one of the small, old buildings built by the Japs, but, for all that, it was the best house I had ever known.

"Things got worse and worse. We were beaten, kicked, and starved, and every day truckloads of corpses were taken out of the city.

"Then the Japanese were defeated and we thought things would be better. But after the Japanese were thrown out the Kuomintang came. They were worse than the Japs. Then came the Liberation."

She relaxes and for the first time takes a sip of the tea that has grown cold while she talked. Her face clears.

"A whole new life opened up for us. My son was admitted to a primary school. He was a very bright boy, and although he'd had no previous education he soon got double promotion. He did very well at school. He was a fine boy in every way—not like his father. But, because he had been so starved and ill-treated as a child he suffered from heart-trouble. When he was excited his lips would go blue and his heart beat like a bird's. He could not play, though he loved life.

"They took him into the hospital and tried to cure him. Never in my life did I think people could be so good to anyone as they were to him. But he did not improve, so they sent him to the hospital at Shenyang where he could get new treatment." Her voice drops very low, I can scarcely hear her.

"He was there for months. But though the doctors did everything possible he died. He was seventeen."

She sits staring into the past, her face heavy with sorrow. Tears fill her eyes and she dashes them away abruptly. She does not weep. I have a feeling that her grief is of the kind that never found solace in tears. She turns to look directly at me, and her eyes are blazing.

"When I think of the past I am filled with a deep anger. For a while I felt I had nothing to live for. But I have. I have work to do. My husband and I are both working hard in our own way.

"I was elected a group leader in my district, though I was still illiterate. Then I was elected to the Street Committee and finally, although I was still illiterate, I was elected to the District People's Congress.

"It was an awful moment when I first went on the platform to make a speech. My mouth dried up and I couldn't utter a sound.

"I joined a literacy class and now I can write and read newspapers. My work is particularly in the literacy drive among housewives. Now I am director of the Street Committee and, remembering my own unhappy life, I do all I can to see that the people in my area have happy homes.

"Last year I went to Peking, and when Premier Chou En-lai came to Anshan he came to visit me in my own house. I, who in the past had been a beggar, despised by everybody! Do you wonder that I am prepared to give my life to ensure a new world, a peaceful world, though my heart is full of sadness always for my son?"

She puts her hand upon her heart as she leans towards me, her plain face transfigured.

"Though it hurts me I tell you my story. Not because I am proud, but so that you can tell it to women everywhere in the world. Tell them we all have work to do to build a world in which no mother will lose her son as I lost mine."

CHAPTER XXX

Harbin: the Director of the Flax-mill

HARBIN is one of the places I've always wanted to visit. And here I am on my way to Harbin through rich plain land that extends on either side interminably till it is lost in the approaching dusk. Rich and vast under its ripe crops it glows with a strange golden light. Low three-horse carts jingle homewards. A scarlet tractor gleams deserted and solitary in a field. Stooks of sheaves make grotesque patterns against the yellowing stubble. An aeroplane drones over us on its way to Vladivostock.

It is all so vast, so empty, that again it reminds me of home. In the dusk all human differences are obliterated. The earth and the sky might be those I knew as a child.

I get my first glimpse of Harbin through the double panes of my hotel window. (From Shenyang the windows are double to combat the intense cold.) The double glass distorts the view slightly so that I have a picture that reminds me of a French provincial town and a Russian village. Pedestrians hurrying across the wide intersection move like figures in a puppet-film and the painted onion-domes of the little wooden Orthodox church have the air of being tossed on the green foam of the tree-tops. For a city I've hankered after, I feel it's all as it should be.

Kuo Tsin-yuan welcomes me in her attractive office at the modern flax-mill in Harbin. Except for the large managerial desk the room is essentially feminine with its pastel carpet, its tastefully arranged flowers, its lace cloth on the table. Mrs Kuo herself is a plump, well-proportioned woman about forty. Her neat grey woollen slacks are well tailored; her grey striped blouse matches them. The only touch of the feminine appears in the lattice-work grey shoes and matching socks and in her glossy hair turned under at the nape of her neck. If ever a face showed clearly its complete competence to run a large, up-to-date factory, it is hers, though she has a ready laugh and an easy manner.

From the window she shows me the stretches of well-planned garden where workers sit between the brilliant flower-beds and toddlers, whose mothers have taken them from the nursery at the end of the shift, play on the lawns.

"Thirteen hundred of our four thousand factory workers are women and many of them are only in their teens, and it's important that we provide them with all facilities. They're first of all human beings, then workers. It's a lovely place for lovers to wander after work," she adds, "and they make good use of it."

We can hear shouts from some distant sports-field and down in the garden someone is strumming the folk-song that has followed me all over China!

Mrs Kuo's secretary, a bright-faced young man, serves us jasmine-scented tea in fragile bowls.

Briskly, Mrs Kuo tells me the story of the mill which I have just been through. We went from one huge bay to another, seemingly interminable, filled with the latest machinery, seeing the progress of the endless piles of raw flax in their dirty brownish tangles through rows of machines that combed and cleaned and spun and wove and washed and dyed and bleached, till it finished up as canvas, as bagging, as heavy linen, as the finest snow-white cloth that seemed to pour endlessly from washing, sizing, ironing machines until I was lost in a maze of impressions that were still confused as I returned to her office. A mill-worker's dream, anywhere in the world.

I listen to the story of its erection, the installation of the latest machines from the Soviet Union, the training of technicians, the rising output.

Then she gives in minute detail the welfare arrangements for workers, with special emphasis on those for women. Nothing is forgotten. Flats for the workers, a crèche, kindergarten, free medical service, sanatorium, a special clinic as well as a general clinic.

As she talks I find myself devoured with curiosity to know more about her as an individual. The flax-mill is remarkable, up-to-date, efficient. But I soon tire of the most remarkable mill.

Remembering my director of the blast-furnace, I wonder what problems faced her when she took over the post of director, and ask, "Did you have any trouble when you took over?"

She looks at me sharply. "Trouble?"

"Yes. Did the men object to your appointment?"

"Object? Why should they?"

"No reason except that men in the West—"

"You sound like the Member of Parliament from West Germany who came to inspect the mill," she retorts. "He was very much upset when he found me in charge. 'How will men obey women?'

he kept saying. I thought that was his particular hang-over from the teachings of Hitler, but you ask the same question. Surely in British countries where women have been free so long . . . ?"

I skip that one and ask, "But how did you come to be appointed to such a responsible position?"

"I studied under Soviet experts for eighteen months to arm me with the knowledge of the latest machines and methods and all the details of management." She dismisses the subject brusquely.

I am persistent. "Surely it must have taken time to re-educate Chinese men?"

Mrs Kuo laughs—rather pityingly, I feel—at anyone coming from a world with such out-of-date ideas.

"Don't people in foreign countries know that the Liberation wars knocked the stuffing—" Young Chen, the interpreter, has studied a book called *400 Idioms and Slang*—"out of those old feudal ideas? Women worked beside men, fought beside them. They even marched beside them on the Long March. We also shed our blood for Chinese freedom. Is it strange that we should take our place with the men in rebuilding our country?"

That "we" strikes me.

"What part did you play in the Liberation war?" I ask directly. Mrs Kuo calls for direct methods.

She sits silent, looking at me with eyes that are almost hostile. The amiable director has vanished. It is clear she considers me impertinent.

"My past would seem to have nothing to do with the story of the flax-mill," she says, ice in her voice and not even bothering to counter my question with the traditional Chinese courtesy.

"Not with the flax-mill, perhaps, but with your position here."

"I was appointed here because it was considered that my work in the past equipped me to deal efficiently with any problems that might arise in establishing a mill of this type."

From the look she gives my guide and interpreter and from the face she turns to me it is clear she considers the interview closed.

It isn't—for me. I say boldly I am interested in her personal story.

When that is translated her eyes shoot sparks. She restrains herself and merely remarks that she cannot see what her personal life has to do with this at all. She is angry.

I am angry, too. I haven't come across oceans and continents to be satisfied with mills, no matter how modern nor how efficient. I've come to understand Chinese women—yesterday as well as today. I tell her so. I hope Young Chen doesn't water it down. I add for good measure, "You are contemptuous because people in other countries don't understand what has happened to Chinese women and why, but you refuse to help them to understand."

From her expression I think it goes over straight. Waving a ridiculously feminine handkerchief, she shrugs a plump shoulder.

"If that is your reason then I am willing to tell you what I can."

She sits gazing at me for seconds, her keen eyes fixed on mine as though weighing me up. Am I one of these glossy women from glossy magazines she met in the past (I learn this later) trying to glamorize women soldiers, or am I honest?

She frowns. "I will tell you my story on one condition only. When you tell it you must make it explicit that nothing that I have been nor have done has been due to me alone. It is due to the Communist Party of China to which I have belonged for twenty years. My strength and achievement are theirs, my weaknesses are my own. You understand?"

I understand.

She relaxes a little and settles back in her chair, reluctantly preparing to tackle what she obviously considers a distasteful job.

"My 'past', as you term it, really began back in 1935 while I was still a student at Peking University. My father was a public servant in the Railways Service at Harbin. My ambition was to be a doctor or an engineer, but the Japanese invasion of the Northeast put an end to that. At first students like me didn't realize what it meant, though we were very much worried about what they would do to our homes and families. We began to grow more and more disturbed as news filtered through of cold-blooded massacres of innocent people, of every form of robbery and oppression.

"At first it was a personal worry to me—my home-town, my people—but as the Japanese made more and more encroachments I began to realize that what older students said was true: this was a threat to China's existence as a nation.

"Students of eight universities and colleges in Peking began to organize a movement among students and a great demonstration was prepared for 9th December. Very few of us had any politics, but we were patriotic.

"It was bitterly cold midwinter weather. We were very young, but although there was a great deal of excitement among us, deep down we realized that we were protesting against something evil and harmful to China.

"We concentrated near the ancient Drum Tower. The Kuomintang closed the gates to prevent the students from Yenching University, outside the city, from joining us. When this became known the students within the city began to demonstrate.

"One of the leaders from Chinghua University was a girl, Liu Tsai. She rolled herself under the great Hsunchih Gate which was closed against them. Police beat her with the butts of their rifles, but she didn't stop shouting our slogan, 'Stop the Civil War! Unite to resist Japan!'

"They arrested her but when she came out she continued to agitate. On 29th February General Sung Chih-yuan sent a full regiment to the university to arrest her! But I'm running ahead."

She is sitting with her elbows on the table, her face in her hands. It is a young face again. Her voice is deep and vibrant.

"Whatever they did they couldn't stop us on that December day. We marched twenty abreast, arms linked, singing:

> *"We are the rank and file that march forward.*
> *Our wills strong as steel,*
> *Our hearts beating for China.*

"Then we would shout in unison, 'Turn the guns on the invader!' We passed by Tien An Men."

She pauses. I think we're forgotten.

"It all came back to me as I stood in the ranks of the Liberation armies on 1st October 1949 and heard Chairman Mao proclaim the People's Republic of China and watched the red flag with its five golden stars unfurl. . . . It was a long time from the long line of young students I remembered, a long and bitter fight and a lot of them did not live to see the triumph."

She pauses and for a moment I think I see the glitter of tears in her eyes.

"All the fire-engines had been brought out to deal with us that day. The water hit us again and again, knocking us over with its force. It froze on us, but we got up and marched on, our clothes stiff with ice.

"Three times the police dispersed us with fire-hoses, but we broke, went down side-streets, and re-assembled as we had arranged. We were totally unarmed. We were not hooligans or riff-raff. We were students demonstrating to free China of the invaders. We had no guns, no weapons of any kind. But the police struck about them and many among us were hurt. This infuriated the ordinary people. As we came down through the Wang Fu

Ching we were met by soldiers. Though they had orders not to fire they were not gentle! The street was littered with fallen students. Then, strange in a Peking that was not really politically minded, all kinds of unexpected people joined in. In its small way it was a symbol of what was to happen later all over China. Pedi-cab drivers picked up the fallen and drove them to hospitals, refusing to take money for it, even though most were close to starvation. Poor pedlars, who depended on their small sales to live, took the frozen winter pears from their baskets and threw them at the soldiers and the police. They were like stones! I remember seeing one policeman, hit on the forehead, fall with an air of surprise on his face." Her eyes are shining and she laughs infectiously at the picture it brings back.

"Unarmed as we students were, by sheer force of numbers we surrounded the firemen, wrested the hoses from them, and turned them on them to give them a taste of their own medicine."

She is silent for a moment, her eyes far away.

"We were beaten, of course. No!" She brings her small fist down on the table. "No, we were not beaten. It might have looked like defeat. Many students injured, fifty to sixty arrested, others running everywhere to escape, and the streets a shambles with hats and clothing and broken bicycles. But the demonstration influenced all China, and not long after students in Nanking, Shanghai, Tientsin and other big cities did the same. But it was not until long after we realized what a significant part our student protest played in the war against Japanese aggression, since it started a nation-wide protest that used our slogan: 'Stop the Civil War! Unite to resist Japan!'

"It was interesting, too, that it was in no way politically based. For me and most of the students, it was simply patriotic. We wanted to free China. But it taught us that we must fight to attain our objective.

"All those who took part in the student movement were victimized, thus bringing many people into the movement who otherwise would never have thought of it. My father, who was only a liberal, was dismissed from his job on my account. As a result he joined up with the underground movement in Harbin!"

She looks at me with a malicious twinkle in her eye. "And now I've told you all that for your book are you satisfied?"

"Not a bit!" I retort. "There are eighteen years unaccounted for —1935 to 1953 when you came to the flax-mill."

Mrs Kuo sits looking at me with a quizzical expression, tapping her fingers on the table.

"All right," she says at last. There's a look on her face as though she is saying, "Now you're in for it!" I am. For the next two hours my pen races.

"As it was impossible for me to continue my studies at the university after the student rising I left Peking and went to regions occupied by the enemy, where I took part in underground work. My work was to organize the women and mobilize them to take part in the struggle. Generally speaking, our work was to disrupt enemy movements.

"Ours was a People's Army and it could survive and win only by the closest co-operation with the people. We had to explain to the people—especially the women—that we were all one family sharing the same troubles and successes. This was an unknown idea in China. In the old days soldiers were despised; they were known as 'bad iron'. But our army was a volunteer army and people began to be proud of their sons. When they saw the village militia drilling they used to say, 'Look at them beating the good iron into nails!'

"Used to the distinctions in the K.M.T. armies—Chiang Kai-shek used to say, 'Lower rank should not enjoy the same things as higher rank'—they began to realize that ours really was a People's Army when they saw that officers and men dressed alike, lived the same way, and ate the same food. Used to the corruptions of K.M.T. officers who used to embezzle money intended for the food and medicaments for the troops, they were impressed when they saw that in our army everybody received only food and a small living allowance. They had a saying that the relation of our army and the people was that of fish and water.

"To get the maximum of support the villages had to be organized into self-defence corps. This meant that when the army was fighting the village fought, too. At first it was difficult to persuade some of the village women that this war concerned them. As far as they were concerned this war didn't seem very different from what had been happening for the greater part of their lives, with first the armies of war-lords overrunning their villages, robbing and raping, then the Kuomintang and now the Japanese. But they learnt and learnt quickly when they found that we meant what we said and that by organizing they could save themselves from the worst.

"The guerrilla strategy was that when the Japanese came to a village, if it was a superior force the peasant armies disappeared. If it was inferior they attacked. The Japanese didn't know what

to do with these armies that just melted away. They forbade planting of crops along the edge of the road to prevent ambushes.

"At that time the situation was very grave and many women
underground workers were tortured and murdered, but my section
was lucky enough to escape. There are some heroic stories from
those days. Tso I-man organized a guerrilla troop in 1935. She
was shot in the leg, captured, and taken to Harbin where she was
tortured to make her give information. She told nothing. They
sent her to hospital to recover so that they could torture her again.
With the connivance of the hospital staff she escaped, but she
was captured and executed.

"Another time the Japanese hemmed in eight women members
of a guerrilla troop led by Tsung Tse-ming and drove them back
to a steep cliff overlooking the river. They fought till they had no
more bullets left, then they broke their guns and leapt into the
river."

There is a tremor in her voice which she soon controls.

"You cannot defeat a people," she continues. "And new re-
cruits, mainly students, were coming to join us every week, so the
numbers increased in spite of losses. As I heard one of our commanders say in Yenan, 'As individuals we are nothing but as part
of the revolution we are invincible! No matter how many times
the Chinese Revolution dies it will always live again. Only China's
death can kill it.'

"This was about the time of the Sian Incident when Chiang
Kai-shek was kidnapped by his own rebel patriot officers. But even
the proclamation of a united front didn't make much difference.

"At first we made many mistakes. Many of us were city girls like
myself, but we were learning, and learning fast.

"Everyone in the village was given a job. Young men were
trained in guerrilla warfare. Old ones looked after essential village activities such as organizing a general exodus from the village
when they heard from their own espionage that the Japanese were
approaching. Then everything would be collected—all their cows,
their chickens and pigs, their portable valuables and their young
daughters, and they would be sent to hiding-places arranged with
the local partisans. Grain would be buried. If there was a battle
stretcher-bearers would collect the wounded, who were hidden
and cared for by the women, many of whom were trained as nurses.
Other women were trained as teachers and organizers, while old
women were formed into groups to make uniforms and shoes for
the troops.

"Women did all they could to release men for the armies and in doing it learnt to organize themselves democratically. Old women minded babies to release young women for field-work—something previously almost unknown in the conservative North. Younger women acted as transportation workers and scouts. Even children acted as messengers, carrying false-bottomed baskets through enemy-occupied country to deliver messages to fighting units.

"The enemy used to send a lot of spies and secret agents to the villages and usually the first to discover their presence were the women and children who then arrested them and kept them till our army units came.

"When the enemy realized how strong the relationship was between peasants and guerrillas they tried the plan of shifting peasants from their homes to try to starve out the guerrillas. They forced them to burn down their own homes and if they refused they killed them. In one area they built a wall round the new settlement and put guards on the gates. Curfew was imposed. The partisans were forced into the woods, but the peasants still maintained contact and supplied them with food. Sometimes they would carry it to the fields in their baskets and leave it there in pre-arranged hiding-places. Sometimes at night they made a diversion in one part of the village to attract the guards while others crept out with food. It was very risky. The Japs had a regulation that if one family was caught ten families suffered.

"All kinds of tricks were played by the peasants. The Japanese soldiers had a habit of running down girls in the fields, so young peasant boys would dress up as girls, attract the soldiers' attention, and when several chased them run shrieking away, taking care to keep just far enough ahead to entice their followers and lead them into ambushes.

"If you had seen the makeshift weapons our forces had you would have thought it hardly possible that they could fight against an enemy equipped with up-to-date weapons. I've seen men with hand-made guns, old fowling pieces that had been used in the Taiping Revolution a hundred years ago. Improvised workshops learnt to make mortars. Every bit of metal was cherished—a destroyed Japanese plane, an old truck. They learnt to make substitutes for gun-powder.

"And their clothes! I have seen partisans who harassed the enemy in rough and terrible country, their only foot-covering straw sandals or home-made moccasins of goatskin. Men came into us literally in rags. North-eastern peasants were reduced to wearing cloth woven of grass. It looked all right, but it tore in a week.

"I've seen families of four and five with no clothes at all for the children and one pair of trousers between mother and father so that when one went out the other stayed at home. They had no bed covering at all.

"Gradually I moved out of the occupied areas into the liberated areas and finally to Yenan.

"When the Women's University was established I became the General Secretary. Our aim was to train women to continue the struggle for China's liberation.

"As more and more people came to Yenan accommodation problems became acute. So we dug into the surrounding hills to make tiers of caves in the traditional style with connecting stairways zigzagging from one level to another.

"We built everything with our hands—the Yenan University, the Medical University, the Institute of National Minorities, the University of Resistance, the National Political University, and the Women's University."

Looking at her well-manicured hands I can only gasp, "In caves!"

"In caves," she repeats, her eyes twinkling. "It sounds much worse than it was. They were very nice caves. Our university consisted of about two hundred caves connected by a small road and with stairs leading down to the valley. Our living quarters consisted of domed caverns, lime-washed inside to improve the lighting, each about twenty feet deep, ten feet high, and fifteen feet wide. A door and a window fitted into the front and these were chimneys to carry off the smoke from the stoves.

"We had about four hundred women- and girl-students who had come from all over China. Hundreds of patriotic students had hiked through the Japanese-occupied areas and Kuomintang lines to join us."

"And what was your curriculum?" I asked, deliberately choosing an academic word to try to relate this Alice-in-Wonderland University with my own student days.

"It was a mixture of the usual academic courses and emergency education to fit our particular needs. There were courses in foreign languages—English, Russian, and Japanese—in literature and music, in philosophy, history and political economy, social problems, political training courses, public health, accountancy, weaving, spinning and baby-care!

"They were very necessary. The town was surrounded with Japanese forts and pillboxes. We couldn't get food, cloth, or medical supplies through. Everyone had to plough, spin, or weave. Each government worker and student had to reclaim a quarter acre of land and harvest a hundredweight of grain a year. Life came down to its simplest. Agricultural implements were hard to get and blacksmiths made them from poor-grade iron soldiers brought in and the implements were exchanged for hand-woven cloth. Each cave got only a cigarette tin of paraffin for lighting each night and that was our only light apart from candles of goat lard.

"Actually, when you look at it objectively, conditions were bad, but we were so filled with hope and enthusiasm that we hardly noticed that. Our students were of all social backgrounds and educational levels. We demanded only as entrance requirements that a girl should be co-operative and ready to fight for the emancipation of women. The majority of them were from peasant and working-class homes, again pioneering a new field. The aim of our university was to train local leaders.

"An interesting point in the development of China's revolutionary ideas was the fact that most of our students were from Northern China. This was something new in China's history. It used to be said that revolutionary ideas belonged to South China, and you'd never change the conservative North. All the great revolutionaries were southerners, from the leader of the Taiping Rebellion to Sun Yat-sen and Mao Tse-tung. And the first women revolutionaries, like Chiu Chin, came from the South. But the greatest number of our students came from Shantung—the first province conquered by the Japanese! It used to make me think that it's only necessary to tread on people's national pride and the rest follows. I began that way myself.

"It was a hard life, but a very full one in spite of the hardships, the cold, the shortage of clothing, and food. For a long time our only food was millet. We had no salt or vegetables and for a while we lived on prunes, but they were so sour they were practically inedible.

"Yet it was a good life, for we knew what we were fighting for and in spite of everything we never doubted we would win. The people were with us, as we had seen in the villages, and unless you have the people with you there is no lasting victory."

She pauses a moment, her eyes soft and shining, looking back into the past. They harden again.

"The Japanese were beaten. I came back from Yenan to a liberated Harbin—but only to find new and equally bitter struggles awaited us against the Kuomintang. They were as brutal as the Japanese and more corrupt. Among their atrocities was the murder of a fifteen-year-old peasant girl, Liu Hu-lan, in a village they captured. They beheaded her—and many others of her companions—with a primitive guillotine used for cutting grass into chaff.

"During their long occupation the Japanese had done all in their power to corrupt the Chinese youth, but they hadn't succeeded. Altogether they killed a hundred thousand resistance workers. Now, the Kuomintang turned on the Chinese nationalists, accusing them of being Communists. The struggle now was even worse than against the Japanese, because the Kuomintang were armed with up-to-date American weapons and had many more planes.

"One of our leaders, General Lei Tsao-lin, was caught by them. He had fought the Japanese for fourteen years. He was a good man, a good soldier, a patriot. But he was betrayed by a local spy. They killed him. We found his body with eight knife wounds in his chest. The K.M.T. announced that if they found his followers they would be killed in a worse manner."

She looks beyond me, her face stern: the face of judgment.

"We tracked his betrayer down and executed him before Lei Tsao-lin's grave.

"On 2nd November 1948 the whole North-east was liberated."

When she looks at me at last she is Kuo Tsin-yuan the director. She smiles.

"And now China is free at last. And I, who all these years since leaving the university have been a leader of the Women's Movement, am now director of a flax-mill. Are you satisfied?"

Next evening at my farewell dinner-party, for the flash of a second I don't recognize my efficient factory director in the gracious, smiling woman in a long *chi-pao* of turquoise brocade, from beneath which peep embroidered satin slippers. She is a good dinner companion with a quick wit and ready laughter. She spends a lot of time telling me about her three children. . . .

CHAPTER XXXI

Harbin-Peking

UP at 6 a.m. for the plane. The legend of my fragility has revived—a train-trip back to Peking would be too much for me!

A sparkling morning, dew on the grass and the sky flecked with cloud.

I stammer my farewell and a welcome to Australia in uncertain Chinese. My friends understand. Their smiles are also a little strained. I have a lump in my throat as I wave from the window, watching the two figures recede against the green of the airport. Never have I left a place so briefly known with so much regret.

This is no luxury plane. Half passenger, half freight, but comfortable and clean, with a solicitous crew that insists I share its tea though ordinarily none is provided for passengers on the short trip.

Prominent among the freight are piles of mail, bags bearing—like all postal material in China—the words *"Postes Chinoises"* under the Chinese inscription. No one has ever explained to me why all Chinese postal material bears French as well as Chinese.

There are only five passengers to share the pile of green blankets.

Below, endless villages like clumps of building blocks are scattered over a patchwork quilt of fields.

Changchun, like a park among its trees, its new buildings raw against the gashed earth.

Shenyang, where the cloud-shadows lie bruise-blue on the green and gold and beige-coloured fields and the smoke-stacks scrawl untidy arabesques on the sky.

I look through a pile of illustrated periodicals. My companions read daily papers, each one different.

That, and hunting an amazingly agile fly that got on at Shenyang, keeps everyone occupied.

I marvel once more at the high quality of the publications as well as their variety, with their fine colour printing. Then I settle down with the cartoon-weekly that satirizes everything—domestic and world affairs.

We fly low over black crenellated ranges gashed with scored cliffs and crags, above yellow rushing torrents that foam into open valleys looking like crazy pavements with their intricate terracing.

The Great Wall rides a razor-edged range 1200 feet high. Eastward the coastline—an indented matrix edged with turquoise waters lost in haze. Westward, a backdrop from the mountains of the moon.

An island rising like Capri, the waters of a fan-shaped delta sprinkled with sails of junks, like sharks' fins. Walled towns like something out of the Middle Ages. Villages beginning where the last village leaves off. The crowded life of the coastal areas. Tientsin, enormous, modern, a blur in the midday heat.

And in the early afternoon, the Western Hills, the Summer Palace, the Jade Fountain, Peking.

CHAPTER XXXII

Mist and Flower Maidens

IN the old days Chinese and Westerners alike wove romantic tales round the "Mist and Flower Maidens", poetic euphemism for licensed prostitutes.

Folk-songs and stories and poems and plays enshrined their fame and their sorrows. Westerners, seduced by the quaintness of the exotic façade, painted a flattering portrait of "Willow Lane" —picturesque term for the segregated brothel areas of Chinese cities, whose 2700 years of existence ended only with the abolition of prostitution in 1949.

There, in licensed houses with alluring names—such as "The Band of Kingfisher-coloured Fairies", "The Band of Literature and Flowers"—"Precious Pure One", "Flying Cloud", "White Jade" and "Peach-blossom", to give only a few samples of their professional titles, enchanted all comers with their charm, their beauty and their accomplishments.

Today, from Harbin on the fringes of Siberia, to Canton in the tropic South, in Peking and Shanghai, Tientsin, Nanking, Wuhan, and Tsingtao, in large towns and small villages over seven thousand miles of China, I heard the same tremendous claim: "We have abolished prostitution."

It set me wondering. How had China achieved what the West cynically regards as impossible? What kind of life had replaced the old?

I recalled the warning of the Old China Hand before I left London: "You don't want to believe what they tell you out there about the horrors of the brothels in the old days. Very well run. Very clean. Nice atmosphere. Happy girls, always smiling. Accomplished, too. Singing, dancing, and all that, you know. Entertaining. Communists talk a lot of nonsense. Bad as the missionaries."

I had a vague memory of Pierre Loti's *Les Amours des Chinois* in my mind, and I reread the report of a French journalist who a year or so before had visited a reformatory at Shanghai and written a depressing account of the former prostitutes he had seen there—poor, spiritless creatures who, he implied, would clearly be happier back in their old lives.

Then I read a carefully documented social survey made in pre-revolution Peking under the auspices of Princeton University and the Young Men's Christian Association, factual, objective and horrifying.

I found that figures given by reliable authorities after the First World War estimated that Shanghai and Peking had the highest number of recognized prostitutes pro rata of any great city in the world. Tokyo was third.

I discussed the subject with Lao Sheh, author of the famous *Rickshaw Boy*, who is said to know more about old Peking than anyone alive. He told me that in the two decades before Liberation, warlordism, Kuomintang corruption and Japanese occupation had intensified the poverty and the demoralization that the Princeton University Survey showed to be at the root of what it delicately called "the Social Evil". His powerful novel *Yellow Storm* gave me a glimpse of what happened in Peking during the ten years of Japanese Occupation when the number of illicit "half-closed doors" increased greatly.

An American woman and a New Zealander who had known Shanghai for thirty years told me what conditions there used to be.

I began to suspect that the Old China Hand and the French journalist had a rather superficial view of the subject and decided to find out for myself the truth behind the exotic façade of Willow Lane from the women who had provided the "entertainment" and those who had helped them to take their place in the new society.

Gradually I pieced together from interviews and old documents the story of the sing-song girls, the dancing girls, professional entertainers and prostitutes who flourished in close connection with brothels, their badge—in keeping with the poetry—a spray of peach-blossom, age-old symbol of "loose" or "light" women.

Their history goes back a long way. Two thousand seven hundred years ago Kuan Chung, Minister at the Court of one of the Emperors of Wu, established the system of licensed houses limited to certain districts. His object was to encourage visiting traders to leave behind a proportion of the money they made in the State of Wu—a method of indirect taxation guaranteed painless. The taxes collected from the brothels were used to repair the roads and maintain the police. (I think of the Ponte Sisto in Rome built from the Papal taxes imposed on prostitutes in the fifteenth century.)

A study of the police regulations before 1949 shows that the traffic was organized to the last detail. Intending brothel-keepers had to obtain a permit from the police, first providing proof of their "good" character and suitability to conduct a house of public entertainment.

The fee for the licence depended on the quality of the house they intended to establish, whether first, second, third, or fourth class. The lines of demarcation were strictly observed. The number of girls permitted to each house was carefully set down and a set amount of tax paid per inmate, graded according to their class and whether they were adult professionals or little slave-girls serving a type of apprenticeship.

According to the police regulations, foreign brothels were not permitted in Peking, but they existed. The police were afraid to interfere with them since they were largely patronized by the soldiers and staff in the Foreign Legations. Though there were some Chinese inmates, most were Japanese and there were also European women, chiefly White Russians and Austrian Jewesses.

Apparently there was nothing to distinguish these brothels from their counterparts anywhere in the world.

Willow Lane, however, presented a different face. Higher-class girls (generally known as sing-song girls) resented being classed with prostitutes and protested, unavailingly, after the First World War at being obliged by the police to wear the peach-blossom as a badge, declaring loudly that they were not prostitutes but professional entertainers.

Leaving aside romantic stories, everything I read and heard concurred to show that the licensed segregated areas were quite unlike the red-light districts of Western countries.

The brothels *were* orderly and well run. Police regulations ensured it. The drunkenness and rowdiness that characterizes such areas in the West *were* absent. Prostitutes were not allowed to drink. (They often took drugs.) On the surface everything—at least in the first- and second-class houses—*was* clean. (In 1949 over ninety per cent of the licensed prostitutes were found to be suffering from venereal disease!)

"Precious Pure One", "Flying Cloud", and "White Jade" *were* always smiling. They knew what awaited them if they were not, because "public women", whether famous courtesans or worn-out drudges, were virtually slaves who had no hope of escape except by death or purchase as a concubine.

Always smiling, too, according to an anonymous enthusiast, were "the doll-like little girls who flitted like gorgeous butterflies about the public entertainment rooms, learning to sing and dance from their older sisters".

He forgets to mention that they were slave-girls purchased

young to serve an apprenticeship in the brothel till they were old enough to be initiated into the profession.

The houses provided a variety of services, in addition to those normally associated with brothels. Food, drink, entertainment, gambling. It is interesting that gambling, encouraged in the first- and second-class houses because the house got its percentage, was forbidden in the third and fourth class, since it was considered that their *habitués* could not afford to risk a penny.

One list of "services" and prices I have beside me records these items:

> *Dinner-party.*
> *Sitting and talking.*
> *Serving melon-seeds.*
> *Playing dominoes.*
> *Spending the night.*

Prices were graduated according to the class of brothel.

In Peking there was little soliciting. There was no necessity. The traffic was so accepted that the daily newspapers made large profits from advertising the houses, and pictures of the girls were placed beside the advertisements. In some of the old Peking newspapers whole pages were filled with prostitutes' advertisements. These gave the girl's photograph, her name, address, telephone number, and a flowery description in keeping with the poetic nomenclature that traditionally glossed over the reality of the profession. "Her face is like a flower and her body like a jewel." "She is as lovely and beautiful as the moon." "She is seventeen years old. Though she is not beautiful she is able to act dramas. Mr Chu An loves her very much and sends this picture to us."

Restaurants and tea-shops also displayed advertisements and second-class women frequently sang in lower-grade theatres.

While police regulations forbade houses to have windows or porches facing the street, the entrances to the courts were distinguished by electric lanterns and the class and name. In the evenings the girls' professional names, written on glass or wood or embroidered in silk, were hung round the front entrance.

The type of women naturally varied with the type of brothel. In the first-class houses girls were rarely more than eighteen years old. They were attractive and beautifully dressed in rich clothes. Many were accomplished, having been trained for years as entertainers. Unless a girl married or was bought as a concubine— remote dreams for most!—her period as a star attraction was short. Her tragic progression was sale to the second, then to the third, then to the fourth class, to be thrown out when she was "old" and useless—if she lived as long!

It was not unusual for rich officials to give feasts in their own homes for famous courtesans—feasts from which their wives and families were excluded. As a Chinese said to me, "The moral standard was very strict for women and very loose for men—just as in your countries!"

The less expensive brothels provided warmth and light and entertainment as well as more obvious pleasures, and a considerable proportion of the population, whose hopeless poverty made it impossible for them to marry, found their satisfaction there for a few coppers. It is easily understandable why venereal disease was so widespread.

Nowhere in the world perhaps, did the general term of "Social Evil" describe it so accurately, for Chinese prostitution was the direct product of a series of factors inherent in the old semi-feudal society.

A basic factor was the low status of women. The old family system with its emphasis on the seclusion of women and their exclusion from any educational facilities made it difficult for any real companionship to develop in marriage. And with four or five generations living under one roof, home life could hardly have been described as restful.

Under the rigid system of seclusion the female members of the family were not permitted to meet male strangers. Thus it was customary for high officials and rich business-men to entertain their friends in a licensed house, not necessarily with sex as a primary attraction. Important dinner-parties were held there.

And the girls who provided the entertainment? Whatever the minor differences between individual life-histories, behind the charming, talented creatures in their rich silks and satins lay the same sordid reality. Poverty! The overwhelming majority of them were sold into the traffic when they were young, sometimes only infants. In the years of flood and famine little girls were sold openly on the streets, though theoretically the sale of children was prohibited. Others were kidnapped; there were gangs who specialized in this. In the brothels they became habituated to the atmosphere, and, according to talent and looks, were given courses of singing and dancing, conversation, and the art of entertaining. And then?

Let an old folk-song tell the story:

Mist and flowers in Willow Lane,
Faces bright with harlot's rouge,
I seem among fairy maidens.
I am imposed on, wronged by father, mother,
Who, grasping, greedy, covet silver, gold.
They sell me.
Tears stream. Body is lowered, dishonoured.

Age ten and three; ten and four;
Ten and five; ten and six.
Slave is compelled to be gay,
Selected for lust.
Ten and seven; ten and eight—
I strive to please,
Lead guests to my bedroom.
Am flattered, caressed, receive money.

Don woman's skirt and hairpin.
Three inch, gold-lotus feet
Lie upon ivory bed;
Flowers-of-ecstasy-bud
Man's lust envelopes me.

Gifts are bestowed—silver, gold.
If gifts do not come of silver or gold
Leathern whip descends.
Tears stream down little face.

Years of youth may be bright spring
But sad years of age of the courtesan—
Everyone, everyone scorns me;
Eyes of contempt regard me.

Years pass—three tens,
Am withered and worn.
Can withered flower bloom?

Desire all day, every day,
To be led by the hand;
Desire a pillow in common, desire to share a bed
United behind a bridal curtain.

Oh! Vouchsafe this forthwith.
Would follow a husband;
Would escape, go out, from Mist Flower Lane.

The director of the knitting factory met me at the arched gate of a typical Peking house. As she led me across the first court where scarlet zinnias blazed in the sunshine, she explained that only the offices of the factory were located there; the factory, a modern building, was situated behind.

"A makeshift," she explained, "but we are expanding so fast that the builders cannot keep up with our needs."

I was not interested in the factory. I was to meet a reformed prostitute who was working there.

I tried to keep a purely objective attitude, but a faint sense of guilt nagged me. Was it fair to ask an unfortunate woman to recall the past from which she had escaped? From my experience in other countries, I knew only too well how reluctant women are to be reminded of it. Would I, perhaps, damage her newly found confidence? Who knew what ghosts I might set walking?

But how, I asked myself, was the miracle wrought? For I must know. And here I was to have the chance.

I hardened my heart as the director led me into a low, lime-washed room.

A young woman rises from a desk and comes to greet me. Tall for a Chinese, she moves with the grace of an athlete in her dark-blue woollen slacks and crimson cardigan. Her skin is a clear light brown, her eyes are full, though obliquely set, and it is the first time in China I have met eyebrows that actually slant upwards at the corners. Smiling, she takes my hand in both of hers—well shaped, strong—and her beautifully moulded lips reveal perfect teeth. Two small plaits reach to her shoulder and give her an air of a sixteen-year-old.

"This is Chen Chin-yang," the director explains. "She was on the looms for six years and was recently appointed to an administrative job. She has many distinctions and last year she was chosen to go to the Advanced Workers' Conference of All China."

Chin-yang blushes and smiles as she asks me to sit down. The director inquires, "Where is Huang Su-yu?"

"She's not come yet," Chin-yang tells her.

The director goes off to make inquiries.

The thought strikes me that perhaps my "victim" has had an attack of stage-fright at the last moment. I shouldn't blame her.

The telephone rings. With a gesture of apology Chin-yang takes up the receiver. She deals with the call promptly and efficiently; a veteran executive could not do better. Then she comes back and sits down beside me at the low table and pours the flower tea.

While waiting I make conversation.

"Were you born in Peking?" I ask, wondering from what part of China she came, since I had never previously met her type.

"No. I came from Shanghai," she replies, busy with her duties as hostess and opening a packet of cigarettes for me.

Still making conversation, for my interest today is not this efficient, charming executive, I ask, "How long have you lived here?"

"Since 1948."

I am interested. I sense a story.

"And how did you happen to come from Shanghai to Peking at the worst phase of the Civil War?"

The packet of cigarettes in her hand, she pauses a fraction of a second, her eyes gazing directly into mine.

"The landlord sold me."

I put down my cup.

She goes on rapidly. "My father was a peasant on the outskirts of Shanghai. He was landless, got into debt to the landlord, and the landlord insisted that, as surety for the debt, I must be sent to his house as a maidservant. I was not yet fourteen.

"When I had been there a few months the landlord sold me to a trader who went round the villages looking for girls for brothels. My value was a picul of rice for each year of my age. He brought me to Peking. I thought I was going to a factory. It was a brothel. I never saw my parents again, and although I've made inquiries I've never been able to trace them." Her voice drops and tears glisten in her eyes.

"I was a year and a half in the brothel. It was terrible. I was in one of the hutungs outside the Chien Men and, from what I've heard from other girls since, I was treated comparatively well. But we were slaves, and our treatment depended on how much money we could hand over to the brothel-keeper. If you handed over as much as he thought you could make, he laughed. If you handed in less he beat you. Always there were sounds of beatings. Because I was too independent I was beaten more often than some of the others. Actually we were well fed, had plenty of rich clothes, cosmetics, everything to make us attractive. But physically and mentally, I suffered terribly." Her face expresses her disgust and she makes a gesture as though to put it all behind her.

"Once I appealed to the police. But the K.M.T. police were hand in glove with the brothel-keepers." Her voice is low and intense. "It's very hard to bring back those days. Now it's all like a bad dream. I had to receive customers, no matter how I felt. Once I was pregnant and the brothel-keeper gave me some medicine to bring on an abortion. And a week after I was forced back to work."

She has given the story breathlessly as though to get it over. She pauses and sighs. When again she looks at me directly the strained expression on her face has gone.

"When the Liberation came lots of the girls were terrified. But I felt that nothing could be worse than what had happened to me. Our brothel-keeper was taken away. After a trial he was imprisoned. He had been a brute, but he had never murdered anyone. Our house was one of those that was turned into a reformatory.

"I was four months in the reformatory—four months of the happiest time in my life until then. A funny thing, although the food wasn't as good as that we had had in the brothel most of us grew fatter. We were divided into groups of eight, and, after morning drill, we had classes that taught us the history of our country and explained to us how it was that landlords could sell us, and of the corruption of the police which prevented us from escaping. And we had literacy classes. I soon learnt to read.

"I like novels best," she added, and I hid a smile at what sounded so inconsequential.

"In the evening we had recreational activities. After four months I asked could I go to work in a factory. It was here that my new life began. I was keen to learn. Other workers helped me. They were very good to me. In my spare time I continued to study." She laughs in what plainly is sheer happiness.

"It would take hours to tell you the good things that have happened to me. Now I'm an administrative worker, and my aim is to help make the factory as good as possible and to continue to improve my educational standard. New China has given me a new life and I must do all in my power to build a better country for us all.

"It is a good life. I like sports and I was soon good enough to qualify for the basketball team. We have dancing every week, and sometimes we go to the cinema and the opera. We never tire of talking over our plans and hopes in our little flat in the big block belonging to the factory."

"We?" I query.

"My husband and I."

"You didn't tell me you were married."

She sparkles. "You didn't ask me. In the spring of this year I married one of the technicians in this factory."

There is a timid knock at the door. She calls, "Come in!" and it opens slowly. A woman enters. Mrs Chen crosses the room and puts her arm across her shoulder, and presents her, saying, "My very good friend, Huang Su-yu. Her husband is also a technician here."

Although the new-comer looks considerably older Mrs Chen has an almost protective attitude towards her. This time I am prepared. I move quickly to her and take her hand. I see the shadow of her past upon her—something indefinable, a look in the eyes. In spite of the permed hair she is unmistakably one of the peasant women I have met in so many villages, though her blue woollen jumper and brown woollen slacks show that she earns much more than the average.

Mrs Chen tells me proudly that Huang Su-yu, too, has received awards three years running for her excellent work. Only then does a smile break Su-yu's heavy look, though nothing can take the sorrow from her eyes.

It is some time before she is at ease with me. We talk about her work in the factory. I ask about her husband.

She clasps her hands and sits nervously on the edge of her chair, as though screwing up her courage. She looks at Mrs Chen, who nods encouragingly as though to tell her that although I'm a foreigner, I really am a nice person.

I begin in a voice which I hope truly reflects the sympathy I feel. "Mrs Chen has been so good as to tell me her story. If you feel that you can do so I'll be grateful if you'll tell me yours."

She is silent and my heart falls. Then she bursts into rapid speech as though speed makes what she has to say less distasteful.

It is an unusual opening: "That's what made me study and work so hard. It doesn't seem possible I can be so happy after the nine dark and terrible years I spent in the brothels."

She is silent, breathing fast. She looks at her hands. Her voice drops to a whisper. "I sometimes pinch myself to see whether I'm awake and it's all true."

Then once more she bursts out: "My father was a peasant in Hopei Province. My mother died when I was very young. It was a famine year in our district and she gave the food that might have kept her alive to my sister and me. After that, I lived with my grandmother and my father. Then my father fell in love with another woman and he didn't want two daughters around the place with his new wife, and a distant relative came to the village and said she would look after me. I was then fourteen. She said she would take me to a town near by where I could get work. Instead, she brought me straight to Peking, and when we got here she told me: 'I've got no more money and I've sold you to a brothel.'

"That was almost fifteen years ago in the midst of the Japanese Occupation. I was taken to a brothel somewhere near the Temple of Heaven. For nine years it was hell."

A flush rises to her high cheekbones and the broad jaws set hard. Her hands are squeezed so tightly that the knuckles show white. She raises eyes full of suffering.

"We were worse treated than girls in the high-class brothels, where she was," she says, nodding towards Mrs Chen. "Ours was a poor-class brothel and therefore it was harder to earn enough money to satisfy the brothel-keeper. We had to receive so many men that most of us were in bad health. Sometimes I was so sick that I simply couldn't receive men and then the brothel-keeper would rage and beat me with bamboo cane and give me very little food.

"There were a dozen of us there and we lived in a state of constant terror, fearing that what had happened to one of the girls when she was sick would happen to us, for we'd heard the lid of the coffin being nailed down while we knew she was still alive."

She looks at me and her face shows indignation, hatred. "Animals would have been treated better. I was sold from one brothel to another, each worse than the last. They didn't care whether I was sick or died. All I was frightened of was of being buried alive.

"Then one day some police came, closed the brothel, arrested the brothel-keeper and took us girls away. I thought, 'This is the end!' and I hoped it would be quick. I was so near the end of life, anyway, that I didn't care.

"We were taken to one of the big reformatories and then doctors came. Now I was sure. 'I'm so sick they'll just get rid of me, I'm not worth putting in prison,' I said to myself. I realize now that I must have been as near to the end, so far as my sickness was concerned, as I really thought I was. Once when I wakened and found them bending over me with a hypodermic syringe raised, I screamed with terror and fought. They were very patient and explained that what they were doing would cure me and bring me back to health.

"They were so kind and gentle that gradually I lost my suspicions and fears, though I couldn't understand why anyone should take so much trouble with me. Never since my mother had died had anyone shown me any kindness or love. My health improved slowly. When I was strong enough I went to a literacy class. I'd never been to school before."

A slow smile transforms her face. "Then there were the other classes. The teachers explained that what had happened to us wasn't our fault and we must not be ashamed of the past, but try to get happiness out of the future.

"I had a lot of handicaps, but I determined to study hard. I simply lived for the day when I should be well enough and educated enough to go out and earn my own living and at last be like everyone else.

"Do you wonder that I work hard? And not only me, but all the other women with me? More than half of the women who came from the brothels to this factory are model workers. They feel that this is such a small return for the new life given them. I've been given a new life in more ways than one. All the care and treatment gave me back my health and now. . . ."

She doesn't finish the sentence, but the smile has come back to her face and the light in her eyes makes it unnecessary.

Arm in arm, the three of us went out through the courtyard, talking and laughing. At the gate, after a moment's hesitation— I'm a foreigner, should they do it?—their arms went round my neck, their cheeks were pressed against mine.

I looked back at them waving at me from the archway, smiling in the bright sunshine. Why worry about ghosts walking in a country that no longer believes in ghosts?

The story of one of the greatest social experiments in history was told to me in Peking by two of the women who were actively engaged in the work from the first, and in Shanghai by the director of the Women's Centre. Except for local details, the stories follow the same course, so I shall tell them together.

Liu Mai is now director of the Women's Federation in a district of Peking, a plump, dark-faced woman with great strength in her face, brilliant eyes with a glint of humour in them, and a bush of springy hair.

Chin Sin-lien, secretary to the director of the Women's Federation in Peking, is a complete contrast. Small and vivacious, with a pointed face framed by straight glossy hair, dancing almond eyes, and a smile that reveals perfect teeth—nothing less like the conventional picture of a reformatory director could be imagined.

They both looked so young that I was astonished that such a tremendous task should have been entrusted to them.

"How did you come to be appointed to the job?" I asked.

"Looking back on it, we sometimes wonder ourselves," Liu Mai replied. "I was only twenty. I had been a student in Peking till my appointment, and as I wasn't married at the time, I really had little idea of what the problem of the prostitutes was."

"It was the same with me," said Chin Sin-lien, "but when we realized the real horrors of the prostitutes' lives we both felt we had a responsibility to help them take their place in the New China we all wanted to build.

"The Republic was proclaimed on 1st October 1949, and a month later the provisional Congress adopted a resolution to close all brothels. All licensed brothels in Peking were closed in one night. The larger houses were turned into reformatories and the Government told the prostitutes that the houses now belonged to them, since they had bought them with their flesh and blood."

"The first days were very difficult." Mrs Liu shook her head at the memory. "The girls had been told terrifying stories by the brothel-keepers about what would be done to them, and when we came to take over it was sheer pandemonium. Some tried to escape, others shouted and fought, others had hysterics, and others sat, hopeless and sullen and suspicious, waiting for the worst to happen."

"Could you blame them?" Mrs Chin broke in. "We learnt later, when we had won their confidence, that they were all expecting death in one form or another."

"The high-class prostitutes were naturally the most difficult problem," Mrs Liu said. "I still remember one. She wore a tight satin dress and had her hair elaborately done and stood with the tears rolling down her carefully rouged cheeks, packing her personal goods into a bundle and casting a last regretful look at the room she had occupied for so long.

"A few hours later I went with her to the room she was to occupy in the larger house that had been turned into a reformatory. The furniture from her old room had been moved to her new one. She came in, looked round as though she could not believe her eyes, went up to the cage in which her pet bird was chirping, opened a few drawers, and when she found everything intact sat down at the table, put her head on her arms, and sobbed as though her heart would break. All of them were very touched when they found that their personal possessions, instead of being confiscated, were all in their new rooms."

"Since Shanghai presented quite different problems from Peking," the director of the Women's Centre there explained, "we had to tackle it differently. Besides, we had additional urgent social problems, such as our many beggars and vagabonds, so it was thought that our best approach was to educate the brothel-keepers first. So, soon after Liberation it was explained to them—except those charged with murder—that there was no place in the new society for their 'profession'.

" 'In the past,' they were told, 'you were able to exploit human beings because the old society condoned it. But no one will support you now. Besides, the prostitutes are free to leave your houses. They are already leaving in large numbers.'

"By the end of 1949, seeing that what we said was true, all but seventy-two brothels closed down. In November 1951 the Shanghai Municipal People's Congress banned prostitution entirely, and the seventy-two brothels were closed.

"All the bad brothel-keepers were given public trials, as in Peking. We brought the worst of the old brothel-keepers to the reformatories and told the girls that they could say in front of them what had been done to them.

"At first no one would speak. Then one started, telling about a sick girl she had seen nailed in a coffin while she was still alive. Another told how she had seen a girl branded with a red-hot iron. This punishment for those who tried to run away had not been unusual, but all the girls to whom it had happened were dead at the time of Liberation. Then everybody started pouring out the horrors of their own lives and the hate in their hearts till I thought it would never stop.

"If you could have seen those scenes! The brothel-keepers—men and women—on the platform, arrogant at the beginning, certain that they could dominate the girls as they had always done. The girls below in the hall, growing more and more angry and excited as one accusation led to another.

"One after another they would rush up to the platform, eyes blazing, fingers pointed accusingly, the words pouring out in a furious torrent. Sometimes they would break down and weep. Other times they would be so carried away that they would surge forward in a mass prepared to deal out justice themselves.

"Often we had to protect the brothel-keepers. You see, this was not a trial. It was a method of giving the girls confidence in themselves and in us, and of collecting evidence.

"It had a triple value. Telling their stories cleansed their hearts of guilt and bitterness and released them from their past. It freed them for ever from the fear of the master. It gave us the information we required. This was sifted and, if verified, used as evidence when the brothel-keepers appeared in the ordinary court of law.

There, sentences were imposed according to their offences. Those who had blood-crimes were executed. Others were imprisoned and those who had no crimes against them were given land and sent back to their villages to be re-educated by labour, according to the old Chinese saying: 'Using your own fist to slap your face.'

"A film was made which showed the life of a fourteen-year-old girl whose mother was forced by poverty to bring her to the city to find a job. She was tricked into signing a form which she thought was for a factory, but found it was a brothel. This was something familiar to them all. All the incidents in the film were taken from actual stories told by the girls. When it was shown to them it was heart-breaking to hear them sobbing their hearts out, for there wasn't a thing in the story that didn't touch them one way or another."

When later I saw the film, preceded by a documentary on the reform of Peking prostitutes, I understood. I have never seen a film of such moving sincerity. Simple, factual, it omitted nothing of the horror of the girls' lives. Nothing was done to exploit the merely sensational. There was no vulgar scene, none sexually titillating. Terrible always, sometimes heart-rending, it rose at times to high levels of beauty and dignity, and finished with a song, "Stand up, Sisters!" that must have moved the prostitutes to the depth of their hearts.

Mrs Liu gave me further details of the way in which the girls were led to a new life.

"It was not easy," she said, "for staff as well as girls had to learn as we went along. From the first we tried to make them feel they were our sisters and by our love and sympathy to win their trust and affection. Never was there any touch of moral reprobation or condescension in our attitudes, and gradually, because they were unaccustomed to disinterested kindness and consideration, they began to respond.

"Since there was no line of demarcation between staff and girls in our reformatories they got on very well. They worked together and played together. We impressed upon them the idea: 'It is not your fate to be a prostitute. If you try to make a new life no one will look down upon you. It was not your fault, but that of society.'

"In order to make them feel that they had come back into a world that loved and cared for them, we encouraged relatives and friends to come and visit them. If any of the girls had children they had lost touch with, we tried to find them and bring them to the mothers, who most often were young widows forced into brothels by debt.

"At first we gave them a uniform, but when we found that had a bad effect on them we let them choose their own clothes.

"Because most of them were young—prostitutes did not live long," she explained, "their recreational life was important. So they were taught to play games and do physical culture and dancing. Choral groups were formed and they composed songs themselves. They made up short plays and performed them. Since these plays dealt mainly with incidents familiar to them from their own lives it helped to work out their bitterness. After they were played we would organize discussions, and they would tell their experiences in the past and their hopes for the future.

"Sixty per cent were illiterate when they came in. All finished by being able to read simple books and write simple letters. Some of the highly trained first-class girls—sing-song girls and entertainers—went into opera troupes and song and dance ensembles. Many girls have married, since men don't despise them, saying it is the present that counts, not the past."

"What conditions were necessary before they could leave?" I asked.

"Before they could leave they must be cured of their diseases; they must really understand the reason for their past life and have no desire to return to it; they must be able to support themselves, or, if not, have some relation they could depend on to support them.

"One after another applied to work in factories. Out of one hundred and fifty in Mrs Chin's section, thirty went to factories, forty joined sewing co-operatives, some became nurses, and some went back to their old villages where they were given land."

Here are a few snapshots of some of the girls who passed through the Women's Production and Education Centre in Shanghai. I tell the stories unadorned.

Nothing about Chu Yu-yin indicates the past from which she has escaped as she stands, surrounded by small children, on the lawn of the kindergarten where she is a governess. She is a beautiful woman, slim, of moderate height, with big eyes that dance in her pale face.

"I was born in a village, daughter of peasants," she says. "My parents were murdered during the first years of the Anti-Japanese War when I was not yet fifteen. I was taken in by another family. The man pretended he was going to find work for me in a factory and brought a contract form, which I signed with my finger-prints since I could not read or write.

"When I reached my new 'home' in the Foochow district I was told that it was a brothel and the contract that I had signed bound me to stay there. I was ordered to receive a man in my room. I refused. The brothel-keeper forced me to kneel on a ribbed washing board while she beat me with split bamboo laths until I was unconscious." She broke down and wept bitterly, as though even the memory was too much for her.

"I tried to run away and appealed to the police to help me. But the police were in collaboration with the brothel-keepers, who bribed them with a good sum each month. The contract was produced. They brought me back to the brothel. I was warned what would happen to me if I tried to escape again.

"I did try. I was captured and beaten until I could not walk. And when I had recovered I was put back into the brothel. I was there for twelve years. I don't want to speak of those years. When clients found I was diseased they refused to lie with me. I was so terrified of the brothel-keeper that I would go down on my knees and beg them to take me.

"The brothel-keeper gave me cocaine. At the start I did not know what it was.

"When I was brought to the reformatory after Liberation I thought they were going to kill me. I thought the lack of cruelty was a trick. I tried to run away. I had venereal disease and tuberculosis, I was a drug addict. They sent me to a clinic, despite my protests. They were so kind that my suspicions vanished. I had never known such kindness. When finally I was discharged from the hospital as completely cured my whole life was changed. I realized I, too, had a chance to lead a decent useful life."

Chou Yin is a governess in a kindergarten. She is plumpish, and when I met her wore a blue *chi-pao* split to the knee. Pretty, with big eyes in an oval face, she spoke in a quiet voice and in a tone as if discussing a clinical case, something far removed from her.

"I came from a village and it was the poverty of my parents that sent me to the brothel. I spent many years there. At one stage I became pregnant. The brothel-keeper forced me to have an abortion. The next day he sent men to me as usual. I had three abortions in all. Many prostitutes in Shanghai in those days died from abortions. The third time I had a haemorrhage, a very serious one.

"I was in one of the brothels that did not close down voluntarily when the People's Government came, and when I was brought to the reformatory in 1951 I had two small children, born after Liberation.

"I was allowed to bring my babies with me to the reformatory. They were put in a special nursery and I could see them while I was undergoing treatment for my various diseases.

"Today I have not only the happiness of a new life for myself but the knowledge that my children will never suffer as I did, but will grow up into well-educated, honoured citizens in a New China that respects women and prizes children."

Li Lan Yin is a secretary in an office of one of the giant industries in the North-east Province. She is a tall, young-looking woman of twenty-nine. There was still something naïvely girlish about her in her dark-blue pantaloons and tunic as I saw her first. She rose from the piano where she had been playing a folk-tune and leading the singing of the girls of the factory choir.

"I learnt to play at the Centre," she explained. "I've always loved music and one of my greatest joys is to sing and dance.

"My parents died in the great floods of 1931 when I was a child," she told me, when we had seated ourselves in her room. "I went to live with an aunt who was also poor. When I was sixteen I had to go to work as a maidservant. The master of the house raped me, and then, because I became ill from shock, dismissed me." She dashed away the tears that came to her eyes. "I had no one to turn to for help and was nearly starving when a woman offered to find me work. She took me to a house where I put my finger-prints to an agreement. Then I found I was in a brothel.

"When I was taken to the Centre in 1951 I soon realized that here was the chance to study and improve myself that all my life I had dreamt of but never expected to have. To me, life at the Centre was sheer joy and now my life is all happiness."

The snapshot of the young man in a soldier's uniform that is pinned above her bed may have something to do with it.

Today Lu Li-chuan is twenty-four—a grave, slender girl with two long thick plaits. She works in the co-operative farm of her native village. She tells me her story as though it were someone else's, her eyes fixed on the fields that stretch away to the horizon.

"My mother died when I was still an infant and my grand-mother reared me. My father married again and when I was twelve years old he moved to Shanghai. My stepmother made me wash the clothes, look after the house and cook, and both my father and stepmother would scold and kick and beat me if the slightest thing went wrong. I was never properly fed or clothed.

"One day my stepmother dressed me up better than I had ever been and told me I was going to visit a relative. I found myself taken to a hotel room. There was a man in the room. He forced me onto a bed. I fought and tried to escape, but he was too strong.

"I found out that the man paid my stepmother four hundred dollars because I was only twelve years old. I was so roughly treated that I could hardly walk afterwards. My stepmother continued to scold and beat me and forbade me to tell other people of the incident, otherwise she would kill me.

"But 'fire can never be wrapped in paper'; my misfortune was soon known to the neighbours. They sympathized with me deeply and, knowing the cruelty of my stepmother, they offered me financial help secretly and advised me to go back to my native village. But I was not careful enough in my attempt to escape and my stepmother discovered me as I was sneaking out and she beat me severely. A few days later she took me to a brothel where I became an unregistered prostitute.

"For five years I lived this life. I am sure that but for Liberation I would not be alive today."

Pao Yu-ying was only eighteen when gathered in by the Education Centre—a tiny, graceful creature with a delicate face, big eyes and two long pigtails. Her story is one we know well in the West.

Daughter of a poor family in Shanghai, living in an overcrowded, bug-ridden, one-roomed mat shelter that served her family for a home, she despaired of ever enjoying anything better.

"I wanted clean, pretty clothes instead of the filthy rags which were all my parents could find for me. I wanted some brightness and pleasure. Older girls—'black prostitutes', as they were called —got to know me and they told me how I could get them. They told me how sometimes rich men fell in love with a girl and made her his concubine so that she had a rich home, luxury, and plenty of clothes.

"I was only fifteen when I began frequenting the streets around Foochow Road. It was always brightly lit, not like the dark lane where we lived. I had to pay a big proportion of what I made to the police. And besides, I lived in terror that the neighbours and my family would find out what I was doing. I knew my father would kill me if he knew.

"Shanghai was a terrible place in those days with its procurers and gangsters and soldiers, and, worst of all of them, the police who would force you to lie with them for nothing and then take what little money you had made.

"When I was taken by the new police to the Centre I was physically sick with fright. But it soon disappeared when I saw I was in clean, warm, nice rooms, nicer than anything I'd known, and had kindness and no cruelty.

"I soon found that if I studied hard I could get a job that would keep me clothed and fed and with something to spare—better than that for which I had had to sell myself. And I would be respected instead of despised.

"It was not long before the Centre gave me the opportunity to start in a hosiery-mill. The older workers helped me and I got on very well. I made suggestions for improvement in operating the machines which the management considered very useful. I was given prizes for my suggestions. It was there I met my husband. We have two children and live in a lovely new flat."

It was the director of the Shanghai Centre who told me the stories of White Peony and Black Jade.

Black Jade was a kind of good-time girl we recognize from our own wartime experience in the West, swept off her feet by the glamour of the uniform, particularly when it has a lot of red tabs.

Daughter of a rich business-man, she was well educated, high-spirited, spoilt, the leader of a set which prided itself on being the fastest and the best dressed in Shanghai.

Father was complaisant and turned a blind eye when she became the mistress of a high-ranking officer. What surer way to get juicy contracts?

When the officer passed out of the picture Black Jade went from one conquest to the other, adding American officers to her "bag", and demanding only that the newest comer should be able to give her a gayer time than the last.

Her idea of a good time ended with the Liberation. She resented it. She resented everything that happened to her. Taken to the Centre, she refused to co-operate in any way.

The director sighed. "She really was a difficult case. She despised everybody, staff as well as girls, because she was a college girl. It took a long time before there was any change in her at all. But patience, patience, patience! There is no other method.

"After two years she was won over and today she is a popular schoolmistress in a secondary school."

More fascinating still is the story of White Peony, a *Dame aux Camèlias* with a different ending—the kind of story that would throw film producers into ecstasies and romantic novelists into purple patches. Indeed, "purple" was the epithet that applied to White Peony, for in Chinese it implies "famous". She was a high-class courtesan. For many years her beauty was renowned through-out Shanghai. Poets sang of her face, the "shape of a watermelon seed", her almond eyes, her "eyebrows the shape of a willow-leaf". She was tall and very slim; the ambition of every sing-song girl was to walk as gracefully as White Peony. Her clothes were the talk of the town, rich, elegant, the height of fashion; her taste was envied by respectable women as well as "the others".

Among all Shanghai's famous courtesans, White Peony was out-standing. A brilliant conversationalist, she had all the charm and ease of a sophisticated woman. When conversation palled she sang excerpts from Peking opera as well as any actress. Not surprising that her favours were eagerly sought after. White Peony could pick and choose and had a select clientele of wealthy Europeans as well as Chinese.

Not surprising, either, that such a combination of beauty, brains and elegance commanded high prices.

She was rich. She even had gold bars! (Nice touch, that!) She owned her own house, decorated and furnished as a foil to her personality, and was served by skilled discreet servants.

It was not till 1953 that she was brought to the Centre—against her will. It was not till 1956 that she changed.

All her sumptuous possessions were carefully kept for her; her valuables were put in the bank. She was allowed to keep her clothes. When she came to the Centre she wore rich silk brocades made in the traditional fashion. Her make-up was expertly applied and she spent hours each night setting her hair. At first she refused to do any work at all. She was even reluctant to make her bed. She was completely unco-operative in every way, but never unpleasant. In fact, she was always very charming. It was not that she despised everyone as Black Jade did, but her life had been one of luxury and pleasure and she had suffered none of the hardships of the other prostitutes, so it was difficult to make her see why her life had been wrong.

After a while she found that doing her share of things and taking her share of the dormitory duties was a relief from the monotony of doing nothing. The process was slow, but gradually she began to take part in the recreational activities, where her knowledge of music was very useful. Strangely enough, everybody liked her. In her old life, her ability to adapt herself to people's moods had been one of the secrets of her success, so, long though the process was, she eventually adapted herself to the new life.

(Maybe in that quick mind of hers she realized that, whatever might happen in the future, at thirty-five a courtesan's life has seen its best days.)

Her intelligence asserted itself, and she began to take a keen interest in what was happening outside. The type of contacts she had in the old days gave her a wider picture of the world than the other girls had. She was no fool and knew that, though Western men had come to her, they really despised her. She was only a prostitute! She knew, too, from their talk that they had a tremendous contempt for China itself. She was passionately proud of being Chinese. She began to take pride in her country's achievements. She began to say "we" instead of "I" and took pleasure in helping the other girls to read and write and sing. At the end of three years she was ready to go out, since she had fulfilled all the qualifications.

I asked where she was, thinking that with her accomplishments she had probably joined an opera troupe, and determined to go and see her play as soon as possible.

"Oh, no!" The director smiled at my suggestion. "She was not interested in that. With her educational advantages it was easy for her to learn accountancy and now she is in charge of the office of a State farm."

Dumas, with all his imagination, would never have thought of that!

Back in Peking, I asked Mrs Chin if there was any prostitution today in China. She shook her head. "Prostitution is illegal. There are no brothels. It is not possible for anyone to exploit a girl's body and there is no need for parents to sell their daughters. Since all the world is open to girls and they can keep themselves by working at a job they like there is no reason that they should be forced to earn a living that way. In the Old China a great number of men could not marry because they could not support themselves, much less a wife, but since there is so much employment today they can marry and live normal lives. And the terrible, degrading poverty that was at the root of it all has gone for ever."

"Besides," Mrs Liu added, "the new society has completely altered the pattern of Chinese home life. In the old days companionship as you in the West have known it for a long time, and as we know it today, did not exist. The old sages said that ignorance made a woman virtuous; they never thought it made her interesting! So, naturally, men sought their social enjoyment outside their homes. Now, with the equality of women and educational facilities for all, the home is assuming a new significance for husband as well as wife, and in consequence for their children. Today Chinese home life in its real sense is more soundly and sanely based than it has ever been in our long history."

In Shanghai the director of the Centre smoothed out a letter written on notepaper overprinted with a faint design of plumblossom, herald of spring.

"I think you would like to hear a letter from one of our former girls," she said. "She learnt to write at the Centre." She showed me the page with its vertical lines of spidery characters.

" 'You will forgive me for not writing for so long,' " she read, " 'but so many wonderful things have been happening one after another that I seem to have no time. First, my husband was sent to the new factory and we had all the fun of moving into our new flat and getting to know people. Then my baby was born. She is a beautiful baby and weighed seven pounds. My husband says he has never seen a prettier baby. . . .' " The director laughed. "I'll skip all that about the baby. You have probably heard it many times. She finishes: " 'I never thought I could be so happy. In the old days society turned us into ghosts. The New China has turned us back into human beings. Each day is better than the last. I really understand at last what we meant when we used to sing, "The future belongs to those who fight for it." ' "

Postscript

SUMMER has come and gone again. In the year and a half that has passed since my plane first dipped over the Western Hills the scene I found so strange at first has become familiar and the impressions of those first months when I travelled from one end of the country to the other have deepened, not changed.

Throughout summer and winter I have walked alone through the back-streets of Peking, savouring the exuberant life of the Chinese crowd. No mere anonymous mass, this crowd. Each unit is individual, stamped with the dignity that comes of an age-old civilization and has nothing to do with literacy or material possessions.

Nowhere in the world have I met such honesty and law-abidingness, so that one plunges alone into the narrowest, darkest street without a second thought.

In uncountable hutungs I have seen the Street Committee at its work of inculcating a sense of civic pride and responsibility from the smallest local unit upward.

I have been a guest in many homes and nowhere have I seen family ties—now robbed of their despotism—sounder, more closely knit. In every city street, in every village, grandfather and grandmother wander, holding their grandchildren—and sometimes great-grandchildren!—by the hand, secure in the consciousness that they, too, have a place in the new society, that they are *needed*.

Summer and winter and spring and autumn, I have watched in innumerable villages the unchanging cycle of the seasons go their way in a setting that, practically unchanged for three thousand years, is changing so fast that one can scarcely keep up with it. Even in my brief time I have seen in so many places the single-bladed plough with its plodding oxen give way to the tractor, the primitive oil-lamp to electricity.

The women who have told their stories in this book are only a small part of the countless women I have met, during the year and a half I have watched the greatest social movement in history widen, deepen, strengthen and accelerate. Recently at the All-China Women's Congress I mingled with the thirteen hundred delegates of forty nationalities, come from all parts of this vast country—larger than Australia, Europe, or the United States!

I admired their bewildering variety of national costumes and fantastic head-dresses. The translation was made in ten languages, for many, though members of the Chinese Republic, do not speak Chinese, and over the earphones I heard them recount the progress made by the women of their villages and towns and cities, from Tibet and Sinkiang to tropical Hainan; from sampan-dwellers in Canton to herdsmen's co-operatives in Inner Mongolia.

There, as though stepping into another age, I walked hand in hand with a Buddhist nun and a woman of the Yi nationality who till last year was a slave in the literal meaning of the word, as her ancestors had been back into the mists of time.

There I heard the past evoked, the present debated, the future planned—planned like a giant housekeeping budget that takes as its primary duty the harmony of the home, the welfare of women, the care of children.

Scenes flash across my mind, symbolic of the change.

A rocky village behind Tsingtao I have just visited, nestling beneath the Laoshan Mountains, with their saw-toothed peaks piercing the sky, ancient Taoist temples in luxuriant valleys. And along the village road, grandson proudly riding his new bicycle with bound-foot grandma sitting equally proudly on the pillion.

Young lovers wandering hand in hand along the painted colonnade that was once the Empress Dowager's favourite walk. Swimming side by side in the East Lake at Wuchang. Skating together on the frozen moat in Peking with the towers of the Forbidden City glittering golden against a high blue sky.

Girl athletes practising for an international contest.

A young girl floating from the parachute-tower.

A literacy class for mothers who sit poring over their books on a winter afternoon while their babies sleep on the heated kang.

A group of girl geologists setting out to prospect for oil.

These are only symbols of the profound transformation that has taken place in the lives of Chinese women.

The reality is deeper. Perhaps it could be written only by a Chinese woman who has herself experienced it. Only she can know the inmost truth.

"It was not easy," they say to me, with staggering understatement. Always "was". Sometimes I wonder if it is easy yet. How can the prejudices of several thousand years be uprooted in less than a decade?

Sometimes the Women's Federation protests against discrimination in industrial and political organizations. Village women complain that some of the older men are still "feudal-minded".

Hardly strange when one remembers that China has the influence of 2500 years of feminine suppression to wipe out!

That they *protest* is itself proof of the profound change. In the past their role was to *accept*.

But they have stood up, and in their standing up millennial burdens have slid from their backs. They are free now to make of their lives what they will.

Already freedom has released potentialities in the older women they did not know they possessed. For the younger, it is part of the air they breathe.

ACKNOWLEDGMENT

I WISH to thank most sincerely the innumerable people in China who made it possible for me to write this book. My thanks in particular to the Chinese Peace Committee, the Women's Federation, the Commission for Cultural Relations with Foreign Countries, the Writers' Union, all of whom gave me their fullest co-operation wherever I went in China. To my untiring interpreters Chang Sou-tien and Cheng Wan-chen who accompanied me on my long voyages. To Yen Ching-hung of Shanghai, Ling Shan-tsen, and Yang Li-i of the Women's Federation, Peking. To Sun Tse-chio (Secretary of the Women's Federation) and Chao Sun of the Foreign Languages Institute of Harbin, and Chang Ping, our guide and friend of that city. To Rewi Alley, not only for the privilege of reading and publishing his translations of Chinese poetry, but for the insight he gave me into thirty years of China. To Lao Sheh, novelist and playwright, for sharing his profound knowledge of Old and New China with me. To Hsieh Ping-shing, writer. To Betty Chang and to Talitha Gerlach. To Pang Tao-hsiang, of the Peking National Library and to Chang Hsin-lien.

To Liu Feng-yuan, my housekeeper beyond price, who has shown me every day, for eighteen months, how Chinese women have "stood up", and how they use their new freedom. To the innumerable and unnamed people I have met in hundreds of back streets and villages throughout China who have given me the warmest of welcomes, courtesy and kindness, and the ever-deepening conviction that all women are sisters.

D. C.

74 30/F

ofm x5610

24.95

2/5-87

50/886v